MISSION CRITICAL

MISSION CRITICAL

REALIZING THE PROMISE OF ENTERPRISE SYSTEMS

Thomas H. Davenport

Harvard Business School Press
Boston, Massachusetts

Library of Congress Cataloging-in-Publication Data

Davenport, Thomas H., 1954–
   Mission critical : realizing the promise of enterprise systems /
Thomas H. Davenport.
      p. cm.
   Includes bibliographical references and index.
   ISBN 0-87584-906-7
   1. Management information systems.   I. Title.

HD30.213.D38 2000
658.4'038'011--dc21

99-051644

CONTENTS

PREFACE

I'M ASSUMING THAT YOU ARE A MANAGER OR AN EMPLOYEE in an organization that's putting in a mission-critical enterprise system, or perhaps a consultant to such organizations, or maybe someone who works for a vendor of these systems. You may be well down the road of implementing a system, or only be considering getting involved with enterprise systems as an organization or as an individual. You may have even implemented a system that hasn't really delivered the benefits you expected. In any case, you'd like to make yourself more successful by helping your organization or your customer's organization be successful with this technology.

I want to help you by providing a better understanding of what enterprise systems are and what they can accomplish in an organization. I'll describe how other organizations have done well and done poorly in their own implementation efforts. The emphasis throughout the book will be on achieving the business objectives that these systems make possible, not on the technical aspects of a project. For that type of advice you'll have better luck with books that address specific types of enterprise systems. (For example, Nancy Bancroft's 1996 book *Implementing SAP R/3* [Greenwich, CT: Manning Publications] is a good source on SAP implementations.) Here I'll take the high road and not delve into technical details concerning any particular vendor's system.

A word about my experience and biases. I am a researcher and consultant who works at the intersection of information systems and organizational behavior and change. I've led or participated in three different multicompany research projects on enterprise systems management, and consulted with many individual firms on how to get value from them. At the time of this writing I've done research or consulting in over fifty companies that are implementing these systems.

My general perspective is that information systems are worthless unless they lead to better information or better ways of doing business. I think that enterprise systems are without doubt an impressive technical feat, but I am primarily concerned that organizations get business value from them. I work for an organization that makes a good deal of money from implementing enterprise systems (or "Enterprise Business Solutions," as the practice is called within Andersen Consulting), but this is not a book designed primarily to promote my employer's services (though I do think highly of them!).

I will address the messages in this book primarily to the organizations that want strategic change and competitive advantage and are willing to take the time and spend the money to achieve them. However, if you're looking for a fast, strategic implementation, most of the advice I provide will still apply. You'll just have to decide what's most important to you and limit the breadth of your ambitions. Everybody has to compromise with enterprise systems; it's just a matter of how much.

One cautionary message: In some cases it's still too early to tell whether these systems will be successful within a given organization over the long term. Given that virtually no organization is finished with its project, it's still early for dispensing advice. On the other hand, people working on these systems need help. It's surprising to me that there aren't more books on this very important topic, given that many organizations have been working on enterprise systems for several years. Although no one has completed a broad business transformation based on an enterprise system, many have made substantial progress. To me it's worth dealing with a bit of uncertainty in order to get some sort of message out while many people and companies can still benefit from it.

THOMAS H. DAVENPORT
NOVEMBER 1999

ACKNOWLEDGMENTS

THIS BOOK IS IN MANY WAYS AN EXTENSION OF MY WORK ON business process reengineering. When I became aware that companies were adopting enterprise systems in order to achieve their reengineering goals, I couldn't resist finding out how it worked. I had done considerable work on reengineering at the Center for Business Innovation, and that's where my earliest research on enterprise systems began. I worked with Rudy Ruggles on a multiclient project there; I'm grateful to him and to all the firms that participated in that and subsequent projects. I think enterprise systems are one of the greatest business experiments of the late twentieth century, and the managers of the firms implementing these systems are the scientists.

When I moved to the University of Texas, we installed SAP for instructional purposes, and I began to discuss enterprise systems often with two faculty members there, Larry Leibrock and Judy Scott. While I was at Texas, I began to work with SAP AG on research and educational projects. During that time, SAP sponsored my research on how companies use the information from their SAP systems to manage their businesses, the result of which became the nucleus of chapter 7. I am grateful to SAP for its support and to Caroline Sayre of Waggener Edstrom, SAP's public relations firm, for arranging the project.

While at Texas I was drafted as a subject matter expert for two studies on enterprise systems implementation—one at the American Productivity and Quality Center (APQC), and one at the Concours Group. I would like to thank Carla O'Dell and Jack Grayson at APQC, and Ron Christman and Bob Morison at Concours.

Shortly after I actually started to apply graphite to cellulose for this book, I moved to Boston to direct Andersen Consulting's Institute for Strategic Change, and to teach at Boston University. At Andersen, Peter Fuchs graciously consented to support this "legacy" project. Under the auspices of the Institute, I completed the book with help from several people. Julia Kirby wrote the first draft of chapter 8 and helped with the marketing of the book. Jeff Brooks and Susan Cantrell, then students at Boston University (and now Institute researchers), helped considerably with chapters 9 and 4, respectively. Bob Baginsky gave me access to the experience and resources of Andersen's Enterprise Business Solutions line of business, and connected me with its leaders, Karl Newkirk, Hap Brakely, and Eileen Basho. My assistant, Noelle McDonough, assisted with checking quotations and with final preparation of the manuscript.

This is my fourth book with Harvard Business School Press, and I think they're the best publisher around of serious business books. I greatly enjoyed working with Hollis Heimbouch, my enthusiastic editor. The Press sent the book to Gary Banks (then of Xerox), Gerry Coady of J.D. Edwards, and a third reviewer whose identity I couldn't deduce. All reviewers were helpful, but Gary Banks's contributions were truly extraordinary.

My wife, Jodi, helped me in a number of ways with this book, including interviewing some managers of enterprise systems projects and reading several chapter drafts. I know she had no interest whatsoever in the topic, so her contributions were heroic. My sons, Hayes and Chase, are becoming quite blasé about seeing their names in print in my books, but if I left them out they'd be outdone.

MISSION CRITICAL

1

WHAT ARE
ENTERPRISE SYSTEMS
AND WHY
DO THEY MATTER?

AROUND THE GLOBE COMPANIES ARE QUIETLY AND STEADILY
becoming more connected—one business function with another,
one business unit with another, one company to another. They
are putting information systems in place that will yield more and
better information more quickly than they have ever known. For
the first time since large businesses were created, managers will
be able to monitor the doings of the company in near real time,
without having to wait for monthly reports that must be cross-
referenced with other monthly reports, all of which may be out
of date—or just plain wrong—by the time managers receive
them. Managers will also be able to sit in front of their workstations and know what is happening at every point around the
globe.

For the first time ever, information will flow seamlessly
across diverse business functions, business units, and geographic
boundaries. What the Internet is doing for communications between organizations, these systems are doing within companies.
For better or worse, no business transaction—no customer

purchase, no supplier invoice, no product produced—will go unnoticed by these systems. Ultimately, every bit of computer-based information used for running a company's operations can be supplied by these systems. This situation sounds utopian, but it's actually available today if companies can master a relatively new type of information system.

Let's call such information systems enterprise systems (ESs). Also known as enterprise resource planning (ERP) systems, these are packages of computer applications that support many, even most, aspects of a company's (or a nonprofit organization's, university's, or government agency's) information needs. The ERP name reflects the manufacturing roots of these systems—it's a modification of "MRP" (manufacturing resource planning)—but in my view these systems have so transcended their origins that the somewhat clumsy ERP name is no longer appropriate.

From accounting to manufacturing, from sales to service, ES modules support thousands of business activities. Aside from personal productivity applications such as spreadsheets and word processors on personal computers, highly specialized production systems such as process control, and Internet-based systems for information and knowledge access, an ES may be the only business information system an organization requires. This breadth is one of the key factors that distinguishes enterprise systems from earlier systems.

Enterprise applications started out as "back-office" systems, automating the workmanlike business transactions that customers never saw or cared about. Sure, ledgers needed to be updated, suppliers paid, and employee vacation balances debited, but accuracy and speed in this type of transaction rarely led to any competitive advantage or increased customer satisfaction. Although back-office systems may not offer competitive advantage, they do have important implications. Poorly functioning back-office systems can lead to dissatisfied customers, suppliers, auditors, or regulators. If a company can't generate an accurate invoice, meet a promised delivery date, find a missing shipment, or properly account for costs and revenues, it can get in big trouble quickly. Well-implemented enterprise systems can make well-executed back-office transactions a reality.

More recently, however, ESs have moved into the front office, supporting supply chain optimization, sales force automation, and customer service. These new functions have been achieved either by installing more comprehensive packages from ES vendors or by installing complementary software applications—sometimes called *bolt-on systems*—from third-party software companies. Because the goal is to have added capabilities connect smoothly with the core ES system, I'll refer to the entire entity as an ES, even though it may consist of several different components.

Even more recently, a new technology has largely erased the distinction between front and back offices. The Internet, and associated internal networks called *intranets,* is the ideal tool for distributing and providing access to information. With just a browser, employees, suppliers, and customers can all access the organization's information. But where will that information come from? Internet technology itself is not suited for processing business transactions or for storing key data—it's an information access technology. Enterprise systems are, of course, perfectly suited for information transactions; they're the underlying information factory producing the information for internal and external Internet consumption. Using the Internet to give employees and customers access to poor-quality, unintegrated information is like opening more bank branches when the currency is worthless. You have to work on both access and high-quality information simultaneously. The combination of enterprise systems as the primary platform for organizational information and of Internet technology for providing access to it will be the hallmark of leading organizations in the new century.

Whether front office or back office, by themselves or in combination with other technologies, ESs are distinguished by their information commonality and integration. It's great to have the entire business supported by a single type of information system, but what if the information differs from one part of the organization to another? For the most part, this is prevented in ESs through the use of a common database for the entire organization. Not only can one track customers through marketing, sales, and service activities, but the customer's identification number and address are constant across those different applications and business functions. The Babel-like information environments of most large organizations, in which the same term might mean different things in different parts of the company, can be avoided altogether through the use of an ES.

In short, these systems offer just about everything businesses want from a computer. They serve up information in a format that anyone—not just technologists—can understand. They employ client/server technology—the state of the commercial art in information systems. They even work well with the Internet. If these systems are so good, why wouldn't every organization want one?

In fact, they do. With a few exceptions I'll discuss later, large, medium-sized, and increasingly even small organizations are installing enterprise systems: from Iowa Spring, which has about $11 million in revenues, to its customer General Motors, which is more than ten thousand times larger. Public-sector organizations ranging from the "city" of Round Rock, Texas, to the Victoria Department of Education in Melbourne, Australia, have them. In some industries, such as petrochemicals, every company has an ES. In others, such as the electrical utilities business, ESs are being adopted at a rapid rate. Even in financial services, one of the industries in which these systems have been less popular, hundreds of organizations from Bank One to Dai-Ichi Life Insurance have them in place.

The software and hardware spending alone for ESs is well over $15 billion per year worldwide, and professional services fees add another $10 billion. Revenues for ES vendors have grown between 50 and 100 percent a year. Very large companies, such as Hewlett-Packard, Procter & Gamble, and Intel, speculate that their ES expenditures will easily top $1 billion before they are finished. (As I describe later, they will never be finished, so their total costs will ultimately be even higher!) In such firms the cost of implementing an ES is orders of magnitude higher than, for example, the money spent on the Internet, Web sites, and electronic commerce.

Of course, with every benefit there is risk. A few companies have failed at implementing ESs; many more have spent more than they intended or encountered resistance from managers and workers who were unprepared for the changes ESs bring. Companies are willing and correct to take these kinds of risks because of the impact the systems can have on quality, cost reduction, and customer satisfaction and loyalty.

Enterprise systems offer the first great opportunity to achieve true connectivity, a state in which everyone knows what everyone else is doing in the business all over the world at the same time. And because they represent the first great opportunity for connectivity, they pose one of the greatest threats to the status quo that companies have ever faced. Because companies are made up mostly of people, ESs mean you will have to change people and the way they do things at the same time that you change all the computers and the software. That is why ESs may be more rewarding—and more challenging—than any computer system a company has ever tried to install.

Big Systems, Big Change

Being successful with enterprise systems is not simply a matter of writing big checks. What's really important—and difficult— about these systems is the dramatic change they bring to a business. I'll argue throughout this book that an enterprise project is as much about changing the way a business operates as it is about technology. Successful implementation of an ES does involve probably the greatest technological change most organizations have ever undergone, not to mention the largest employing client/server technologies. Even more difficult and important, however, are the major changes in business that come with an ES project.

Business processes, the way work gets done in an organization, change dramatically. Organizational structure and culture, the behaviors of workers throughout the company, and even business strategy all have to be restructured. The reengineering movement of the early 1990s, with all its radical approaches to reorganizing companies, turned out to be a mere preamble to the ES era, which has brought even more ambitious (and complex) changes. In fact, the business process reengineering movement has largely been replaced by ES initiatives. Given their breadth and technical complexity, ES projects are even more difficult and consuming of time and resources than the largest reengineering projects. The most ambitious ES projects can take a decade or more of a company's time.

Implementing new mission-critical systems, then, is hardly just a matter of installing an ES. Business processes and information must be made common around the world within the implementing organization. Idiosyncratic ways of doing business must be abandoned. Informational linkages between business functions and units must be tightened. Employees must be educated about the broad implications of simple actions like pressing a key within an ES. Perhaps most difficult of all, senior managers must be persuaded of the wisdom of changing virtually everything in a company at once. In short, organizational change represents a huge part of a successful ES project. Managers at Steelcase, for example, estimate that up to half of the company's project resources went for organizational change issues. A Monsanto manager felt that change management activities constituted 75 percent of the total project effort there.

Despite these difficulties, ESs are the answer to the Information Age's wildest dreams. The concept of an integrated set of information technology (IT) applications that could meet all of an organization's information needs has been with us since the beginning of information systems in business, but has been unrealizable before the modern ES. We have gotten what we wished for; now we only need to make the business and organizational changes necessary to take advantage of our fulfilled dreams.

BUSINESS BENEFITS OF ENTERPRISE SYSTEMS

I've already pointed out that ESs are difficult to put in place from both a technical and business change standpoint. Why go to all the trouble and expense of implementing an ES? In an ideal world, ES-enabled organizations would be seamlessly interconnected both internally and externally. Excess inventory and waste would be nonexistent. Demand and supply would be perfectly coordinated. It would be just as easy to transact business with suppliers and customers as with another department of your own company. Customers would have perfect information about not only the products and services they've ordered from you, but also about how every aspect of your business affects theirs. Managers could understand any aspect of a company's operations and performance with a few clicks of the mouse.

These benefits aren't purely hypothetical. Many companies have already realized substantial business benefits from their ES projects, even if they are not completely finished installing them. Several examples of these benefits are described in the following paragraphs.

1. *Cycle time reduction.* Autodesk, a leading manufacturer of computer-aided design software, has achieved substantial benefits in terms of cost and time reductions in key business processes. Whereas the company used to require two weeks on average to ship to customers, 98 percent of products are now shipped within twenty-four hours. Financial closing times were cut in half, from twelve days to six. Autodesk calculates that it has saved more on reduced inventory alone than its SAP system cost to install.

2. *Faster information transactions.* IBM's System Storage (disk drive) division achieved a reduction in the time to enter pricing information from five days minimum to five minutes, replacement part shipping went from twenty-two days to three, and credit checks that previously took twenty minutes

are now accomplished in three seconds. Crediting a customer for a returned disk drive used to take three weeks; it now happens immediately. The division once spent thousands of hours reconciling management reporting data; this now happens automatically. IBM in general has twenty-one SAP projects underway, covering 80 percent of its core business; eight projects are up and running.

3. *Better financial management.* Microsoft is installing an ES to bring about common financial and procurement systems worldwide. The fast-growing software company has already saved $2 million in equipment depreciation (it previously took three months to start the depreciation schedule for a new asset; now it can begin immediately). The company's ES has allowed it to receive $14 million per year in early-payment discounts from vendors. Microsoft's managers also report substantial benefits in improved management and reporting systems, and the financial closing cycle has been reduced from twelve days to four.

4. *Laying the groundwork for electronic commerce.* Cisco Systems put in an ES to structure and rationalize its back-office business transactions systems, which were previously unable to support the company's rapid growth. Without the system, Cisco also wouldn't have been able to offer customers Web-based access to product ordering, tracking, and delivery processes. Cisco's system cost it over $15 million, and the company spent another $100 million connecting it to the Internet. Today, however, Cisco believes that the combination of its ES and its Internet applications yields more than $500 million in annual operating cost savings.

5. *Making tacit process knowledge explicit.* Monsanto was concerned that decades of knowledge about plant operations existed only in the minds of an aging workforce. After successfully implementing its ES, company managers now feel that key processes, decision rules, and information structures are well understood and documented in its sys-

tem. Furthermore, the knowledge is now more common to the industry, so that new employees are more likely to understand the work process. Support of the process and the system can also be outsourced to external suppliers.

The primary lesson from these examples is that key business processes can be improved dramatically through the implementation of an ES. Whether the process is financial, managerial, or operational; whether it involves internal activities or customers and suppliers; whether the process runs faster or leaner—enterprise systems are the primary vehicles for making business processes better. It's virtually inconceivable to try to reengineer today without them.

Business Life before Enterprise Systems

In order to better understand the value of ESs, it's useful to contrast them with the way that organizations previously met their information needs. In 1954, when the first business application of computers was developed (by what is now Andersen Consulting for General Electric), and for most of the following forty years, when a business function needed computerized information it used a stand-alone application. The first application created was for payroll processing; later ones would be created for general ledger, accounts payable, inventory management, or customer billing. Each system had its own application logic, its own information, and its own user interface. An individual company might have hundreds of individual applications. Even when software vendors began to sell application packages of broader functionality in the 1980s, they were almost always within individual business functions, for example, finance and accounting. We haven't totally left this approach behind today. Companies that don't have an ES still have a variety of standalone systems.

Chopping up information systems this way makes it impossible to coordinate planning across different business functions. Say, for example, that a company wants to compare information from its manufacturing and sales functions so that it doesn't produce more inventory than it can sell. The information is there within the company, but it's not accessible or comparable—making things frustrating for those who need it. In most cases in the past, this coordination simply couldn't be done in any automated fashion because companies' manufacturing systems were separate from their sales systems. The sales force didn't know what manufacturing had produced recently, and manufacturing didn't find out until later what the sales force had sold. The idea of "available to promise" inventory (i.e., stuff a company has made or could make that isn't promised to anyone else, so is available to be sold) just didn't exist. Connections between functions—and often between different geographical areas—were loose and slow. When connections did take place they involved many middle managers, whose jobs entailed collating and passing this information around the organization.

The most insidious aspect of this problem involved different interpretations of the same information entities. The term *customer,* for example, might appear in many of these disparate systems around a firm. In one system it might include distributors, in another only end customers. In one version it would incorporate prospects, in another only existing customers. If the CEO asked for a list of the top 100 customers, it could take weeks to come to consensus on the list (as happened at one computer company with diverse systems around the organization). Having diverse forms of information has some positive attributes as well (e.g., every part of the organization gets the interpretation of *customer* that best suits its needs), but there is no doubt that the proliferation of information meanings can cause considerable confusion. One department's interpretation of how much has been sold through what channels may differ from another's. Every department could have its own interpretation of how much money was passing through based on what information they each believed described a customer. Obviously, this disparity made it difficult to make good decisions about which customers to serve, which selling approaches were most effective, and whether to build the business or hold back.

Having multiple systems that could not talk directly to each other was—and still is for those organizations who haven't moved fully to ESs—a maintenance nightmare. Managing hundreds of different systems means managing tens of computer languages, hundreds of different maintenance and update schedules, and thousands of pieces of documentation. In most organizations there is literally no one who understands how all of the pieces fit together. When one system needs to be connected to another, ad hoc connections must be made, the maintenance of which becomes another problem. Because of these difficulties, many companies spend more than half of their information systems budgets on maintenance. Managing communications between computer systems that were never designed to talk to one another requires enormous, continual work on interfaces. When any of the systems is changed, all of the interfaces have to be changed as well.

If a major problem occurs in these multiple standalone systems regarding system design or functionality (say, purely hypothetically, of course, that the date field in many systems held only two digits as the year 2000 was approaching), finding and correcting the problem across so many systems is extremely difficult. In fact, the Year 2000 (Y2K) problem has been a major driver for many companies to install an ES. Companies adopted a "kill two birds with one stone" approach, solving their Y2K problems while installing a more functional and integrated system. Current versions of ESs from major vendors can all deal with 2000 and subsequent years (at least until the year 10,000!). Another example of this "simplification through integration" approach is conversion to the new common European currency, the euro. Those organizations with multiple nonintegrated systems need to incorporate the new currency across each system; companies with an ES need only install one system (or a new release of their existing ES) that can handle the euro.

It is possible, of course, for companies to build proprietary ESs just as they have written proprietary standalone software programs. A few companies have succeeded in this regard.

VeriFone, for example, which provides banks and retailers with transaction automation via its card-swipe devices, has long had its own fully integrated system for internal business transactions using a common database. VeriFone's managers and programmers designed and built the system, and it works well. However, the success rate for companies trying to build their own systems is quite low, and the price quite high. Many large banks, for example, have attempted to build integrated systems only to fail. Even at VeriFone, the company's system runs on an obsolete computing platform and needs to be rewritten. Further, the company has been acquired by Hewlett-Packard, which is implementing an ES from a large vendor. Hence the future of VeriFone's home-grown ES is in doubt. Most organizations should not even consider developing their own system. Few companies do business in a unique enough fashion to benefit from such a move.

BUSINESS LIFE TODAY WITH ENTERPRISE SYSTEMS

With ESs, you don't have to build your own integrated system. You can buy it from one of several vendors. Each vendor offers more or less the same overall product: a set of application modules that all fit together. Each module includes a variety of functions; for example, the accounting module from almost every vendor includes general ledger, accounts receivable and payable, funds management, financial consolidation and reporting, foreign exchange, and cash management. Most of the information produced by these modules is already Internet or intranet accessible; all of it will be before long.

A company need not install all possible modules. Some modules (e.g., those for finance and accounting) are implemented by almost all firms; others (e.g., human resource management) may not be included in a particular ES project. The company may already have serviceable systems in that part of the business, or it may choose to use standalone "best of breed" functionality rather than a somewhat less functional ES module that is fully integrated with other systems and business processes. The greater the number of modules selected, the greater the integration benefits, the more need for business change, and the higher the cost and the risk of the implementation project.

Companies assemble their choices of modules and install them as a complete system, perhaps adding one or more additional applications from third-party vendors. All of the applications work with the same data, defined in the same way and stored in a common database. A business transaction recorded in one application ripples through the entire system, and all relevant data values are updated.

For example, let's assume that a South Africa–based salesperson for a U.S. multinational computer firm prepares a quote for a customer using an ES. The quote specifies a legally binding product configuration, price, delivery date, shipping method, and so forth, all determined in real time from the system. When the customer accepts the quote (via the Internet, let's say), a sales order is recorded. The system schedules the shipping (including shipping points and truck routes), then works backward from the shipping date to reserve material availability, order needed parts from suppliers, and schedule the computer assembly in manufacturing. The customer's credit limit is checked. The sales and production forecasts are updated. MRP and bill-of-materials lists are created. The salesperson's payroll account is credited with the correct commission, and his or her travel account credited with the expenses of the sales call. Actual product cost and profitability are calculated. The division's and firm's balance sheets, accounts payable and receivable ledgers, cost center accounts, cash levels, and any other relevant financials are automatically recalculated in an instant. Virtually every information transaction resulting from the sale of the computer is taken care of except for the impact on the company's stock price (alas, ESs cannot yet calculate investor psychology).

A KEY CHOICE IN IMPLEMENTING ENTERPRISE SYSTEMS

All ESs work in roughly the manner just described, but companies can implement them in several different ways. The two key dimensions that differentiate approaches to ES implementation are the time it takes to implement, and the amount of business change and value to which a company aspires. These dimensions, when combined, form the matrix of approaches in figure 1-1.

Enterprise systems can be implemented quickly or slowly, depending on how ambitious the company's goals are, how pressing any deadlines are, and how well implementation proceeds. A fast implementation might take as few as six months; a slow one can take up to five years or more. Enterprise systems can be installed for technical reasons or to enhance strategy and competitiveness. A technically focused implementation is intended only to provide core information systems functionality to an organization, with as little business change as possible. A

FIGURE I-I

ALTERNATIVE IMPLEMENTATION APPROACHES

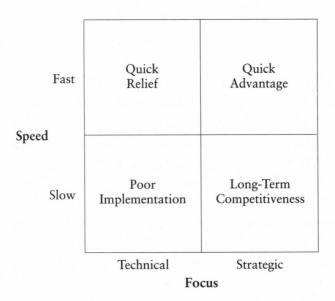

strategic implementation attempts to maximize positive business change and business value.

The only combination of these dimensions that it makes no sense to strive for is the slow, technical option. Since the technical focus provides little business value, it makes sense to complete it as quickly as possible. If you find yourself in this category, it probably means you've just experienced a poor implementation.

A fast, technical implementation can mean quick relief from pressing technical problems or inadequate legacy systems. This approach is probably the least expensive implementation option. It provides no direct business value other than removing any technical barriers to business effectiveness. Some companies say that they are starting with a fast, technical approach but are planning to later achieve significant business value from their systems. ("We'll put the system in quickly, and then later on optimize it to fit our business.") I wonder just how many will ever get around to the optimization phase. It's too early to say whether this is a valid approach, but I don't really advocate it unless the organization is truly threatened by its technical problems.

Instead, I advocate that companies strive for business value in their ES implementations. It's only logical that when a company spends the millions it takes to put in an ES it should try to achieve as much business value as possible from the project. And evidence from an Andersen Consulting survey of 200 CEOs of companies that have implemented ESs suggests that projects viewed primarily as business initiatives are more likely to be perceived as leading to satisfactory business results. Fortunately, 85 percent of the CEOs in this survey, at least, did view their ES projects primarily as business initiatives.[1]

In an ideal world, companies could transform their strategies and enhance overall competitiveness while completing ES implementations within a few months. However, the comprehensively strategic and fast project probably doesn't exist. It is possible, however, to adopt a quick approach and achieve some competitive differentiation. This simply means that the implementation must be heavily focused on a specific business process or means of competitive advantage—for example, the supply chain or customer service. Most of the remaining business processes would have to be viewed in the same terms as when considering a fast, technical implementation.

Companies don't like to admit that their implementations are slow, but it may be worth a drawn-out implementation if it leads to considerable business benefit or competitive differentiation. In fact, if you're looking to change a broad range of processes, improve the way you relate to customers and suppliers, create a new organizational culture, and modify the behaviors of many workers, it's going to take a long time. Don't worry about it.

CRITICISMS OF ENTERPRISE SYSTEMS

From both the technical and business perspectives, ESs have their faults. If you are trying to decide whether to implement one, you should be aware of both the opportunities they provide and the problems they portend. Even if you've already committed to an ES, you should read this section because you may discover difficulties that lie down the road. On balance, however, I believe the criticisms can be overcome and that some ES is a good fit for most large organizations.

Inflexibility. Some would argue that today's enterprise software offerings are too inflexible. It is just too difficult, this viewpoint would have it, to fit an ES to a business—both for the first time and for subsequent changes. Further, many times companies end up doing business in a way that they don't really want just because the system requires it. Another aspect of this supposed inflexibility is that once an ES is installed in your organization, it's too difficult to change how you work and are organized. ESs are like cement, the critics say—highly flexible in the beginning, but rigid later.

There is some truth to these criticisms. One of the greatest difficulties in any ES project is to match the system to one's preferred ways of accomplishing a business process or activity. And most companies have only experienced this problem once; future updates of the system to meet changes in the business may be as difficult as the first go-round. Intel, for example, has already found that it needed twelve additional people to adapt its SAP system to day-to-day changes in its organizational and financial structure.

In response to this inflexibility charge, I ask companies "Compared with what?" A hypothetical object-oriented, highly modular system may someday provide greater flexibility than today's ESs, but no such system is available today, or even on the immediate horizon. Another answer to the flexibility issue is that some ESs are more flexible and easily modified than others. In general, there is a trade-off between the comprehensiveness and breadth of an ES package and the ease with which it can be configured and modified. Thus, organizations do have a choice, obviating some of the criticism. And it is certainly true that today's ESs are more easily configured than those of the past: ES vendors and third-party firms have both developed tools to help companies tailor a system to their businesses. Finally, there are a number of companies who have argued that putting in an ES actually made them more flexible in response to a changing business environment simply because they have only one system to change, not many.

Long implementation periods. A related criticism is that implementing an ES simply takes too long. There's a factual basis to this assertion as well. A three- to five-year project duration is fairly common for implementing an ES in a large company, and for many firms that is overly optimistic. Critics of ESs charge that in the rapidly changing business world we inhabit, five- and even ten-year projects are insupportable.

Again, what's the alternative? To build one's own system from scratch would almost certainly take longer. Even to assemble a collection of "best of breed" software programs and install all of them would take several years, and then they wouldn't be integrated—or if you could connect them through interfaces, doing so would take years. Further, it should be pointed out that what takes such a long time is not installing the system (at the University of Texas business school we installed a fully functional educational version of SAP over a weekend!) but making the required business changes. It's very time-consuming to define and adopt new business processes, to establish common definitions of key information entities, and to set up desired reporting and information aggregation structures across business units. The systems themselves thus shouldn't be blamed for tardiness.

For those companies that are obsessed by speed (rather than achieving business value), it is possible to ram in an ES in a matter of months. Because ES vendors have been criticized for the length of implementation projects, they have created "preconfigured" versions of their systems that can be installed out of the box. One of the first companies to install SAP rapidly, for example, was the *Seattle Times* newspaper, which installed the SAP R/3 system (largely restricted to financial modules) in six months. Many other companies have done so since then.

Of course, such rapid installations mean that a company has to forgo a good fit between their system and the way in which it would like to do business: It has to adopt out-of-the-box business processes as well as a system. In other words, it's a "fast, technical" implementation. But the fact that these implementations are possible blunts this criticism.

Overly hierarchical organizations. A third criticism of ESs is that they impose a hierarchical, "command and control" perspective on organizations. According to this argument, centralized monitoring and control of information is an outdated perspective in organizations in this era of empowerment, employees as free agents, and bottom-up complexity theory.

This characterization is true to a greater degree than the other criticisms. Enterprise systems do presume that information will be centrally monitored and that organizations have a well-defined hierarchical structure. For better or worse, however, most organizations I have encountered in the world are still quite hierarchical. It's fairly clear who reports to whom, and the carpet is thicker and the money a lot better in the Executive Suite. Such concepts as bottom-up complexity theory, self-organizing systems, and empowered employees are intriguing, but few large organizations have adopted them in large measure. There are, of course, truly decentralized companies that do allow their business units the freedom to do as they wish (as long as they make money!). In this kind of company, the obvious answer is to give each business unit its own ES, as some companies have done.

Antiquated technology. A last criticism of ESs is that most are based on obsolete technology; that is, that they are thinly disguised mainframe programs ported into the client/server world. It's true that virtually all ESs have some degree of mainframe-derived program code in them. Further, it's true that the user interfaces of most of these systems is not as graphic and up-to-date as one might like. However, again there is no obvious alternative to the situation; more modern object-oriented systems don't yet offer the breadth and integration of ESs. Furthermore, the practical implications of this issue are negligible.

WHY ARE ENTERPRISE SYSTEMS PARTICULARLY IMPORTANT TODAY?

In an important sense, organizations have currently arrived at a watershed with regard to ESs. Those who had to install them for Year 2000 compliance have now done so. These companies and many others have now installed at least some components of an ES in some parts of their organizations. Now is the time to do something useful with them. Companies must begin to turn the major investments they have made in these systems into improved performance, better decision making, and competitive advantage.

In addition to this general need to take better advantage of ESs, companies face a business environment that makes this technology essential for almost every firm today. Some aspects of the business environment are new; others are simply continuing. There are several general business issues driving the need for ESs: globalization, overcapacity and reengineering, the rise of electronic commerce, and constant change.

Globalization. Globalization, as anyone other than Rip Van Winkle surely knows by now, is a powerful force in first-world economies. Companies are increasingly likely to cross global boundaries in their operations; those that have been global for a long time are trying to coordinate their actions better across geographical boundaries.[2] Enterprise systems are a natural response to this situation: They allow managers to keep much closer tabs on far-flung operations than they would be able to do otherwise. As one manager in a chemical company with an ES noted, "Country and business unit managers that are far from headquarters can no longer hide behind poor information systems."

Indeed, ESs may lead to such close monitoring that they violate basic management principles of granting some autonomy to far-flung managers; it's too early to tell exactly how they'll be used in this regard. In principle, senior executives could fight the impulse to micromanage from behind their ES screens. With the availability of up-to-date, accurate information about the business performance of remote operations, however, they may not be able to resist.

The widespread adoption of ESs in global firms may even lead to new organizational forms. Perhaps firms will need fewer in-country managers because headquarters executives are able to check on production, inventory, and sales results from their desks. But managers who rely too heavily on ESs could lose track of the human side of remote offices. The real feelings of employees, customers, and suppliers are not easily detected—at least in their early stages—in data provided by ESs. There are thus some risks involved in using ESs to manage global enterprises, but the greatest risk of all would probably be not employing an ES at all.

Overcapacity and reengineering. Most manufacturing industries today have substantially more capacity to produce than there is global demand. As a result, they have to continually improve their products and processes in order to compete effectively. In the early 1990s the need to improve took the form of business process reengineering. This top-down, start-from-scratch approach to radical process change became somewhat discredited when companies discovered how difficult and expensive it was.

Because of their business environments, companies still need leaner and faster processes. However, managers' thoughts on how to go about reengineering key business processes have changed dramatically. Instead of viewing process designs as a blank slate to be designed from scratch and then supported by information systems, companies now think about new processes and new information systems at the same time.[3] Now when companies want to reengineer, they view ESs as a means of doing so. Instead of starting from scratch, they start from what is possible or easily accomplished in SAP, Baan, Oracle, or PeopleSoft.

This trend, which I'll describe in greater detail in chapter 5, has both positive and negative implications for the business world. Let's get the bad news out of the way first. No longer are companies likely to dream of visionary process designs and then make them a reality. One company's processes are likely to be similar to another's. The process designs that best fit a company's strategy and business environment will fall prey to those that best fit a system created by a far-off software vendor. Firms that do have radically different processes from the rest of their industry—Dell and Amazon.com come to mind—are likely to have competitors who feel constrained to respond.

Is this process sameness a tragedy for mankind? Not really. Many visionary process designs in reengineering projects were never implemented anyway, which is why firms have moved to an alternative approach to improving their processes. The process designs that are supported by ESs are perfectly respectable; they are based on a generic set of "best practices" that are better than what most firms employ today. Businesses are more likely to achieve better processes when they simultaneously reengineer and support those new processes with new systems. As I'll discuss later, there are good ways to go about ES-enabled process change and poor ones, but the impulse itself is fundamentally sound.

Laying the foundation for electronic commerce. Most people don't think about ESs when they think about e-commerce. They view Internet access, Web servers, browsers, and so forth as being front-office technologies, and ESs as residing in the back—and never the twain shall meet. Life might be easier for technologists if this were true, but it's not. If you want your customers, your suppliers, and your employees to have easy Web connections to your most important information, you're going to need both a good ES and Internet/intranet connections to it.

What do customers do with your business on the Web, for example? Place orders? Then they'll need to go into the ES to make sure that you have the right shipping address, that their credit has been checked, that products are available in inventory, and so on. Arrange shipping? That goes through the logistical modules of the ES. Check whether their bill has been settled? They have to have online access to financial systems. Virtually all Internet transactions have to be connected with basic transaction systems and databases, and it won't do if they are unintegrated and unresponsive.

Many companies are planning close electronic interfaces over the Internet with supply chain partners, including customers, suppliers, and distributors. These relationships will be much easier to build and maintain if the underlying transaction systems are in order. It may even come to pass that companies share ESs across an industry or a supply chain; anyone who doesn't have one—or even some who don't have the right one—may be left behind.

Dealing with constant change. It's certainly a cliché that change in business is constant today, but a cliché can be true, and this one is. Virtually every company has to be prepared for rapid changes in strategy, organizational structure, alliances, and market relationships. And since information and IT are becoming increasingly integrated with business activities, companies will require flexibility in their information systems as well.

As I mentioned earlier, ESs have been criticized for being inflexible, and they can be difficult to change. However, there is a paradoxical aspect to the flexibility issue: Standardization can lead to increased flexibility. Many companies feel that by having a single, logically structured, and common information technology platform worldwide, they can more easily adapt to changes in their business environments. Certainly a well-implemented ES will be more flexible than a hodge-podge of legacy systems with complex interfaces between them. And ES vendors are working on making their systems more flexible. I believe strongly that having an ES in place will be a considerable advantage to companies that need to change their ways of doing business frequently and rapidly.

There's every reason to believe that ESs will be even more valuable in the future than they are in the present. Just in case you're not yet sold on the importance of these systems, I'll give you a quick preview of what I think will be the future of ESs and the businesses that use them, which is the primary focus of chapter 9 as well.

WHERE ARE ENTERPRISE SYSTEMS LEADING US?

Let's think big for a moment. What are the business and economic implications of ESs? Other than a massive shift of resources from industrial firms to software and consulting organizations, what difference does it make that ESs were invented? Most of the news, I believe, is positive.

Enterprise systems can lead to greater productivity and efficiency in advanced economies. They can help companies squeeze out unneeded inventory, cut time and cost out of core business processes, and produce only what the market demands. Call it what you want: "lean production," "mass customization," or "just-in-time" manufacturing. And when companies figure out how to employ the information resident in their ESs, they'll be able to manage better, making changes in reporting and other management processes, with fewer managers. Companies and economies that make broad use of ESs can expect to grow faster, be more profitable, and increase their productivity more than those that don't.

Enterprise systems can also lead to interorganizational transformations and empires of business alliances. Today firms implementing ESs are largely internally focused; tomorrow they can be directed to creating linkages between firms. Enterprise systems can lead to closer, more efficient relationships among companies and their customers and suppliers. New clusters of organizations and new forms of relationships between firms will emerge. ES-enabled *keiretsu*—the tight relationships between customer and supplier firms long admired in Japan—can occur on a different basis in the West.

There is a possible downside to these changes, however. The greatest risk is to the people who work in the companies and societies transformed by ESs. Such organizations may require substantially fewer employees because they are more efficient. Employees who do remain will probably be asked to master a broader range of information-enabled tasks. This learning will be beneficial for them, but difficult to accomplish. I hope that companies will grow sufficiently rapidly because of the positive benefit flows from ESs that any negative effects on employees are minimized. Because increasing skills can take a long time, companies need to begin planning for the impact of an ES on people at the earliest opportunity.

New "virtual industries" formed by ES connections may lead to inflexibility. When customers, vendors, and vendors' suppliers are all linked electronically, they may find it difficult to disentangle themselves. Japanese keiretsu networks, once praised, are now being pointed to as a reason behind the country's extended downturn.

Another scary long-term outcome of the enterprise application movement is that the basis for competition in industries will change dramatically. Today, most companies compete on distinctive business strategies and processes. One company in an industry might offer high levels of customer service, for example, whereas another focuses on product innovation. In industries in which every major company is adopting an ES, or even the same vendor's ES, it's quite possible that identical strategies and processes will result. Every company will be focusing on leanness and don't-make-one-until-we-sell-one efficiencies. Every company will be focusing on getting better information about what's happening in its distribution channels. Everybody will be trying to be the most integrated, cost-efficient producer in the industry.

Some data exists about what happens when everybody in an industry has roughly the same information-enabled business strategy and capability. The airline industry—at least in the United States, but increasingly worldwide as well—offers an interesting case study. When every airline got hold of the same basic reservation systems, yield management systems, and frequent-flyer programs, the basis for competition changed quickly. The companies that succeeded were those that reduced service, went to hub-and-spoke distribution networks, and managed costs down. The near-perfect airline ticket information market, in which every competitor knows through their information systems what everyone else is charging, shrunk margins considerably. Only one airline—Southwest—departed from that strategy, and it is the only airline to remain consistently profitable over the past ten years.

Unless companies are smart about how their ESs support their strategies, and vice versa, they may find themselves in the same situations as the major U.S. air carriers (which, thanks to a booming economy, are doing well today—but no one knows how long this situation will last). There may also be opportunities to prosper through the avoidance of industry-wide systems, as Southwest did with its minimal airline reservation system and its manual, but highly efficient, business processes. What is clear over the long run is that companies will have to devote considerable thought to how ESs affect the basis for competition in their industries.

THE STRUCTURE OF THIS BOOK

In this chapter I've introduced you to why companies adopt ESs and given an overview of how these systems work. More detailed information about the technology itself can be found in the book's appendix. This chapter was largely at the big picture, strategic level. However, if you're going to discuss how to really get value from enterprise systems, at times you have to get specific concerning what works and what doesn't. In this brief overview I'll identify which chapters are more strategic and high level, and which get into lots of detail.

In chapter 2 I discuss, also at a broad, strategic level, the promise and peril of ESs, using examples from firms that have implemented—or in some cases, attempted to implement—them. In this chapter I discuss in detail the types of business benefits that are available from ESs and begin to lay out how to achieve them. In chapter 3, the focus is whether to implement an ES within your organization, with detailed discussion of doing a business case and selecting a specific vendor's software. Note the word "detailed"—if you've already decided to put in an ES, a quick skim of this chapter will probably be all you'll want.

In chapters 4 and 5, I continue the thread of how organizations need to think about ESs before implementing them. Chapter 4 addresses strategy and organizational structure issues. Chapter 5 is directed at process and information change within ES-enabled firms: Are these systems being used to change how firms do their work and how they communicate with common information? Both chapters are written at a high level and shouldn't bog anyone down.

In chapter 6 I assume that you've decided to go for it and actually put an ES in place. The chapter is all about the implementation process itself. A variety of implementation options and issues are addressed, with several in-depth examples of company experiences. As you might guess, it's a topic that requires a lot of detail; again, if your system is already more or less in place, skimming is recommended.

The next several chapters discuss specific aspects of the organization that need to change if an ES is going to bring business value. Very few firms and managers can say that they have mastered the subjects in these chapters, which are generally high level and future oriented. In chapter 7 I focus on needed changes in how managers use ES information to actually manage differently. Chapter 8 addresses some actual and potential changes to supply chains—a key potential benefit for many firms.

Chapter 9 looks into the future—both of ESs themselves and of organizations that use them. After reading it you may not know whether to buy stock in ES vendors, but you'll have a better idea of why they'll be selling their wares in the next five to ten years.

An appendix discussing how ESs work and describing some of their more technical aspects is, well, appended at the end. It's intended for nontechnical readers who want to learn a bit more about the technology.

2

THE PROMISE AND PERILS OF ENTERPRISE SYSTEMS

ENTERPRISE SYSTEM PROJECTS CAN YIELD DRAMATIC BENEFITS, mostly in the form of more efficient business processes. Or they can yield no benefit at all while still costing hundreds of millions of dollars to install. The choice is yours. What will it be?

Most companies would, all other things being equal, choose the benefits. But all other things are not equal. Choosing to get business benefits from an ES project means treating it as a business project, not a technical one. It means setting up clearly defined objectives at the beginning, and monitoring their achievement throughout the life of the project. It means putting business executives in charge—not technical managers—who can make the organizational changes necessary to achieve benefits. And like all business projects, achieving benefits from ES projects requires a tough-mindedness: When benefits aren't achieved, paychecks must be smaller and heads must roll. Put more positively, there must be incentives for the project to be successful, and they must affect all managers, not only those involved in the project.

There is an equally clear recipe for benefits disaster in ES projects. First, make the goal of the project just to get the system in. Justify the lack of business benefits with reference to Year 2000 problems or an impending merger or whatever works for you. Don't even think about what kinds of business processes you need or want; just adopt those that work most easily with the system. Keep senior management out of the whole process—involve only IT people. Turn everything over to consultants, and don't provide them with incentives to finish quickly or to share their knowledge with you.

I'm making it sound as if it's easy to stay on the side of business benefits. But often it isn't; the waters get muddied quickly. Most companies have multiple objectives in mind when they implement an ES, objectives that are both business and technically oriented. They want better business processes and to survive Y2K. They want to link up with suppliers and also to replace that antiquated billing system. Because focusing on business benefits means redesigning processes, organizational structures, and strategies, it can take substantially longer to implement an ES when business objectives are the primary focus. But what's the alternative? Spending millions for purely technical benefits is not very appealing either.

CASE STUDIES OF ENTERPRISE SYSTEM PROMISE

Most companies must keep a fine balance between getting the system in and getting benefit from it. For some companies, success might be defined as getting the system in quickly with minimal business disruption. For others, substantially improved business processes or the ability to conduct business in an entirely new way would be necessary for success to be declared. Let's look at three concrete examples of how companies have wrestled with these objectives. Keep in mind that even the most promising ES implementations can feel perilous at times.

BAY NETWORKS

Bay Networks, a large networking equipment company formed by the merger of smaller firms and recently acquired by Northern Telecom (forming the new company Nortel Networks), illustrates the fast implementation scenario.[1] The professed objective of the project was not any specific business or process goal, but rather putting in the system quickly and operating the merged business on one system. The company's previous systems were stretched to the limit by 1995 and were perceived as a barrier to future growth.

Bay's managers made an explicit decision to deemphasize process reengineering in favor of a fast installation. As the project manager put it, "We took SAP and made changes [to our business processes] as required by SAP. If SAP was lacking in some areas, we made some minor tweaks to it, but mostly we kept to what SAP could do." This strategy is not recommended if you want a unique operations strategy or order-of-magnitude process improvements, but it is probably essential if you want to install a complex ES quickly—and Bay's implementation was partially completed (installed and working in several geographical areas) in only nine months.

Bay Networks did have some subsidiary business goals, primarily in the area of order management and customer service. The company did improve its ability to schedule orders and match them to production capabilities—a common goal for a high-technology ES implementation. Order scheduling had previously taken four to five days, but after SAP was installed, a same-day turnaround in this process became routine. Because of system constraints, the company had previously been unable to generate financial reports at busy transaction times (e.g., ends of financial quarters), and that constraint was eased with the new system.

Of course, just as companies seeking business benefits need to manage their achievement carefully, you don't put in SAP in nine months without careful project management. Each phase of the project was carefully planned, and scope changes were resisted. Modifications to SAP were minimized. "Friday night fights" addressed any outstanding scope issues, since no one could go home until they were resolved. And Andersen Consulting, Bay's systems integrator for the project, was given special incentives to get the system in on time.

ELF ATOCHEM

Elf Atochem North America, an $11 billion petrochemical branch of the French oil giant, struck a compromise between a reasonably fast installation and a strong focus on measurable business benefits.[2] In fact, the company's ES project is one of the strongest I have seen with respect to benefit management and measurement. Elf is in its fifth year of work with SAP's R/3 and is approximately 90 percent complete with its project. Its primary focus has been on process improvement benefits. The company defined four new business processes and set up improvement goals for them. In several cases, the cost of doing business before the new system was calculated. For example, reconciliations among the several different cost systems across the company cost $3.4 million per year. Underleveraged purchase agreements, the company figured, were costing it $200 million per year. Eliminating these costs became a big part of Elf's justification for the new system.

Perhaps the most important benefits to Elf, however, involved customer service issues. The company competes in many commodity chemical markets in which service and price are the only possible sources of differentiation. For example, it previously took several calls for an Elf customer to place and confirm an order; now "one call does it all" in most cases. This is expected to lead to both better customer retention and slightly improved sales.

Each of the process benefits was converted into a financial return. No individual category is overwhelming in terms of the level of benefit, but overall the benefits from changed processes and the new system that supports them are expected to increase net earnings by more than 20 percent, or $45 million. The company is already saving more than $10 million per year and has already paid back its investment before finishing installation.

Surely one reason why Elf has achieved these benefits thus far is its approach to managing benefits. The money and other organizational resources required to put the ES in place are viewed as an investment like any other. Every cost and every benefit is itemized and tracked. New metrics have been developed to assess things that were previously unmeasurable, such as forecast accuracy. A full-time project team member is devoted to cost and benefit measurement issues. Executive compensation is tied to achievement of benefits.

DOW CHEMICAL

Dow Chemical's SAP implementation is one of the earliest, longest-lasting, and most global ES projects in the United States, but the company has clearly achieved a commensurate level of business benefit to show for its efforts. Dow's objective was to achieve common processes and information worldwide in its financial and administrative processes. It replaced a hodgepodge of existing systems with a single global one and created a platform for the integration of many acquisitions.

In customer-facing processes such as order management, Dow managers relied on the ES project to support a new set of customer service concepts called "Diamond Service." Substantial improvements in service processes have resulted and are visible both internally and to customers.

Dow has also achieved one of the greatest ES-enabled transformations of any company I've seen in terms of using its SAP data to manage the company. Enterprise system data has been used to stock a broad set of data repositories supporting a process view of the organization. It has also been used as the basis for information support of a new management approach called *value-based management,* in which shareholder value and profitability are emphasized. Literally thousands of users have been trained in the use of the SAP data to understand business operations and to make better decisions.

In short, although the ES implementation at Dow was quite expensive and time-consuming (due in part to the company being an early adopter of the technology), the company's managers are quite pleased with the results. The ES initiative involved substantially successful changes in business processes, a tighter, more integrated organizational structure, and much better management information. Managers at Dow recently finished a postimplementation evaluation (a rarity in itself) that took a conservative approach to the issue and didn't consider costs averted, only actual cost savings. The analysis still found that the project achieved a 15 percent return on investment (ROI) and a positive net present value. Dow expects that the project will lead to hundreds of millions of dollars in free cash over the life of the system. The project is clearly a success story and an illustration that success doesn't come easily.

CASE STUDIES OF ENTERPRISE SYSTEM PERILS

The case studies that follow are of organizations that achieved no positive business outcomes from their ES projects. They are dramatic cases in that they involve outright failure to complete large ES initiatives. However, keep in mind that there are many less dramatic examples of companies that did put systems in but achieved little or no benefit from their efforts. These quiet failures are just as worrisome as the more visible ones.

A EUROPEAN OIL COMPANY

Euroil (not its real name; I promised the company confidentiality), the European refining and marketing entity of a large U.S. oil firm, had a model implementation of its ES underway. The business unit had previously been a loose collection of twelve country-based organizations, with little coordination between them. Some of the twelve needed new systems, and some had adequate information environments. Coincident with the rise of Europe as a single trading entity in the early 1990s, Euroil's management team decided to "merge" the different countries into one highly coherent operation. They realized that they needed new software to support the integrated organization, and began a pilot project with the mainframe version (R/2) of SAP's ES. In the course of the trial, Euroil managers realized that the system needed to be highly similar throughout Europe to achieve efficiencies of scale and commonality in business processes. When country-level variations in how SAP was being implemented began to occur, Euroil senior managers reasoned that if they didn't have country managers anymore, then those managers wouldn't try to customize the ES to their needs. So they simply eliminated the country management role.

Things were going fairly swimmingly in the company until 1996, Euroil's eighth year of SAP implementation. Almost all of the European business was now supported by SAP, and common data and processes had been propagated throughout the continent. Euroil began to see cost savings from some of these large-scale common processes, such as purchasing for example, which could now be handled on a centralized basis. But in 1996, executives of the parent company decided to combine its European refining and marketing business with another oil company's in Europe. Apparently the negotiations about which system to use were brief. The CEO of the other company was on record as being very negative about large, complex ESs, preferring smaller, interconnected applications. And his technical staff argued that its own homegrown client/server systems were technically superior to Euroil's mainframe system. If Euroil had insisted on preserving SAP, one manager told me, "It would have been a deal-breaker." So eight years of work and about $250 million went down the drain with this merger.

It would be difficult to say that long-term business benefits were achieved in the project. I should point out, however, that the combined firms say they expect to achieve about $500 million in annual cost savings from the merger overall, so perhaps the monetary loss is not as troublesome. Interestingly, when the combined firm acquired a third firm, another SAP user, a new study was undertaken (not yet complete as I write) about whether to use the package throughout the firm after all.

So what's the lesson here? We know that all sorts of things change dramatically when companies decide to merge. Could the problem with the merger have been anticipated? Some managers told me that the pending merger had been discussed at high levels for several years, but the systems implications were never addressed until the merger discussions were very far along. In the past, postponing the discussion of systems issues until the last minute may not have been wise, but it was rarely a fatal error. Now, however, with ESs the ante has been raised considerably. If a company doesn't foresee organizational changes that might threaten its ES project, it risks losing thousands of person-years and hundreds of millions of dollars.

However, there is some ground for optimism in this story. When firms with different ES packages merge and one is thrown away, all is not lost. It's likely that the two firms share similar beliefs about the value of an ES to a business: integration across functions, common data and processes, and the value of real-time information availability. Achieving similar views of these issues in a merged organization can be much more difficult than replacing one ES with another, even if the costs of achieving consensus are much less visible than the writeoffs resulting from cancelling the installation of a particular package.

A PERSONAL COMPUTER FIRM

Unknown Computer (an alias by request of the company), a successful manufacturer of personal computers, has been somewhat less successful in the realm of enterprise systems. In 1994, Unknown joined the first wave of U.S. companies to adopt SAP's R/3 enterprise software. The "BigSys" project (not the real name) called for the software to be installed in three successive phases in each of Unknown's geographic units: first Europe, then the Americas, and finally Asia-Pacific.

The business justification for installing an ES was that Unknown was a global company with consistent business operations around the world that could all benefit from the integration that an ES offered. In a letter to employees, the senior vice president and chief operating officer, the primary sponsor of the project, wrote, "[Project BigSys] is a cornerstone of two of our corporate priorities—infrastructure and systems, and globalization." The COO and others at Unknown imagined being able to assess worldwide inventory positions and forecast product needs using a single view of all the company's different regions. To help create that single view, Unknown would try to standardize its business processes around the world and capture them in R/3.

Though a worthy and ambitious goal, it was mostly technical. Aside from creating a global view through SAP, Unknown didn't declare any operational goals other than a general desire to support its growth. The prevailing sense that Unknown needed to replace its current computer systems also distracted the project leadership from a firm business rationale. The existing manufacturing system, for example, was limited in its ability to handle large numbers of digits in part numbers. As Unknown grew, the system ran out of available part numbers, forcing managers to retire old part numbers to handle new components.

Making matters worse, Unknown's overall business strategy shifted during the course of the SAP project. The COO, who had come to the company from another firm with a highly decentralized structure, dropped his original goal of achieving globalization through common processes and began focusing instead on a more decentralized approach in which geographic and product units retained their autonomy. He didn't reconcile the new vision of Unknown with the continuing SAP project, at least not for several years.

Without clear business goals, the SAP project team had difficulty focusing on clear, achievable benefits. Project memos spoke of vague outcomes without defining clear metrics to track progress toward those outcomes. "[BigSys] will result in significantly reduced expense, increased revenue opportunities, and improved customer satisfaction," said one project memo. "Additionally, [BigSys] will provide more accurate and timely information about our business, and will establish an environment that can more readily adapt to change." Unknown didn't attach any specific numbers to its expected financial, process, or customer satisfaction outcomes. Very specific, however, was the dramatic level of resources devoted to the project: 160 people total (100 internal, 60 consultants), all working full-time. The cost in actual dollars approached $225 million, but that didn't factor in the losses from taking all those people away from their regular jobs at a very fast-growing company. In addition, that cost was to finish what was estimated to be only a third of the project.

Meanwhile, most of Unknown's competitors were already using or installing SAP. "How does [Unknown] gain a competitive advantage if other companies are using the same software to do the same thing?" asks a member of the Sales and Distribution module team in a project newsletter. "To leverage [Unknown's] strengths and maximize our competitive advantages, we must use the software to uniquely design and support our business." True enough, but there was no clear idea of how to do that.

Finding and expressing those unique processes took a long time. Unknown's consultant recommended that the company undertake three different analyses of the relevant processes: where they were now, where they'd like to be optimally, and where they could be with the capabilities of SAP. The plan was to evolve toward the optimal state over time. It took more than a year to do all these analyses on paper, however. Translating them into SAP-compliant processes within the software promised to take even longer.

As Unknown began building those processes into the software, it ran into another common problem with ESs: The system put an extraordinary load on the company's networks and computer servers. The greatest blessing of ESs is also their worst technology curse: As employees enter transactions into the system, the system begins automatically routing that information all around the company, setting off a kind of information explosion that can wreak havoc on the network and an underpowered computing architecture. Unknown upgraded its servers twice (even eschewing its own products to handle the tremendous loads), but the response time of the application remained very slow. By the end of the project, there was some optimism that the current European transaction volume targets could be met, but nobody was sanguine about the United States, or future, volume targets.

When employees at the company began to tinker with prototypes of the new system, they didn't like what they saw. Customer service representatives saw the number of screens they used to process an order jump from four to twelve with the new system. That's when Unknown's board began to get jumpy and eventually cut back the project dramatically. Unfortunately, Unknown's project team did not involve actual users in the development process until the last minute. They could have saved a lot of money by thinking about what it would be like to live with the system earlier on in the project.

In December 1996 the project was canceled, although some pieces of SAP had been installed. The Human Resources module had already been installed in Europe and was still planned to be installed in the United States. But as a true ES, the project was moribund.

The lesson from Unknown is not to change business models in midstream. Enterprise systems can be used in highly centralized firms, and they can be adapted to highly decentralized organizations. It doesn't work well, however, to change from a centralized to a decentralized approach in the same project. Even if Unknown had succeeded in putting its ES in place, it would probably not have received real business value from its system because its business objectives for the project were never clear in the first place.

GENERAL SEMICONDUCTOR

General Semiconductor (not its real name) is one of the world's largest manufacturers of semiconductor equipment (i.e., machines to make semiconductors). The company is generally quite successful; it's one of the fastest-growing firms in a fast-growing industry. However, like Unknown, General has not been terribly successful in implementing ESs, having already cancelled a major SAP project and fallen behind schedule on a second project using Oracle software. I'm not privy to all the details about why the project didn't succeed, but I have a pretty good idea.

General has a very distinctive culture. It's one in which the firm's engineers will work hard, think creatively, and jump through all kinds of hoops to make the sale or ship the order. It's a dynamic, aggressive, customer-focused organization—but it's not terribly disciplined. These hard-charging engineers have very little patience for such abstractions as process, infrastructure, or common information. Their work is a mad dash to get the product out the door and get the customer off their backs. No one even wants to spend time telling a consultant or systems analyst how he or she does his or her job so that a system could support it better. Each project is viewed as a one-off exercise, and it predictably becomes one.

I'm sure it was difficult to explain why General was spending over $100 million on infrastructure, commonality, and process betterment when no one really believed in those concepts. Sure, somebody at the top must have believed in them enough to sign the checks, but at General everybody seemed to feel deep down that the organization was successful with its existing culture, so why change it? Of course, General is a technically oriented organization, and the SAP system was criticized internally for being lacking in technical functionality and for having potential problems in meeting technical performance objectives. But my view is that these technical arguments masked an unwillingness to change the organization in the needed ways. Even if the SAP system had been installed successfully, the organization would have surely chafed under its day-to-day use. And I doubt that the somewhat less structured and complex Oracle system will fare much better than SAP R/3 did at General.

The lesson here is that organizations will encounter great peril when the system they seek to install does not fit their culture. If your company doesn't care about business processes beforehand, buying an ES package won't change that aspect of the culture. If your company doesn't care much about information, an ES also isn't a good fit. (The chief information officer of one company now installing an ES, a large apparel firm, once said that his company really didn't care much about information, preferring to "shoot from the hip" in making decisions and taking actions. Any guesses about how that ES project will fare?)

LEARNING FROM SUCCESS AND FAILURE

What can we learn from these cases? How do we generalize from success in creating business benefit and avoid the visible or the quiet failures? The remainder of this chapter will be devoted to the specific lessons of ES implementations from the standpoint of business outcomes and benefits.

MAKE IT A BUSINESS INITIATIVE

In most of the quiet failures to achieve business benefits, the culprit is failing to make the project part of the business's overall objectives and to put business, not technology, managers in charge. This is becoming a shopworn maxim in ES management, but there is no more accurate statement in the ES world. It means that one should give the ES project all the accoutrements of senior executive involvement—time spent, emotional commitments made, and money at risk.

At a biotechnology equipment company, the SAP implementation project was a business project from the beginning. The ES project team worked with business unit managers to define success factors. The division president made it clear that the project was the top priority, not just in a single department, but in the entire division. Many managers' bonuses were tied to the success of the ES project. Of course, some managers were less committed than others, but ES virtue was rewarded. "You could clearly see that the ones who were just paying it lip service or going along because it was politically correct didn't get the same level of benefits as the ones who were committed," the project leader noted.[3]

A STRONG OUTCOMES ORIENTATION

The most important single lesson is the need for an orientation to outcomes and benefits, whatever their specific content. Outcomes include such benefits as financial improvements, process improvements, reductions in inventory, improvements to customer service, or reductions in product or service defects. Outcomes are definable in advance and measurable. They have value to the business or to its customers.

What does the absence of an outcomes focus look like? It's easy to find in companies. First, the only real goal seems to be getting the system in, and even that may not have firm deadlines and project plans. Another symptom is seen when companies justify their ES project on the basis of documented benefits and documented costs, but everyone seems to have forgotten about the documents several years into the project. In one workshop of twelve companies at which ES implementation was discussed, the initial budgets and justifications seemed to be something of a joke in about half of the companies.[4] The lack of outcomes orientation is also notable in companies where vague criteria for success are espoused: "We want our processes to be consistent worldwide"; "We want better information for decision making"; "We want to upgrade our legacy systems environment."

There is only one acceptable benefits orientation that involves simply putting in a new system and not achieving other benefits: the case in which an organization must put in a new ES or go out of business. This logic was most commonly encountered in relation to Year 2000 projects. Perhaps there were companies that would go out of business in 2000 if they did not fix their systems. However, it is normally cheaper to fix existing systems than to put in a new ES package; the added cost of an ES can generally be justified only through improvements in business capability.

If getting the system installed is necessary to stay in business, then its installation should be made an obsession. It should be done as quickly and cheaply as possible. Everyone in the organization should be informed that getting the system in and adapting to its requirements is the first priority; no dissension or discussion can be allowed about modifying the system or preserving idiosyncratic ways of doing business.

For most organizations, however, the system isn't necessary to stay in business, and the emphasis should be on achieving real outcomes. The outcomes must be decided upon in advance by business people who understand what's possible from an ES and what's needed by the business. They may need substantial education on the former set of issues, such as what can be asked of an ES in terms of the better processes it supports or the better financial performance it enables. They should treat the decision to put in an ES like any other major investment: It should meet hurdle rates, be monitored regularly at management meetings, and become an essential part of management evaluation and compensation plans.

In addition to education, there are several other means of articulating an organization's outcomes. Managers can articulate the organization's critical success factors, that is, those things that must go well if the organization is to succeed. That will direct management attention to the key processes that an ES implementation should support. Another approach is to start externally—to survey customers or analyze competitors with regard to business requirements that need to be met. A company could also go through a traditional strategic planning exercise to articulate ES project goals, but in such an effort more energy should be focused on operational plans than financial or business growth objectives, since these may be difficult to convert into the implications for an ES.

The responsibility for achieving these outcomes should belong to every senior executive—otherwise, the pervasive and cross-functional nature of the business change engendered by an ES won't be managed well. However, the ownership for the achievement of results can't be totally diffused throughout the organization. Some senior executive has to feel that his or her career is on the line based on whether the ES project succeeds or fails. Depending on which modules of ES functionality are desired, the right executive may be a chief operations officer, a chief financial officer, or, if the application is sufficiently broad, even the company's CEO. In fact, a survey of 200 CEOs suggests that they are the most likely role to sponsor an ES initiative, ahead of chief financial, operations, or information officers.[5] Of course, different managers may have different notions of what "sponsorship" means.

Though there needs to be a single owner for the benefits, he or she must have the strong backing of the organization. Everyone in the company should feel that this systems-driven reengineering effort is one of the most important projects of the time. Everyone should understand that changes are going to have to be made, not for the good of the system itself, but for improved organizational performance and a better fit between the information system and the rest of the organization. The outcomes should be publicized not only to employees, but also to external stakeholders, such as stockholders and analysts.

At Owens Corning, for example, desired project outcomes for a major implementation of SAP were packaged for internal and external consumption in an initiative called Advantage 2000. The goals were printed on reference cards for all employees, distributed to and discussed with Wall Street analysts, and summarized in the company's annual report. The goal of publicizing the outcomes to this degree was to keep the pressure on company managers to actually deliver what they promised. And if the project wasn't relevant to the company's shareholder value, CEO Glen Hiner reasoned, it shouldn't be done at all. Therefore considerable energy was put into making the project of importance to shareholders; operational improvements were translated into their implications for key financial performance indicators.

Of course, in a project as complex as a large ES effort, changes in objectives may take place over time. It's all right to change goals in midstream as the organization learns more about itself and the system. What doesn't make sense is to quietly forget about goals and to bury previous statements about benefits and their relation to costs. An ES project is certainly a voyage of discovery; no one should pretend, however, that the voyage never had a destination.

A CLEAR VISION OF "WHO WE ARE"

Because an ES is intimately intermingled with the organizational structure and function of a company, it's vitally important that companies have a clear sense of who and what they are before embarking on an ES project. Are they a diversified conglomerate in which business units share only financial information? Are they an integrated business in which functions are tightly knit? If they're in between, where on the spectrum of integration and business cohesiveness do they lie?

At a workshop on ES implementation, none of the managers from twelve companies felt that their executives had a clear view of "who they were" before beginning their ES projects. Six of the twelve noted that the lack of a clear corporate identity had already led to problems in their projects. My work with other companies suggests that this is a substantial problem at almost all organizations. It was a key factor in the failure of Unknown's ES implementation: The company started the project believing that it was an integrated business worldwide, but halfway through the implementation, the management team decided that the company was geographically autonomous.

Before starting to implement an ES, a company should have a good handle on the following sets of issues:

▶ What kind of organization are we today? How strongly embedded in the culture is our current identity, and how hard would it be to change it?

▶ What kind of organization do we want to be when we finish with our ES project and the associated organizational changes?

▶ What factors in our marketplace and business environment are moving us in this direction? What factors might retard our movement?

▶ What specifically would have to change for us to get from where we are today to where we want to be?

In chapter 4 I'll describe some of the key alternatives for corporate organization and structure as it relates to ESs. It's important to say here, however, that the key questions concerning organization involve how much commonality—of information, process design and execution, and business rules—there is across the organization.

If the organization is a conglomerate, the only common element may be using dollars as the common currency for reporting of financial results. One European conglomerate, for example, installed more than 400 different versions of the same ES and couldn't even consolidate all of the corporate financial information without heavy manual intervention. At the other extreme, if the organization is a fully integrated firm, almost everything will need to be commonly defined in order to coordinate operations across functions and units.

A few words about the process for determining identity are in order. Although knowing what you are as an organization seems an obvious point, there are no obvious venues for most organizations to debate and discuss it. An issue of this magnitude should be discussed by the board of directors and the entire senior management team. The discussion should not be high level and abstract; someone should generate a set of specific examples about specific processes or units of information. "What are the implications of having one customer list worldwide?" is an example of an appropriate issue.

STRATEGIC CLARITY

In the same category of "things that need to be settled beforehand if you're going to get value from an ES" is the notion of strategic clarity—certainty as to what business the company is in, how it delivers value to customers, and how it differentiates itself from competitors in the marketplace. We'll discuss the strategy implications of ESs in chapter 4. Here it is only important to point out that the strategic choices must be clearly defined or it is unlikely that they will be advanced by an ES. This is not a new issue: Companies for years have discovered when thinking about IT strategy that they didn't have a sufficiently clear business strategy on which to base IT applications. Enterprise systems only raise the stakes to new levels of cost and interdependency between technology and business.

One of the simpler ways to think about this issue is whether or not there is clarity and broad agreement on the company's choice of *value discipline,* or primary strategic goal. Is the organization devoted to product innovation, operational excellence, or customer intimacy? Aside from the fact that ESs may facilitate some value disciplines more than others (thus far, at least, ES vendors have not developed a high degree of functionality in the product innovation category), what is most important is that there is widespread agreement on the choice. If operational excellence is the goal (a good pairing with an ES in most cases), the company should work with diligence to define, improve, and measure the key processes on which it competes, and strive for a tight fit between the processes it needs and those supported by the system.

If, on the other hand, customer intimacy is the primary goal, the processes on which the organization should focus will primarily be customer-facing (marketing, sales, customer service), and the primary role of the ES will be to act as a repository for customer data. Early on in the history of enterprise packages, there were relatively few capabilities for the front-office activities involved in building customer intimacy. Now, however, several ES vendors have embraced sales force, service, and marketing analytics applications. Another common ES capability, order management, has always been relevant to the goal of customer intimacy.

The value disciplines idea is only one example of a strategic concept the organization can address. It may also be helpful to think about which aspects of an organization's value chain may be most affected by an ES, or how the ES might affect the Porter "competitive forces" model for the business. Looking externally, is the company going to go direct to market or work through distributors? This is currently a major issue in the personal computer industry, where firms like Hewlett-Packard, IBM, and Compaq (all of which are installing ESs) are wavering a bit on whether they should remain with the dealer channel in the face of aggressive direct competitors like Dell. It may be good strategy for them to question the viability of the channel, but if they make a shift it will undoubtedly wreak havoc with their ES projects. Again, the key point for this chapter is clarity, which means the strategy issue must be discussed by senior management, some consensus must be arrived at, and whatever conclusions are reached must be broadly circulated within the organization.

CONSTANCY OF PURPOSE

If an organization is going to receive benefit from its ES project, it appears to be very important to have a long-term constancy of purpose. This virtue is not widely known or celebrated today. Our system for supplying capital to publicly owned companies forces them to take a short-term focus, and nothing seems to be constant or inviolate. Yet an ES requires that an organization take the long view—as long as a decade or more—of its needs for information and its desires concerning how to run the business. It does not work well, for example, for an organization (like Unknown Computer) to decide in midproject that it wants to give substantially greater autonomy to business units. It is not felicitous when a company such as Euroil picks a merger partner after five years of installing a system, and the partner doesn't like that system.

Like strategic clarity, constancy of purpose has always been a virtue from the standpoint of information systems. For decades IT people have spoken somewhat ruefully about pouring "COBOL concrete" around the existing way of doing business, and it's never easy to change after a system has been implemented. But ESs are an order of magnitude more complex than systems of the past, and rarely have companies spent the kind of time and money that characterize today's ES projects on systems of the past. It's more important than ever (and perhaps more difficult than ever) to have a stable foundation on which to erect an enterprise information platform.

Constancy of purpose is a conspicuous aspect of an organization's culture. One can diagnose whether it exists fairly easily. How many major reorganizations has the company had in the past five years? If there were more than one or two, constancy may have been the victim. Has the company changed its basic business in the past decade? Have mergers or acquisitions been undertaken frequently? If the answer to these questions is yes, it's not necessarily a bad thing for the company, but it could be a bad thing for the company's ES project, at least if it's intended to support the entire organization. One approach to dealing with rapid change in corporate structure is to implement an ES not at the corporate level but rather at the individual business unit level. However, this strategy only provides constancy if you are highly confident that the current business unit structure will persist over a long period—an assumption not borne out in many firms.

If your company has relatively little constancy of purpose and you for some reason feel that an ES is necessary anyway, be careful how you go about installing it. If, for example, business units are often acquired and divested, you may want to implement multiple, relatively independent versions of the ES, each in its own business unit. If management teams change frequently, you may want to recruit very broad sponsorship so that if one or more managers depart you will still have the backing of others. If your company intends to acquire many other firms, you may want to discuss with your company's management team the idea that each acquired company will be rapidly converted to your particular brand of ES.

In short, companies should recognize that the demands of implementing an ES are somewhat at odds with the contemporary business environment. An ES needs stability, whereas today's business environment is in constant flux. If your company or industry is particularly change-ridden, you're probably better off avoiding a large, complex ES project in the first place.

Of course, it's difficult to predict the level of change in advance. Sometimes the entire organizational structure can change while an ES project is in midstream. At Perkin-Elmer Analytical Instruments (AI), for example, managers began their SAP implementation with the idea that their system would be largely common with another major division of their company, Applied Biosystems (AB). All of the system design work was done with the idea that AI would share information and processes with AB. However, a few months before they were to go live with the system, AI managers were told that they needed an entirely separate implementation. A smaller business unit was to be viewed as part of AI, but at the last minute it was moved over to AB. The reason for all this structural change was that AI was to be sold to another company, EG&G Inc. (which then recently adopted the Perkin-Elmer name).

Given the close fit needed between organizational structure and the SAP system, it's very difficult to configure this fit when one of the targets is constantly moving. The price at AI—and probably at any company with so much change underway—is that the business had to adopt fairly generic process models and then adapt their processes to the system rather than vice versa. However, at AI managers did succeed in getting the system running, which was a major accomplishment in itself under the changing circumstances.

TACTICS FOR BENEFIT REALIZATION

In addition to these strategic issues in getting benefits from an ES, there are a number of smaller, tactical guidelines that organizations can adopt to increase the likelihood of business value being achieved. Most of these have been adopted by at least one organization already. Each guideline is described in the following list, along with an example where possible.

▶ *Don't view going live as the end goal or the end of the project.* Most organizations with ES projects tend to view the "go live" date (the time at which the system is up and running basic business transactions) as the end goal; many view it as the end of the ES project. But that's indicative of a technical focus, not a business one. The real end of the project is when benefits are actually achieved. It may be that some of the reporting-oriented benefits of an ES will not be implemented for several years beyond when the system is first installed. At Dow Chemical, for example, well after the system went live the SAP team was working on integrating the SAP data with performance reporting systems and on developing measures of shareholder and business value that could be automatically produced by the system.

▶ *Deduct ES-related savings from budgets.* It is easy to put cost savings and other benefits into financial justifications for an ES project, but many times these will not be realized unless there are teeth for the savings. Corporate finance and accounting organizations should simply deduct planned savings—either monetary or head count based—from the operating budgets of units and functions. These groups will then have no choice but to actually implement the planned changes and savings. Monsanto, for example, focused particularly on reductions in plant financial personnel when it implemented a centralized ES. Many plant controller and accounting positions were eliminated on paper, and at the appropriate time were deducted from plant budgets. The plants had no options other than eliminating the positions or redeploying the controllers into other open positions.

► *Provide incentives to consultants to help deliver benefits.* Since consultants do a good chunk of the implementation of most ES projects, it's a good idea to motivate them to help achieve the benefits. Again, the goal is not to motivate consultants merely to get the system in, but rather to motivate them to help achieve business benefits. When process performance targets reach a certain level, for example, consultants could be paid a bonus. This forces consultants to address not only the technical side of the ES implementation, but also the human components and the overall business context of the work. At Farmland, a $10 billion farm cooperative, both project team members and external consultants are motivated with an incentive bonus plan based on achievement of metrics in a project scorecard. The scorecard measures not only project costs and timeliness but also achievement of such business goals as development of a shared services approach to administrative processes.[6]

► *Don't implement the software where benefits aren't high.* Given the all-encompassing nature of a contemporary ES, there is a tendency to put it everywhere within the business that it will fit. While there are benefits to a high level of integration, not every business domain will benefit equally from ES-supplied automation. The most economically beneficial approach is to implement an ES in those areas that are most strategically and financially rewarding and to put the remainder off until later or never. At Owens Corning, for example, the ES project was initially quite broad, involving most major business functions. But when the company ran into financial performance problems, managers concluded that some of the functions already had sufficient information support, and some could be addressed more cheaply and with less complexity through standalone packages. The ES project was reserved for those areas of the business where value would truly be delivered.

▶ *Measure baseline metrics at the start of the project.* As I'll describe further in chapter 5, companies are less likely today to go through a major exercise to understand existing business processes before modifying them with an ES. However, it's still important to measure existing processes before an ES project so that any improvements can be detected. It doesn't make sense to measure all processes, only those that are key objectives for improvement in the ES project.

▶ *Don't upgrade for technical reasons alone.* Enterprise system vendors supply frequent upgrades to their packages. In some cases these supply new business functionality; in other cases the improvements are purely technical. The decision on whether to upgrade should, like other aspects of the project, be based on business benefits. In most cases there will not be sufficient business benefit to justify installing every upgrade. Even in the case of a major technical upgrade— from the mainframe version of the software to a client/server version, for example—it may be wise to delay the upgrade as long as possible. At Dow Chemical, for example, one of the earliest firms to adopt the mainframe (R/2) version of SAP, company managers are resisting the trend to upgrade to the client/server version simply because the expense is high and they see no real business benefit in doing so. They will probably ultimately be forced into the change because of vendor support policies, but they are delaying the change as long as possible.

I'm sure there are other possible tactics for benefit realization. The point is to continually view the project in business terms and to continually ask whether there are better ways to achieve benefit as the project progresses. The strategic and the tactical issues interact; it's much easier, for example, to implement only high-value business domains and to measure baseline metrics when you have a clear business strategy and clear goals concerning where to focus the power of an ES.

Nothing in this chapter is a radical departure from what was presumed to be good practice in the past. Academics and consultants have stated for years that IT projects should be treated as business projects, with concomitant benefit management approaches. Some firms actually followed this advice, but not many. The fact that companies have spent literally trillions of dollars on IT projects with little apparent financial or productivity benefit indicates that benefit realization is insufficiently practiced. With the size and complexity of ES initiatives, it's particularly important to get one's act together in this regard.

3

SHOULD MY COMPANY IMPLEMENT AN ENTERPRISE SYSTEM?

DESPITE THE FACT THAT ALMOST EVERY COMPANY SEEMS TO BE putting in an enterprise system these days, doing so shouldn't be a foregone conclusion. Maybe you've already been scared off by the size, complexity, and cost of these things. Maybe you've heard that some companies have failed. Maybe you don't feel that you know enough to make an informed decision.

Well, you've come to the right place. In this chapter I describe all the factors you need to consider before deciding whether to put in an ES, and provide examples of companies that decided for and against implementing such a system (admittedly, it's been easier to find the former than the latter). But I'm not trying to sell you on the idea. Enterprise systems aren't for every organization, or for every part of an organization. The key, of course, is to think about how an ES fits with your business and its needs for information.

In preparing this chapter I was greatly helped by Susan Cantrell, a Boston University student who gathered materials and ideas for the chapter and interviewed Reebok and Nike managers.

Maybe you've already decided to implement an ES; maybe you're already well along in implementation. Hold on—don't skip to the next chapter. It's likely that you'll benefit by reading this chapter anyway, particularly the sections concerning benefit. Knowing what the possible types of benefit are that can be achieved in ES projects may help you derive some in-process or even postimplementation business value. I'm sure you're a very good manager, but you may have overlooked some possible sources of benefit along the way.

Although this book is primarily oriented to business, not technical, issues, I will consider both business and technical factors in the decision concerning whether to put in an ES. The fact is that many organizations make their decisions at least partially on technical grounds. The issues are not particularly difficult or complex from a technical standpoint, however, so a business-oriented reader should have no problem comprehending them. Throughout the chapter I'll describe the decision process of several companies, including some in the athletic shoe industry, just to compare firms within the same business.

This chapter also addresses the issue of how to decide among the different ES vendors. If you've already made this decision, you can safely skip that section unless you are a glutton for punishment and want to see if you made any mistakes!

ENTERPRISE SYSTEM PREREQUISITES

Before you even decide whether an ES is a good fit for your organization and begin to plan an implementation, you need to have a lot of diverse information at your disposal. Many organizations won't be fully equipped to make an informed ES decision because this kind of big decision doesn't come along very often. It may take several months just to gather all of the needed information; this effort won't be wasted even if you decide not to adopt an ES, however, because most of the information is useful for other purposes. The information is needed to address the following types of questions:

▶ In what shape is your data? How much do key data elements differ across the organization? For example, how many different meanings of the term *customer* can you find?

▶ How strong is your current group of employees in terms of ES-related skills? Can they design new processes, configure new systems, adapt to new ways of working, and manage a high degree of organizational change over time? Do they understand how specific ES packages work? How many "A-level" performers do you have available to work on an ES project?

▶ In what kind of shape is your technology infrastructure? Can your current servers, desktop systems, and networks support a major new application?

▶ What are the key strategies of your business, both at the corporate level and for business units, geographies, products, and so forth? If you can't articulate your strategies, you can't support them with a new information system.

▶ How much could your business afford to spend on a new ES? How would a major expenditure affect your balance sheet?

▶ How do most executives feel about the notion of an ES? Do they understand the nature and purpose of such systems, and do they agree that a more integrated, common, and functional set of backbone applications is necessary? What do they say about the idea, both publicly and privately? If they don't support it now, will they eventually line up behind the idea?

▶ Are there any major organizational changes, issues, or problems that you can already anticipate will take place over the next several years that would make a major ES project a bad idea?

Knowing the answers to these questions will help not only with deciding on an ES, but with implementing one. Make sure that when you address them someone records the answers and conclusions for later access. Monsanto, for example, articulated its basic strategy for data; technology; and the finance, order-to-collection, purchasing, and manufacturing processes in one short document before it began its ES project. The document—called the project "manifesto"—stated, for instance, that Finance would use one ledger world-wide, populated with data direct from its source, in near real time, untouched by local management. The many design decisions covered by this document greatly shortened—but did not fully eliminate—the subsequent debates about implementation details.

WHO DECIDES?

Whether or not to implement an ES shouldn't be a primarily technical decision. Therefore, the decision shouldn't be made primarily by technologists. The decision process should involve investigation by a group of business and technical executives within the company—typically working for several months unless some factor makes the outcome fairly obvious. Ultimately, because of the level of costs and business change involved in an ES project, the go/no go decision should be made by the CEO and the senior executive team, and probably the board of directors as well.

The technologists can educate the business people on how the technology works and the implications of particular technology choices. The business people can determine or articulate where the business is going and what the requirements imposed by particular business processes are. Jointly they can determine how the technology might influence the achievement of business objectives. The small group should present their conclusions to the entire senior management team. The board of directors should also be consulted, not just because the amount of money is substantial, but because of the business changes involved. After making the decision, it should be communicated to the entire organization, but in business rather than technical terms.

But if the decision to adopt an ES should be made by business people, technologists will have to play a much more active role in deciding *which* ES to select. Only hard-core systems experts can evaluate whether certain technical capabilities are really present; only IT people with substantial experience in dealing with software vendors can apply the correct amount of skepticism. Business people should be on the package selection team as well, however, to ensure that the proper high emphasis on business objectives and value is continued.

Both the business- and technology-oriented people who make the decisions about ESs should have the ability to be forward-thinking. As one manager put it, it's necessary to "shoot ahead of the duck" in thinking about ESs. A firm must think about what it will need two years ahead, not what it needs today. It doesn't work to wait for the challenge to be present before beginning to think about an ES project.

Decision makers must also be prepared to decide what not to do in an ES project. Limiting the scope of the work will be critical to the success of the effort. Several managers have told me that agreeing not to implement a particular aspect of the system, or not to attempt some add-on functionality, was one of their most difficult decisions.

To give a quick overview of some of the issues involved in deciding on an ES, I'll describe a case study that is fairly typical of many organizations' decision-making processes.

DECIDING TO IMPLEMENT AN ENTERPRISE SYSTEM: A CASE STUDY

EMC, a manufacturer of leading-edge data storage products, decided in 1998 to pursue an ES. Described by *Business Week* as "one of the hottest growth stories of the hot-growth 1990s," EMC hardly needed to put in an ES to hold its business together. Nor did it have a Year 2000 problem. EMC's decision to adopt an ES is rather a story of opportunity and growth.

In the summer of 1998, an internal "Business Process Development Center" (BPDC) group was chartered to look at the firm's business systems. EMC's information systems had evolved over time with no particular strategy. The company had addressed point-specific problems with point-specific applications; by 1998 there were over 250 different applications being used in the company, 70 of them meeting major information needs. A diagram of the existing applications architecture was called the "spaghetti chart" within EMC. The company's core manufacturing software, installed in 1991, was being phased out by its vendor, and there were two different versions of it for domestic and international business, requiring labor-intensive reconciliations each financial period.

Despite these issues, EMC's systems were not broken and met the company's needs, and any major Year 2000 problems had already been addressed. The decision to adopt a new ES was motivated by the dramatic growth the company's leaders planned. Michael Ruettgers, the EMC CEO, had informed the company and the outside world that EMC would have $10 billion in revenues in 2001, from a base of just under $4 billion in 1998. He felt that the company needed a stronger IT infrastructure to support more than doubling in size.

In late 1998 the BPDC recommended that the firm adopt an ES. It also recommended that the firm have one global ES as a backbone, and that any existing systems that were highly functional (e.g., its PeopleSoft human resources system) or still necessary to meet unique EMC functionality be interfaced to the ES. The company would also likely need, the BPDC felt, some bolt-on applications for some specific processes.

The BPDC commissioned a consultant to do an analysis of available packages. After mapping all key processes and comparing them with the functionality in alternative ES packages, a short list of three systems was selected. EMC also asked another consultant to prepare a business case for implementing an ES. The consultant interviewed all department heads and added together the projected process-by-process savings from implementing a system. The overall return came to $300 million in savings over five years. However, when the figure was presented to Ruettgers, he was not impressed. He pointed out that the savings amounted to only 1 percent of EMC's spending levels over five years.

Ruettgers suggested that much greater benefits could be identified and achieved by making individual managers responsible for them. He asked the financial organization to calculate the remaining funds after deducting a specified gross margin from the $10 billion that EMC would generate in 2001 revenues. The amount would be divided proportionally among departments. With the department heads knowing how much they could spend by 2001, they were then encouraged to determine how they could use the ES system to achieve more effective and efficient processes by that time. EMC's management team was initially resistant to the idea of an ES, but after being educated at a key team meeting in early 1999, enthusiasm levels rose markedly.

EMC managers expect benefits all across the company, but there are some specific areas that are being strongly anticipated. Order processing efficiency, for example, is a key goal. The company also has a strong need to understand global sales for a given customer. Some of these benefits will provide better customer service; others will allow rapid growth with the efficiencies that EMC's goals require.

EMC is now on the verge of selecting a specific package. The company expects to install its system by early 2001 and refine it throughout the year. A new group has already been formed to implement the software, new processes, and needed organizational changes. It will report directly to Ruettgers, and will have the same status as the company's four business units. The company is putting in an organizational infrastructure to parallel its new technical infrastructure.

BUSINESS AND TECHNICAL FACTORS IN AN ENTERPRISE SYSTEM EVALUATION

As the EMC story illustrates, it's impossible—or at least undesirable—to treat business and technical factors in an ES evaluation separately. Business factors create the need for technical functionality; technical limitations create business risk. Therefore, I'm going to consider the two sets of factors jointly, and if you can't tell which I'm addressing at any moment, we could even consider that a good sign.

Cost versus Benefit and the Business Case

Perhaps the most common analysis that companies make is cost versus benefit: Will it cost more to implement these systems than the financial benefits that will be delivered? This analysis is usually done in the context of a business case. The business case may include nonfinancial factors, as was the case at EMC, but financial issues and calculations are generally the stars of the show.

It's a good idea to do some sort of business case. Even if financial justification isn't that important to your organization (and a surprising number of firms feel that way), doing a business case will focus you and your organization on the business value you expect to achieve from the ES and associated business changes. It's in the business case that you specify the types of process, competitive, or financial capabilities the organization will have when implementation is over. If you intend to make better and faster decisions with ES data, that should go in the business case. If you expect that your customers will order more from you because they can place orders from the Internet, order all your products in one transaction, and find out whether items are out of stock at the time of order, then you should say so (and say how much more you think they'll order) in the business case. Granted, it's a lot easier to state these anticipated benefits in a business case than it is to actually achieve them. However, it's not likely that you'll achieve benefits if you haven't planned for them in advance and told the world about it in a business case.

Despite all of these potential benefits, many firms don't even do a formal business case. Just what percentage of firms do and don't seems to vary across samples. When Andersen Consulting interviewed about 200 CEOs on ES issues, 62 percent said their company had developed a business case. This survey revealed substantial benefits from doing one. In the companies that had prepared a business case, 85 percent of the CEOs said they felt comfortable with their understanding of ESs; in companies with no business case, only 44 percent felt comfortable. The CEOs who hadn't insisted on a business case were also 50 percent more likely to express dissatisfaction with ES business results.[1] A second survey of sixty-two companies found an even higher percentage of business cases—72 percent.[2] One researcher, however, reported substantially lower levels of business case virtue. He found that only a third of the companies he questioned who were doing an ES project had a formal justification, and only 39 percent of those who had done a business case felt they had already produced quantifiable business value with their ES.[3]

Even though it's not uncommon to skip it, there are few good reasons for not doing any sort of business case. However, it is possible to do one after you've already decided you're going to implement an ES. In that case, the objective for the case is obviously not to decide whether to implement a system, but rather to understand how to achieve maximum benefit from it. In fact, if you are several years into implementation or even if you have gone live, it can still be useful to formally assess the business benefits you can achieve with an ES.

THE BUSINESS CASE PROCESS

Business cases are usually thought of as taking place before implementation and as being a one-time event. Wrong—on several counts. First, since it's impossible to predict how benefits will be realized over time, the business case should be modified continually. Second, even at the initial stage of an implementation, the business case process should be a bit iterative. Initially you need to assess the basic business requirements of the organization at a high level, without regard to any particular system. It's at this point that you can compare the benefits you anticipate to the ballpark cost of implementing a "generic" ES. The goal, of course, is to decide from a financial benefit perspective whether to implement an ES.

It's not terribly common to decide at this point not to go ahead, but some companies have done so. At a consumer products company, for example, managers decided not to implement the ES considered in its benefit case—including a supply chain optimization bolt-on application—because the financial analysis didn't measure up to the company's benefit standards. Table 3-1

TABLE 3-1

SAMPLE COST VERSUS BENEFIT ANALYSIS FOR AN
ENTERPRISE SYSTEM

Item	Value (millions of dollars)
Benefits	
Savings from applications that would have to be implemented without an ES	7
Savings from not having to solve the Y2K problem separately	1
Savings in infrastructure investments needed if ES not implemented	5
One-time savings from inventory costs	11
Procurement savings	7
Savings from improvements in forecasting and operational planning	5
Savings from improvements in demand planning	4
Annual customer service productivity improvement savings	2
Annual finance productivity improvements	5
One-time savings from accounts receivable reductions	0.3
Total benefits	47.3
Costs	
Labor (internal and consultant)	22.7
Hardware (production, development, and desktop)	8
Software (ES, supply chain bolt-on, middleware tools)	7
Communications infrastructure improvements	2
Total costs	39.7

lists some of the costs and potential benefits the company envisioned in its business case over five years.

In this case, even though benefits exceeded costs, the cost outlays would have preceded the benefit realization, bringing a net present value calculation into play. With time value of money taken into consideration, the costs and benefits were roughly equal, and the investment didn't meet the company's investment criteria. However, my view is that the company had substantially underinvested in information systems in the past, and as a result needed to spend more to catch up with competitors. On a purely financial basis, however, the project was rejected.

If a decision is made to go ahead in principle, it makes sense to assess what ES vendors have to offer and to start a package selection process. When a specific package has been selected, it's possible to start gathering detailed cost information about the software and hardware environment for the ES. Companies also typically select implementation partners at this stage in the process, which yields cost information for consulting and other services related to the ES.

Now it's possible to develop a detailed business case. In addition to the more detailed cost information available at this stage, identifying specific software and consultants helps to flesh out the benefits side of the equation. Other companies can be visited to learn what kind of benefits they achieved. Consultant relationships can be structured partly on the basis of rewards for specific process or financial improvements. This is the point at which all of the cost and benefit information can be brought together and analyzed, and a decision made on whether to proceed.

The analysis of what costs and benefits actually are realized should take place throughout the project, and every stage of the process should involve decisions about how and whether to proceed with the ES. This is usually not an all-or-nothing proposition; with millions invested, it will normally make sense to continue with a project. However, it may make sense to change the scope or scale of the project based on the ongoing business case. I've already mentioned Owens Corning's decision to back off from some aspects of its implementation. Five years into the company's SAP project, the company encountered some financial performance issues. Managers hired consultants to undertake a strategic review of its project. Given the time and money it had invested in the implementation thus far and the progress made to date, Owens Corning managers revisited the question of how broadly SAP should be implemented throughout the company. Certain subsidiaries, for example, could get by with less expensive and less integrated packages. The managers decided that they would get the primary share of benefits from the parts of the firm that were scheduled for implementation early on, and hence they delayed or cancelled plans to install the system where benefits would be more marginal.

One way to build in the approach of ongoing analysis is to employ a *real options* approach to financing the ES work. Real options approaches are analogous to the use of options in the stock market. Instead of financing the entire project at once, an option is bought to evaluate the investment and its risk over time. Real options are a look-and-learn approach to funding investments: You invest a bit, learn something from the progress (or lack thereof) you make, then invest some more and learn some more. Because you have invested in stages, the risk of losing a bundle is substantially less.

Real options approaches are becoming common in industries where firms make long-term, high-uncertainty, big-bucks investments, such as pharmaceutical drug development projects (Merck was an early adopter of this strategy, for example) and mining. Unfortunately, the idea is only being applied to ES projects by a few early adopters, and it's too soon to tell the results. For better or worse, you'll have to be a pioneer to try it.[4]

TYPES OF COST

Costs for enterprise projects fall primarily into three different categories: the software, the hardware, and the people. As you may have guessed, people are by far the most expensive of the three. Nevertheless, I'll describe the other two first just to get them out of the way.

Software costs include licenses to use the ES package, ongoing maintenance and support fees paid to software vendors, and the cost of bolt-on applications used to supplement the capabilities of the primary ES package. Depending on the vendor you select, you may pay by the user, the number of copies of the server software, or by the application module (e.g., if you only use finance and inventory management, you may not have to pay for the human resources module), or you may pay a large fee for a company-wide site license. Large ES vendors have well-established pricing structures; smaller ones will do deals, but you'll pay later on in implementation for anything you save now.

Hardware costs typically involve setting up a new client/server technology architecture. It's unlikely that you'll already have all the hardware and networking capability that you need. Servers for ES packages have to be quite beefy, and for reliability and security reasons you'll probably want your ES machine to stand alone. You will probably want a backup server that can also be used for testing. The major vendors of client/server technology (Compaq, Hewlett-Packard, IBM, and Sun, in alphabetical order) have plenty of experience specifying what you'll need, and will be happy to accept your call (even if it's collect) and purchase order.

Typically far larger than hardware and software costs are implementation costs, which I'll define as the costs to configure the system to your organization, install it in the company, and (most importantly and expensively) to bring about the process, organizational, behavioral, and strategic changes to really make an ES a worthwhile business investment. Implementation costs are generally people costs. The people can come from within your organization or, more commonly, from a consulting firm. Most firms employ consultants because they don't have the internal skills to implement an ES, and in fact don't even have the spare resources to deploy into learning the new skills.

Implementation costs vary widely depending on the amount of business change that you envision, but can exceed ten times the costs of other types. Of course, if you don't plan on reengineering any processes, changing how your organization is structured, improving your competitive capabilities, or acquainting your people with a new way of working, you can probably get by with implementation costs being only double your hardware and software costs. But you'll have to view this spending as a cost, rather than an investment, because you'll be unlikely to see much payoff.

Even if costs are considerably exceeded by benefits, firms must evaluate whether they have the necessary financial resources for an ES project. Unless you're putting in a new ES because current systems won't allow you to stay in business for some reason, this is not a project to be done on the cheap. Make sure you can afford not only the hardware and software costs and costs of pure system installation, but also the costs to bring about business change. Returns won't be realized until

► some of the ERP system is implemented.

► all of the current systems are discarded.

► all new business process designs are implemented.

► all decision makers use the system to plan and manage the organization's resources.

► all transaction processors use the system to process the organization's transactions.[5]

The absolute costs of an ES can undeniably be high, but there are other ways to think about cost. Monsanto, for example, calculated a "cost per user" metric. Project leaders found that when measured on that basis, costs could be one-fourth the cost of traditional, narrower-scope systems. They believe that this beneficial comparison holds for both initial implementation and ongoing support.

The costs of an ES are not just financial, however. Implementing a system and bringing about the associated business changes will also involve substantial human costs. The ES project will monopolize the time of many of your best people for several years. Virtually every person in the organization needs to learn about the impact of the new system and related changes on how their work is done. Senior managers will be busy reconfiguring various aspects of the business. If you don't have sufficient organizational slack—including time and attention—to focus on an ES project, don't undertake one or kid yourself that you'll put in the system now and plan for business changes later. This means that if your organization is planning considerable activity with regard to mergers and alliances, a major financial turnaround, significant geographical expansion, many new product introductions, and so forth, you simply won't have enough managerial attention to deal with all these issues effectively while doing an ES-enabled business transformation.

You can also include the political costs of an ES in your calculations. Will the firm's leaders be active and visible in their support? They can't support everything, you know. Make sure that the consent of senior executives, if you're not one yourself, is more fervid than lukewarm. You may be able to install the system without senior executive support, but you can't change the business without it.

TYPES OF BENEFIT

There are many different ways that an organization can get value from ESs. Each possible source of savings or benefit should be considered by the organization for inclusion in justification and ongoing "benefit management" programs. The following describes a number of alternative types of benefits in a list that draws heavily (but differs a bit) from one compiled by the Gartner Group.[6] The benefits are grouped within three different categories:

Savings from new approaches to work

▶ Savings from automating previously human tasks. An example is moving to self-service querying and reporting by customers and employees.

▶ Savings from data rationalization; that is, no longer having to manually reconcile and aggregate different definitions and values for the same unit of information.

▶ Savings from process changes. Described in chapter 5, these benefits are, I believe, at the heart of the benefits case for ESs.

▶ Savings from organizational changes. An example is adopting a shared-services group for common administrative processes across business units.

▶ Savings from inventory and other factors of production. Many companies find that they can run leaner with an ES, eliminating excess inventory, labor, and plant and equipment.

Savings from dismantling legacy systems

▶ Savings from avoiding ad hoc systems changes. Companies that implement ESs do not have to make Year 2000 fixes, euro currency conversions, and so on; many converted to an ES purely for this reason, although in my view it does not yield sufficient benefits alone to justify the cost.

▶ Savings from legacy systems upgrades and support from contractors. Although ES users incur these costs as well, they may be offset by savings from legacy systems expenditures not made.

▶ Savings from not having to build new systems when additional modules are implemented or become available from a vendor.

Revenue enhancement benefits

▶ Improvements in customer service. Better order interfaces with customers; enhanced availability, pricing, and profitability information; and the availability of improved customer service may lead to increases in revenue and profitability.

▶ Ease of expansion and growth. Implementing an ES may make it easier to accommodate growth in customers, merged or acquired business, or reorganization to better fit a company's markets.

▶ Better decisions. Although this is an unquantifiable benefit, ESs certainly make possible better decision and management processes, as described in chapter 7.

EXISTING SYSTEMS AND FUTURE BUSINESS NEED

One of the most fundamental analyses that any company must make before moving to a new ES is the trade-off between existing systems capability and future business need. Both are slippery concepts. Predicting things is always difficult, particularly when it involves the future—to paraphrase Yogi Berra. There are plenty of reasons to ditch existing systems, including the following:

▶ Year 2000 noncompliance (though if you've made it to now, you're presumably OK)

▶ Redundant or inconsistent information

▶ Lack of integration

▶ Doesn't satisfy all of the decision-support requirements

▶ Not user friendly

▶ Costly to maintain

▶ No longer state-of-the-art technology

▶ Duplicate systems

▶ Desperate need to go to client/server model

▶ Cobbled together systems from acquisitions, growth, add-ons, etc.

▶ No longer supported by vendor

▶ Reached end of useful life cycle.

Virtually all systems have one or more of these shortcomings, but that in itself hardly means an automatic decision to adopt an ES. The key is to think seriously about how problematic these issues are and how they might be remedied. How does the cost of upgrading existing systems compare with those associated with an ES? If you have all these problems, then implementing an ES is clearly indicated. You may have a horrible current systems environment, but at least you have an easy decision!

A few instructive case studies of technology-based justifications for ES projects may be helpful. Cisco, the highly successful manufacturer of Internet telecommunications equipment, viewed its growth as the primary incompatibility with its existing systems.[7] The company's continued and rapid growth (e.g., anticipated fivefold revenue growth in three years) could not be supported by their existing transaction processing system, which typically supported companies with revenues in the hundreds of millions, not billions. Even Cisco's vendors conceded that they couldn't meet the company's needs. Current systems didn't provide the degree of redundancy, reliability, and maintainability needed to support even the current business environment. Cisco could no longer make changes to the application to meet business needs. The system had become too customized and patched, and constantly required new bandages. Cisco executives correctly anticipated that the company would eventually deal with its customers over the Internet, and the existing system also was incapable of allowing customers to place and track their own orders.

Because of the compelling nature of Cisco's business needs and the clear insufficiency of its current systems, the company didn't do any serious business case. Cisco encountered substantial problems when it turned on its enterprise system (detailed in chapter 6), which might have been avoided with greater attention to business change issues. However, the combination of an ES at Cisco and the company's wholesale move to on-line customer transactions eventually yielded considerable business benefits.

At Chevron, the large oil company, the rationale for change was as much the number of existing systems as their poor quality.[8] Chevron had a collection of more than 200 separate, internally developed mainframe systems in the financial area alone. The largest program, primarily a general ledger and reporting database, was written in the 1960s and later converted to the new and exciting computer business language, COBOL. The program code had been modified many times over the following decades and by the mid-1980s contained close to three million lines (for you non-technicians, that's a large number). The main system had many interfaces to smaller systems, which were difficult to maintain and modify. Data extraction for analysis and decision purposes was difficult and required specialized program languages. Data was thus restricted to a handful of IT experts. Chevron did undertake a formal business case, but because of these system constraints the likely outcome was fairly apparent from the start.

A cautionary tale may be helpful here. I've described Unknown Computer earlier in this book as illustrating a failure in ES implementation. However, Unknown is not out of business—in fact, the company is doing well. Like Cisco and Chevron, Unknown justified its ES project on the basis that its current systems (current in 1996, anyway) couldn't handle its growth. At that time Unknown was already having problems with such basic information needs as issuing new product and component numbers, keeping track of diverse customer information, and configuring complex products. When Web-based sales took off at Unknown, the company had to move customer orders from the Web to its internal systems manually; when an automated link was finally developed, it was hardly elegant. Yet the company continued to grow and prosper on these supposedly antiquated systems.

Now, Unknown is putting in a new set of systems employing message-brokering technology that switches information among a set of best-of-breed systems. The company's technical people are still using the argument that existing systems can't handle growth. They're even arguing that the company's growth precludes it from working with a single ES vendor. If I were the CEO of Unknown, I'd be suspicious of this argument. And if you're a senior executive evaluating an ES business case, you should always be careful to confirm arguments that existing systems or current IT architectures won't handle your company's growth.

INFORMATION QUALITY AND VISIBILITY

A related deficiency of existing information systems involves the inability to easily obtain good, clear information about business processes and overall organizational performance. Even if current systems are able to perform basic business transactions, they may not readily yield up information for analysis of the business and for decision making about it. Incompatible systems and databases—with multiple definitions of key information elements—hinder global communications and understanding. You can't manage a global organization as one unified firm when you have a lot of diverse information that doesn't match or agree.

In fact, in the CEO survey I've described, overcoming this deficiency is the benefit of ESs mentioned more frequently than any other. When the CEOs were asked why they were investing in an ES, "improv[ing] information accuracy and availability" was mentioned by two-thirds of respondents. A related benefit, "improv[ing] managerial decision making," was the second most popular, cited by more than 60 percent of the respondents. These and other benefit categories mentioned by respondents are graphed in figure 3-1.

Of course, you don't necessarily need a new ES to achieve common information, and it's entirely possible that even with ESs you'll still have a diverse information environment. Companies can create common, integrated information with old technology. And if you have multiple ESs, chances are good that you'll end up with multiple customer IDs, part numbers, and product identifiers. However, many companies find the essentially centralized structure of an ES, and the "green field" nature of a new system, a good rationale for developing common information across the organization. Certainly the easiest way to implement an ES is to use one instance (copy) of the system for the entire corporation, and that forces a common set of information elements. The key is to realize that the hard work of

FIGURE 3-1

RESULTS FROM CEO SURVEY

Question: "Why did your company invest in an enterprise business solution?"

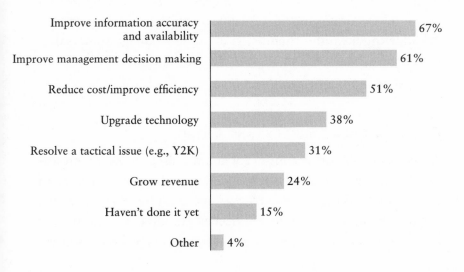

information integration is more a human task than a technical one; various important people around a firm have to be persuaded to mean the same thing when they refer to an entity such as a customer.

The other difficulty about this benefit is that it is hard to measure. Better information quality and visibility primarily benefits analytical and decision-making processes, which are rarely measured in any rigorous way. Few organizations, for example, measure either the quality or the speed of decision making (e.g., how often have that particular decision maker's decisions turned out right?); doing so would require a high level of management accountability. The only alternative to this type of benefit from information access and visibility is simply generating the same information that's available today, but doing it faster and with less human intervention. The information may be produced for analytical effectiveness purposes, but the benefit is in producing it in a more efficient way. This is, in fact, what most companies have done with ES data, as I will discuss in chapter 7 in more detail.

Still, many companies are convinced that they have received substantial benefits from greater information visibility. For example, Productos Corinter, a leading consumer products manufacturer in Mexico, feels that its reputation and relationship with its customers have been enhanced because the firm now has real-time, accurate information on the sales of all products by brand, store location, channel, and region. Managers and salespeople now have time to analyze the effects of new promotions and devise new ones.[9]

ORGANIZATIONAL STRUCTURE AND CHANGE

Another key factor to consider when deciding on an ES project is how the system matches the existing and future structure of the organization. Does the ES package encourage a centralized organization, whereas yours is decentralized? Is your company smaller—or in a few cases, larger—than the typical ES customer, at least for a particular vendor's ES package? Are you now going through, or do you expect to go through, a series of mergers, acquisitions, or divestitures? If so, how easily will you be able to accommodate acquired organizations with your ES, and would a divested organization be able to break off easily? These are some of the organizational structure considerations you should take into account when adopting an ES.

First, a simple, no-brainer example. Bay Networks was formed from the merger of Synoptics and Wellfleet Communications in 1994. Wellfleet, a manufacturer of routers, and Synoptics, a maker of intelligent hubs, had both been investigating ESs. Wellfleet was somewhat further along, having already identified SAP as its preferred vendor and purchased a system. Synoptics had decided on an ES and had narrowed its choice to SAP or Oracle. The obvious question for the combined organization was, why not go with SAP across the board? The company wanted one system so that it could present one face to the customer. If SAP passed a quick validation, they'd go with it. If not, they'd re-open the search. A twelve-week validation process identified Bay's core business processes and assessed SAP's capability to support those processes. There were some gaps, but process support was generally good. Another factor at the time in the ES analysis was what system could best support growth. Bay's revenues, for example, grew 47 percent in 1995. Given these criteria, the company went with SAP.

Bay also was concerned about the ability to integrate organizations it might acquire or merge with. After the merger, Bay acquired companies at the rate of one per quarter, so integrating new acquisitions into R/3 was an important emphasis. Ironically, Bay itself was acquired by Northern Telecom in 1998, forming the new company Nortel Networks. Thus far, Nortel's information systems have remained largely separate from those of the rest of Northern Telecom, which employed some application packages but had no overarching ES in place. The combined company will slowly merge systems and information as business needs require, according to Nortel managers with whom I've spoken. Nortel's experience with ESs through these various organizational changes may be on the more active end of the continuum, but almost all organizations should think in advance about the way they will deal with this type of organizational change relative to their ES.

The worldwide oil industry is currently experiencing massive restructurings due to mergers and acquisitions and is finding out about the ease of turning two or more ESs into one. For example, when BP merged with Amoco in 1998, and then acquired Atlantic Richfield (Arco) in 1999, the combined firm's executives faced important decisions about which system or systems to adopt. BP had developed its own system for all downstream (refining and marketing) operations, now being co-marketed with Oracle as Oracle Energy Downstream. Amoco was largely finished with a broad-ranging SAP implementation; Arco employed a variety of systems, but primarily had Oracle applications in its upstream (exploration and production) business. BP Amoco executives felt that their own downstream system, called ISP, had both a lower cost per transaction and a greater ease of moving into Internet-based electronic commerce than external package alternatives. They decided to standardize on SAP financial applications in the upstream business (and to outsource operations in that area to two professional services firms) and to continue using their own system in downstream operations, while converting it to Internet-based technologies. In the rapidly consolidating oil industry, it's particularly important that senior executives have a well-defined approach to ESs and how to deal with them when another business combination comes along.

Mergers aren't the only consideration in thinking about ESs and organizational issues. Simple size is also a factor. Large organizations—say, $1 billion in revenues and above—have been the most active adopters of ESs thus far. They have the scale, complexity, and global presence to take advantage of the many features and functions of an ES, and are also most likely to need ES-enabled integration. Large firms might have difficulty supporting their complexity with an in-house system (though they would also be most likely to have the capabilities to build an ES-like system in-house). Large firms are also perhaps most likely to have developed their own best practices, which might work against the adoption of an ES with its own set.

Really small organizations (less than $25 million or so in revenues) typically won't want to bother with an expensive, time-consuming ES. So that leaves mid-tier organizations—by my definition those between $25 million and $1 billion—a large and important category for ES vendors to penetrate. In fact, selling to this market is the current primary strategy for most ES vendors, so if you work in such a firm you'll probably be hearing from SAP, Oracle, PeopleSoft, and others soon if you haven't already.

Mid-tier companies could adopt ESs for many of the same reasons that larger ones do, but the most common reason is to establish a platform for growth. These companies may be relatively small, their managers figure, but they won't be for long, and they don't want to run into systems constraints as they grow.

For example, Boston Beer (which in one name combines my favorite city and beverage), better known as the brewer of Samuel Adams beers and ales, decided to put in an SAP system even though consultants told them that the package was designed for companies ten times their size ($191 million at the time of the decision in 1996). Jim Koch, the CEO, decided that a big-company system was necessary because of the expected rapid rate of Boston Beer's growth; at the time the firm already had an annual compound growth rate of 46 percent. Koch felt that the company would be better off in the long term with a more comprehensive system even if it were twice as expensive (and it was, at least). He wanted to avoid the pain of conversion two to three years down the road by acquiring technology that would accommodate the company's growth.

As for current systems, it was patently clear that Boston Beer had outgrown them. So many modifications had been made to the existing system that moving to the newest release would be tantamount to a full-scale conversion. Boston Beer was spending the majority of its IT budget writing code to analyze and understand what was going on in the company. Replacing these systems was a fairly obvious choice, although at the time few companies that size selected a package as large and complex as SAP R/3. Boston Beer did get its system installed, and certainly it has been able to deal with the company's significant growth.

A less positive outcome occurred at Power Computing. Remember that company? It was growing at a rapid rate in the mid-1990s selling clones of Apple Macintosh computers. The president of the company (an Unknown alumnus) told me, "I never want to be constrained in growth rate because of our information systems." So he decided to implement SAP at a time when the company had less than $100 million in revenues.

The company's ES project was relatively quick and successful, and the president got his wish. He was constrained not by his information systems, but rather by the denial of a technology license from Apple. The company was basically given a liquidation payment by Apple and went out of business in 1997. I argued at the time of the decision that Power was too small an organization, with too uncertain a future, to be putting in a large, complex ES. If hindsight proved me correct in this fashion more often, I wouldn't have to be working for a living.

In summary, mid-size organizations usually have fewer budgetary and human resources to purchase and operate an ES. They are usually less tolerant of risk and of ESs that require significant customization or lengthy implementations. They want a near-term return on their investment. Their ES selection criteria are more concerned with ease of use, vendor service and support capability, and product cost, and less with detailed system functionality. Midsize firms should be cautious about the level of business evolution they might experience. With these cautions, an ES can work in mid-size firms.

For example, PC Connection, a $700 million mail-order seller of personal computer hardware and software, decided to implement the J.D. Edwards WorldERP software in 1998.[10] PC

Connection was already using IBM AS/400 hardware, a type of minicomputer known for its simplicity and reliability. J.D. Edwards software ran on the AS/400, unlike most other ES packages. PC Connection managers felt that both the software and the hardware they chose were relatively simple, and they avoided substantial modifications to the ES software. The company didn't have a lot of resources to install and maintain the system, and thus kept everything as simple as possible. The company's managers are pleased with the system, and it has supported PC Connection's rapid growth.

FLEXIBILITY

The degree of organizational change anticipated for an ES environment is, of course, related to the amount of flexibility in the system. There is no doubt that firms desire flexibility in their information systems, ES or otherwise. It's impossible to predict all of the business and technical requirements a system might be called on to fulfill. Whether ESs lead to greater or lesser flexibility is a complex and paradoxical issue, as I discussed in chapter 1. But it's also an issue for this chapter in terms of whether an ES is the right decision for a rapidly changing organization.

Once implemented, an ES and, even more so, the organization it supports can be hard to change. Because ESs are so tightly linked with organizational structures and processes, a change in the business requires a change in the system and vice versa. Further, the integrated nature of ESs makes it difficult to make change in one area without affecting another.

Put more positively, however, ESs do make some organizational changes easier and therefore must be viewed as contributing to flexibility. Because many organizations replace multiple different systems and interfaces with a single ES, a change in business or information requirements may be more easily made with a single enterprise-wide system. Enterprise systems tend to store key configurations and relationships to company structures in tables, which are relatively easy to edit. Enterprise systems may also increase flexibility by providing sufficient functionality for almost any new business an organization might enter.

For example, managers at Fujitsu Microelectronics felt that as a result of having installed an ES, they were better positioned to enter new businesses than they had been in the past. Their lack of capability to build systems quickly enough to support business change was a major limitation, they believed. The fact that their ES supported a very broad range of processes and business models made them confident that they could rapidly have information support for whatever they wanted to do.

Enterprise systems can also make it easier to exit businesses through spin-offs or divestitures. Departing business units can either take the ES functionality with them (buying their own license and configuring the system similarly to the parent system) or outsource to their previous parent. Dow Chemical, for example, feels that its SAP system made it much easier to divest over $10 billion worth of business over a decade. Monsanto managers argue that the company's spin-off of the $3 billion Solutia chemicals unit was straightforward technically because the systems were "clean and well organized in SAP." Further, the new company was almost immediately up and running with fully operational systems—increasing its value to shareholders— and did not have to remain dependent on the parent company.

SUPPLY CHAIN LINKAGES

An aspect of ES decision-making that is related to flexibility is the ease of connecting to customers, suppliers, and channel partners in the supply chain. This subject is the primary focus of chapter 8, but it's worth mentioning here as a rationale for attacking mission-critical business objectives with an ES. For the most part, an ES can easily facilitate supply chain linkages, particularly if other members of your own chain are implementing the same package as you. Even without the same package, however, the overall focus of ESs on supply chain processes and information can help create tight linkages with other firms. However, in times of rapid change in both business structure and ES status, dealing with the supply chain factor can be confusing, particularly since this is the primary area for Internet-ES connections, a very fast-changing technology domain.

Some of the firms we've already considered addressed this issue as well. Not surprisingly, companies that supply equipment for the Internet are among the leaders in using it to interface with their ESs and link to supply chains. Both Nortel Networks and Cisco Systems have implemented impressive capabilities for customers, suppliers, and distributors to place orders, manage inventory levels, arrange delivery and check on shipments, receive software products over the Internet, and generally synchronize their businesses with those of the two communications equipment companies. Both firms have direct linkages to their ESs from the Web—Nortel with its SAP system, and Cisco with its Oracle system.

Nortel needed "integration and synergy between distributors and suppliers, and we would need to share information across boundaries as never before."[11] Managers wanted every customer, employee, and supplier to be able to obtain any information they needed, when they needed it, in the format that they wanted. They viewed their ES, along with the Internet, as helping to enable this level of external information access. Cisco estimates that it spent about $100 million to "Web-enable" its major applications, but the company figures it saves more than double that amount annually in reduced inventory, distribution, and customer service costs. Although these companies are in the business of helping their customers to use the Internet, the only thing that other firms can't do as easily, perhaps, is to ship their products over a communications link.

Boston Beer had the goal of leading the "craft brewing" industry in the use of the Internet as a low-cost network to link wholesalers and contract brewers to speed order entry and plant scheduling. This was particularly important for Boston Beer, which outsourced much of its brewing to other firms. By enabling business partners to access selected portions of the company's SAP database and order on a weekly or more frequent basis, Boston Beer hoped to eliminate over- and under-buying and improve its ability to meet the needs of its customers without carrying excess inventory. Another hoped-for effect of such a system was an increase in sales; out-of-stocks had occasionally prevented customers from getting the Sam Adams they desired. Since implementing the system, the company has experienced increased sales, although it's always difficult to trace such improvements to any particular cause. This is the most difficult aspect of implementing ESs with a supply chain rationale: Many things have to change in addition to systems in order to sell more product, reduce inventory, change customer behavior, and so forth.

One last word on supply chain linkages. If you're thinking about an ES because you want to link to other companies in your chain, it makes a lot of sense to find out what they're doing with regard to ESs. As I'll discuss to a much greater degree in chapter 8, linking one company's supply chain to another's may ultimately be considerably eased if both are using the same ES. Systems that translate from one ES to another are emerging today, but they will add another layer of complexity to an already complex situation.

For example, Elf Atochem N.A., the Americas petrochemical subsidiary of the French oil firm Elf, decided to implement an ES and decided on SAP as its vendor in part because virtually every other company in its industry was doing so. "We thought that at some point it would be very helpful to be able to link our SAP systems with their SAP systems in a relatively seamless way," notes Bob Rubin, Elf Atochem's chief information officer and leader of its ES initiative.[12] Although this sort of linkage may take years to materialize (as it will at Elf Atochem), it's likely that an ES will be in place for a decade or more, and the clear direction in supply chain management is toward interorganizational linkages.

SELECTING AMONG ENTERPRISE SYSTEM VENDORS

Okay, you've done at least a high-level benefits case and for the moment are willing to proceed. Now you're ready to see what particular vendors have to offer. Deciding whether to implement an ES and selecting among ES vendors are pretty much two separate decisions, right? Well, not really. They are two decisions, but they are often linked. I've already mentioned one linkage, in which getting benefits in the supply chain and competitive advantage arenas involves not only whether you put in an ES, but also what type of ES you and your supply chain partners and competitors put in.

Another key linkage between the two decisions involves whether any vendor offers software that is particularly focused on your own industry. Because tailoring to a specific industry can be very expensive, whether a pre-configured enterprise solution already exists should affect not only your vendor selection, but also whether to put in an ES at all.

For example, the retail building materials giant Home Depot will wait to see more functionality before installing SAP Retail in its U.S. stores. The custom industry solution, developed by SAP and some development partners, had gone live with only two companies at the time of Home Depot's decision and lacked key functionality the firm's managers thought was necessary. For example, SAP Retail couldn't handle the company's approach of letting each store place its own product orders with suppliers. Home Depot planned to work with SAP to allow customization of product mixes at stores and to enable tying retail store reporting to financial modules. However, although the package wasn't deemed ready for U.S. implementation, Home Depot did install SAP's finance, logistics, and warehouse management software to help run its stores in Argentina and Chile because these countries' markets are somewhat less demanding and doing so will help the organization's learning curve on installing and using the software. Home Depot can afford to wait on a system that better meets its needs in the United States because it doesn't have an immediate need to replace current mainframe-based systems.[13]

Despite these intertwinings and complexities, let's focus on just the factors that differentiate one vendor from another. The factors to consider aren't terribly different from those used in making other software decisions, but the scale and scope of the decision is usually much greater. Thus effective vendor selection practices make a lot of sense, particularly if you value your career.

FACTORS TO CONSIDER IN VENDOR SELECTION

The selection of a particular vendor's ES package is something over which many firms agonize. However, it need not be that difficult or time-consuming a decision, and to my mind is less important than many other issues regarding implementation and ES-related business change. All of the major ES vendors offer software that works and that allows the possibility of information and business integration; all ES packages are complex and difficult to install. Any differences between major packages are marginal. I believe that you won't get much business value from spending more than a few months on this decision. There are also several gross factors—for example, your industry, particular functions you want to emphasize, your size—that can make the decision process much easier.

In certain industries, it may be a relatively brainless decision to go with a particular package. If you are in the oil or petrochemicals industries, for example, it would require a supreme act of will to resist implementing SAP's R/3, since most other firms in these industries have already done so, and there are many features of the package that have been customized to support these industries. Still, there are segments of even those industries (e.g., the upstream, or exploration and production, business and the retail component of gasoline-focused oil firms) in which there is as yet no clear winner of the selection lottery, and it won't be easy to decide whether to adopt a different system for that component of a large, integrated oil company.

For some industries there are also so-called best-of-breed ESs, which may offer integrated offerings for that industry or may partner with other leading-edge software vendors to offer a suite of applications. In the retail industry, for example, there are several different providers of such software, including JDA and

Richter Systems. Representatives of these firms argue to retailers that generic solutions won't fit their needs well. "By virtue of doing it all, those ERP providers are not focusing on the vertical aspects of retailing. Those solutions don't tend to be as function-rich as industry specific applications. All we concentrate on is retail," explains Brent Lippman, CEO of JDA Software.[14] "It's extremely costly to buy a generic solution and then configure it to suit your specific needs," argues Jim Soenksen, general manager of the Americas for Richter Systems.[15] If you're a relatively small firm that expects to stay within one industry for the foreseeable future, examining best-of-breed packages makes sense. Otherwise, you should stick with the mainstream ESs.

The selection of a package may also be made easier by heavy reliance on a particular module within an ES package. If, for example, human resources applications are your primary drivers for implementing an ES, strong consideration of PeopleSoft would make sense. This is true in many government, service, and professional service industries, for example, and PeopleSoft probably has the lead in those segments. SAP's financial and supply chain systems are very strong; Baan is noted for its flexible manufacturing software.

Functional best-of-breed vendors also exist that encourage customers to buy individual applications for specific functions and then somehow string them together. If you think this is a good idea, I doubt you're still reading by this time. However, with the proliferation of smaller, more focused bolt-on applications, and the embracing of so-called *component assembly* strategies by ES vendors (who portray their systems as the eventual backbones for components to link into), we'll continue to see the spread of functional best-of-breed software, and at some point it may be able to be integrated as well as a current ES. That point is not here today, however. This doesn't mean that good companies don't consider the idea. Cisco originally wanted to go this route and let each functional area choose a system, but because the functional areas felt that justifying a new system was too much work and too disruptive, they never actually chose new functional systems. Eventually, the existing systems became overloaded and malfunctioned, so Cisco managers decided to go with an ES, and fast.

The size of your company may also lead you to choose a particular vendor; SAP is typically chosen by the largest global firms, for example. Smaller firms are more likely to select such vendors as J.D. Edwards, Lawson, and Ross. Oracle and People-Soft are in the middle; Baan has one very large customer (Boeing), and the rest are mostly mid-sized.

DETAILED FEATURE ANALYSIS

In addition to a basic fit with a company's industry, size, business model, and functional emphases, companies often look for specific technical or business-enabling features in their ES. In this section I'll describe some of the features commonly sought. However, it's easy to get carried away in the analysis of specific features. Even if a vendor doesn't offer them, there is usually some way to work around them or change your business processes so that they are no longer necessary. You have to figure that if thousands of companies use a particular ES (as is true for the major vendors' packages), they must have figured out some way to do without the feature. Nevertheless, you may want to ask competing vendors whether the specific desired features are present, and to what degree. Because the presence or absence of features in various vendors' packages is subject to both interpretation and change, I don't describe which vendors have what features.

Data ownership: Central or local? This feature refers to who is responsible for maintaining and updating data worldwide. The key issue is not who can make changes to data, but rather who has accountability for those changes. Many companies have decentralized and heterogeneous IT organizations in which each IT person is responsible for data in his or her area. This practice can continue with some ES packages; others force centralization of data change accountability. The latter arrangement is desirable when changes in key data affect many parts of the organization. It also provides for easy auditing of changes in records, which will appeal to auditors and regulatory bodies.

Procedures: Autonomous or directive? In autonomous systems, work procedures can be adapted to local conditions. This approach allows the user flexibility about which procedures to run and how. In one ES package, for example, corporate policies for paying suppliers cannot be implemented in the software; the supplier payment functions give the user many choices, and the user voluntarily follows corporate policy without enforcement by the system. Companies to which this approach is appealing presumably assume that payment conditions and requirements vary widely, and they want the person managing payments to take intelligent control.

As you might expect, more directive systems largely specify and constrain how a procedure is done. Some systems allow for a mixture of approaches. The ES employed by Chevron, for example, provides the flexibility to follow different centralization/decentralization strategies. Where and how transactions are processed can be determined on a case-by-case basis. In some instances Chevron has chosen to centralize; in others, to distribute. Financial processing for several smaller business units has been consolidated into a shared financial services center that also controls the corporate master data.

Transaction visibility: Aggregated or traceable? This seemingly arcane issue has to do with how easily users of a system can access original data about specific inventory, financial, sales, or purchasing transactions in an ES. Traceable transaction systems allow a user to drill down to any transaction; good implementations of the feature allow easy on-line drill-down access. For example, at Hoechst Marion Roussel (HMR), a global pharmaceutical firm, one Latin American manager reports that "Being able to drill down and analyze the sales by zone, I've been able to reorganize the distribution network and consolidate some pharmacists who were placing low or less frequent orders by zone" and to identify HMR's most profitable customers.[16]

Systems that allow only aggregated data access report only totals to other parts of the system. With such a system in place, you might be told, "You can get the freight charges if you need them, but the on-line report of freight costs in Asia would not let you drill down to that line on the Thai order." This approach to managing information is cheaper and easier to manage, but allows less direct inspection of data (which, depending on how you feel about your boss and his or her proclivity to investigate things, could be an asset).

Global or multilocal structure? How is the company organized regarding national boundaries, and how does it deploy itself to satisfy the requirements of local markets and regulations? Many ES packages claim to be "global systems," including all of the market-leading large systems. They feature user interfaces in several languages and allow transactions to take place in multiple currencies. They are sold and supported in multiple countries and make some attempt at satisfying local regulatory and market requirements. Companies should confirm that a supposedly global ES not only supports displays and invoices in multiple languages (this is relatively easy), but also description fields, address fields, comment fields, and other text fields in multiple languages. Global companies also need multilingual database field names so that programs written in English and programs written in Finnish, for example, are interoperable. Multi-local companies need only to be able to do invoicing in any language or currency, and their computer screens should display labels in the language of the user. Smaller vendors may not have these global features.

Companies can use globally capable ESs in two ways: in a truly global fashion that ignores, at least to some degree, geography as an organizing principle, or in a multi-local approach that organizes the company by country or region. Global companies that ignore boundaries are complex in terms of regulations and management (e.g., how are approvals managed? How are component parts lists managed and routing costs analyzed when conditions in different parts of the world are quite different?) Truly global firms should have one ES throughout the globe, or at least if there are multiple instances they should not be established on the basis of geography. Multi-local firms, on the other hand, are more likely to put different full installations in different countries and run them from each country individually, with one database per country.

Various key business processes can also be treated in a global or multi-local fashion, which also affects ES requirements. In financial processes, for example, reporting entities can take account of legal requirements in a country but still do other financial operations globally, including currency exchange. Multi-local firms treat each corporate national entity as its own reporting unit. Financial closes are done in each country, and results sent to headquarters. Currency exchange management is left to national companies.

Data management: Centralized or distributed? A corporation that wants to manage a single master data repository but finds itself with multiple databases for the same information will be dissatisfied. A corporation that wants each division to set up and manage its own relationships with customers might find that a single customer master file cramps the different customer-facing styles that keep those divisions successful. Another possibility combines central and distributed data management in a federalist approach: Some data is common, and some varies. Most ESs assume a single common database; if you want data to be managed in a distributed fashion across the organization, make sure your vendor supports it. Certainly ES data management and stewardship is more complicated than this, but a simple level of analysis may be sufficient for making the ES decision.

Modifications: Parameter or program? Enterprise system packages allow modifications to their systems in two different ways. One involves setting parameters in a separate parameter file.

When there are several reasonable ways to do things, system designers will program in all of them, then allow the implementer to determine behavior by setting parameters. This slows down development, puts enormous stress on testing and documentation, and makes the system harder to implement. But it brings flexibility, and customers don't have to rewrite software. The other approach involves modifying the program code itself. Companies that purchase this type of system may not view the software provider as the source of much new functionality. Companies may also upgrade less often with this approach, since it is more difficult. Some vendors who offer program modifications spend considerable time and effort making modification tools available.

Best practices orientation: Vendor or customer? How does a company learn and incorporate best practices into its ways of doing business? Some vendors believe they have access to industry requirements and industry expertise that gives them the ability to lead their customers in best practices. They believe their customers expect them to know best practices better than the customers do. Other vendors believe that their customers know what should be done, and these vendors want to give their customers the flexibility to guide the software and to leverage the core business expertise the customers already have.

THE PROCESS OF VENDOR SELECTION

In addition to thinking about the factors by which to decide between one ES and another, there's the process of vendor selection to think about. It's a complicated process involving the establishment of relationships that will likely last over several years and involve millions to hundreds of millions of dollars. It's worth doing right, but not worth doing forever. Most organizations should be able to complete selection of key vendors, including software, hardware, and implementation partners, in six months or less. Making the choice itself is not normally a value-adding activity for your business, so you should try to get it done as quickly as possible. You'll probably find, however, that both the internal managers and the external vendors you want are busy, so you'll have to work hard to move the process along. One other consideration: Don't strive for perfection in the fit between your requirements and what vendors are offering. You will rarely find it.

WHICH COMES FIRST?

Which should a company select first—software, hardware, or implementation partner? Clearly software should come before hardware, since the package chosen affects the kind of hardware environment needed, and client, server, and networking hardware is increasingly commodity-like. The decision about software partner versus implementation partner or consultant is a little more complex. If your goal is a primarily technology-oriented implementation, with little concern for business value and change, then it probably makes sense to select a software vendor first. Your preferred software vendor can probably recommend a consulting firm to help you with implementation.

If your primary orientation is improving your business with an ES (and you may have detected that I think this is the right choice), you should probably select an implementation partner first. The consultant can help you think about what your business change objectives are, and what they mean for vendor selection considerations. You may also find it helpful to employ a consultant in the vendor selection process itself—either a general management consulting firm that can assist in both vendor selection and implementation, or one of the few firms that focus specifically on ES vendor research and selection consulting.

NARROWING THE FIELD

It's usually fairly easy to narrow the field of ES vendors to a small number (two or three) of leading candidates based on the "macro" factors I mentioned above, such as industry, company size, or functional orientation. Coming up with such a short list as quickly as possible saves considerable time and effort in that one does not have to explore detailed functionality and vendor capabilities for many vendors. If your industry is relatively unusual for use of an ES, you may end up with a very short list—that is, one vendor long.

You can also narrow the list of vendors for which to do a careful analysis by identifying which business processes will be the deciding factors in the selection. It's unlikely, for example, that you'll want to use the general ledger function in different ES packages as the deciding criterion, since they are all pretty similar and few companies view general ledger excellence as a competitive advantage. Supply chain functionality, on the other hand, does vary widely across ES vendors and could easily be viewed as a strategic capability.

Do not, however, consider vendor stereotypes as a primary basis for decision making. Some vendors' packages have the reputation of being harder to implement, but it ain't necessarily so. A recent analyst firm study of sixty ES implementations, for example, suggested that packages that have an "expensive to implement" reputation don't always turn out to be particularly expensive, at least when measuring implementation costs as a percentage of corporate revenues.[17] Nor did the supposedly most complex and difficult packages take the longest time to install in the study.

FROM THE SHORT LIST TO ONE VENDOR

As I noted earlier, I don't think that a detailed "feature 'n' function" analysis serves most companies well. If you take this approach, you'll probably endure a time-consuming process of requests for information and requests for proposals, and you'll end up with a long, complex spreadsheet that ranks each vendor on each criterion. Inevitably there will be no clear winner, or the company you want to choose will not come out on top. (Then, of course, you change the evaluation criteria!)

Most companies are better advised to handle the selection process in a bit less structured form. Again, you may want to analyze vendor capabilities in detail for processes you consider critical, but not for all processes. The overall structure and philosophy of the ES package should carry more weight than individual features anyway, since the latter are always changing with time and new releases.

Talking to and visiting vendor reference sites is a very important step. You'll want to interview several sites with characteristics similar to those of your organization. You don't have to just take the references that vendors give you. Go to conferences put on by the vendors' user groups or by third parties. Look in the business press for references to companies implementing ESs. Call the companies mentioned in this book—but don't tell them I sent you!

You'll probably want a demonstration of the leading packages. But unless you deliver to the vendor the specific business and technical requirements that you want to see (the *script*), they will give you a standard presentation that does not address your needs. Preparing scripted demos is a lot of hard work, so it may be difficult to get vendors to do them. You may also be able to convince a vendor to give a demonstration using a sample of your own data.

In addition to functionally and philosophically driven selection criteria, you also have to consider the fundamentals of vendor selection for any kind of product or service. These criteria include the following:

► Cost (but many companies report that substantial sticker price differences erode during bidding)

► Your beliefs about whether the vendor's claims are truthful and well substantiated

► Financing and payment alternatives

▶ Likelihood that the vendor will remain in business

▶ Investment levels by the company in improving its system

▶ Capabilities for customer support

▶ Technical and implementation consulting availability for the system

The criteria for selecting implementation partners are usually somewhat different. This is a touchy subject, because I am employed in part by a consulting firm. But I can tell you what factors CEOs from 200 firms that had implemented ESs said they employed in choosing an implementation partner.[18] In order of rank, these were as follows:

1. Cost

2. Size/reputation

3. References

4. Commitment to your vision

5. Ability to manage change

6. Expertise in your industry

7. Experience with software product

8. Availability of skilled resources

9. Comprehensive knowledge of business processes

The only criterion I object to in this list is the highest-ranked one. Cost is certainly important, but the ratio between cost and benefit is even more so. Perhaps you could say that the other factors are all benefit related, in which case I'd put at least some of them on top if I were doing the ranking.

I'll conclude this chapter with several case studies: one from a company that decided it didn't need to put in an ES, and two from companies that decided they did.

CASE STUDIES OF ENTERPRISE SYSTEM DECISION MAKING

A COMPANY THAT DIDN'T IMPLEMENT AN ENTERPRISE SYSTEM

Air Products and Chemicals is a $5 billion gas and chemical manufacturer based in Allentown, Pennsylvania.[19] Air Products isn't a sexy company, but it's well managed—solidly profitable, with respectable growth. The firm is an innovator in production and environmental technologies, as well as in business information systems. More Harvard case studies have been written about Air Products' information systems than any other company, and not a single one describes a failure.

Air Products' executives, however, are feeling a bit lonely. They are the only major firm in their industry not to have an ES installed or underway (one competitor has a limited ES in place for manufacturing, but not a fully integrated system). Still, its managers believe that they don't really need an ES, and I would agree. The company has effectively developed its own systems and single-function packages in such a way that it has already achieved most if not all of the benefits an ES would deliver.

Air Products simply had no compelling reason to adopt an ES, no burning platform for change. The company had to spend less than $20 million for Y2K remediation, so that didn't provide much motivation for an ES. Shared financial services supported by standard financial applications were adopted in 1982, so enabling new financial processes wasn't a factor. Air Products is particularly focused on procurement as a strategic process, but the company already had a global procurement system.

Air Products' IT managers have adopted a philosophy of "scale, simplicity, and sameness." Almost all applications are common in the United States; Europe has some of its own financial systems, but there has never been a strong need to consolidate them. Customer-facing systems involving orders and sales are in the process of being consolidated. Desktop systems are being standardized throughout the company. Interfaces between systems are minimized. A program of managed reinvestment in business applications kept the portfolio reasonably current and rationalized. There are no real issues involving exchange of data with other companies: Air Products participates in a chemical industry EDI (electronic data interchange) association, and has been able to exchange data when it needed to.

Perhaps the greatest challenge to Air Products' non-ES approach is the difficulty of integrating information across business functions. To address this issue, the firm's IT managers have focused considerable effort on data management and integration. For example, they widely employ data warehouses that pull together information from diverse applications for analysis and reporting. Increasingly, definitions of key information entities are held in common throughout the company. Considerable attention is devoted to data planning.

No one at Air Products is actively opposed to ESs; it's just that every high-level business case thus far has indicated no need for one. But the company's managers are always re-examining their situation with regard to changing business and technology contexts. The most pressing change issue today is electronic commerce: Will Air Products be able to give customers and channel partners access to key transaction data? Thus far the company has made progress in some business units and functions at supporting e-commerce; it is conceivable, however, that an ES might eventually be adopted to improve external electronic access.

Air Products is a good illustration of how information systems that are well managed over time obviate the need for an ES. Unfortunately, few other firms are as well positioned.

TWO COMPANIES IN THE SAME INDUSTRY THAT IMPLEMENTED ENTERPRISE SYSTEMS

For many industries, ESs are becoming more the norm than not. Looking at two companies in the same industry brings a different slant to the question of whether you should implement mission-critical applications with an ES. This section should be particularly helpful in thinking about selecting an ES with hopes of gaining competitive differentiation and the ability to establish strong relationships with ES vendors as selection criteria. The timing of selection is also covered.

The two companies I'll describe are the giants of the apparel footwear industry—Reebok International and Nike.[20] They have fairly similar processes and compete in the value discipline of product leadership. Thus it is not surprising that both Nike and Reebok chose an ES as a way to maintain industry parity in processes that do not provide competitive advantages. Both companies feel that with packaged applications they would be able to concentrate better on their core product innovation processes instead of putting time and energy into writing and maintaining software. Both companies use custom-developed software to support their product creation processes and additional ES bolt-ons to support other competitive-advantage processes.

Although both Nike and Reebok value product creation as their prime competitive-advantage process, some ES-enabled processes are very important in supporting this advantage. Time to market, or the ability to get the product manufactured as rapidly as possible and sent through the supply chain, supports their ability to maintain product leadership through market responsiveness. Due to the complexity and wide range of configuration choices, both companies maintain that this process is likely to be done differently at each company despite the fact that they have chosen the same package. Both companies also maintain that their adoption of the same ES will probably not strongly affect the competitive landscape.

Reebok's decision to implement an enterprise system. Like many companies, Reebok's drive to implement an ES grew out of recognition that its existing systems were inflexible and increasingly unable to handle the company's growth. Most systems had been installed when Reebok was less than a tenth its current size. Since Reebok had grown mainly through acquisitions, it had acquired many disparate and difficult-to-integrate systems along the way. Reebok had become a global company, but existing systems were encouraging islands of automation and a lack of global communications and understanding. A strategic IT plan first suggested looking at an ES in 1991, though no available system was viewed as sufficient then.

Reebok managers looked again to the ES market in 1995, only to find that no ES vendor could support its unique industry requirements, namely, detailed information on size, color, and style. Although they did evaluate building their own systems or patching one together in the best-of-breed approach, Reebok had decided that an ES would allow them to achieve one of their main goals: maximum global integration. Moreover, an ES would allow them to more easily keep up with best practices in the industry. Reebok also considered buying an existing ES and tailoring it to meet its needs. Yet very quickly it was determined that the amount of coding involved and the difficulty in upgrading and maintaining such a modified system was not worth the effort.

Anxious to obtain an ES, Reebok decided to approach SAP with the idea of partnering to co-develop a vertical software capability that would support the unique requirements of its industry. SAP at the time was gaining market share and seemed to have the size and capability to be able to handle such a project. Moreover, SAP had done some custom development work for apparel companies before. In 1995 the Apparel Footwear Consortium was born, consisting of SAP, Reebok, and another apparel company, Vanity Fair (VF).

By working with the Consortium, Reebok claims several advantages. First of all, managers have gained valuable insight into industry best practices through the close relationship with Vanity Fair. Reebok also has been able to leverage its relationships with hardware and third-party vendors, who supply services for a discount in exchange for the chance to gain experience with the software. On the flip side, however, Reebok has had to endure going live on a "beta," or not fully completed and tested, product. Company managers feel that it was Reebok, not SAP, who discovered most of the bugs that SAP then corrected. This caused a month's delay in their ability to go live.

Does Reebok have an advantage over Nike by virtue of early adoption and co-development? Perhaps. Reebok's experience in co-developing the software means that its employees know the system extremely well and can thus maximize the system's capabilities. This is not a trivial advantage. Reebok's executives liken it to playing a piano: "We can both have a piano. But because of practice, one can play it better. We are 18 months ahead of our competitors." How long this first mover advantage will last and its long-term outcome are questionable, however.

Although a little nervous when competitors such as Adidas and Nike started purchasing the same system, Reebok managers felt that this would ultimately be to their advantage. With more companies on board, SAP would have more incentive to continue to improve the product, as well as more experience from which to draw when pursuing industry best practices.

Nike's decision to implement an enterprise system. Four years after the Consortium was formed and well after the release of the industry vertical system, Nike elected to go with SAP to support its reengineering efforts. Relatively late to adopt an ES compared with most companies of its size, Nike chose to wait until the SAP apparel footwear vertical capability was well established. Also, Nike managers felt that their rapid growth spurt beginning in 1992 had put pressure on key processes. They felt that they needed their worldwide processes to mature a bit before analyzing them for their reengineering efforts, which involved not only product development but also extensive change in their international supply chain processes.

Similar to Reebok, Nike's inflexible existing systems and ambition to be a global company drove their efforts to adopt an ES. They felt that their systems' lack of integration contributed to their functional silos. It was agreed that since integration was more important to Nike than functional robustness, Nike would go with one vendor as opposed to the best-of-breed approach. Like Reebok, custom developing new systems was never even considered.

Before determining to go with an ES, however, Nike did consider an ES's effect on flexibility. This was a particularly painful concern for Nike, a dynamic and rapidly changing company that is used to making quick decisions without concern for impact on systems. Ken Harris, CIO, was even quoted as saying that although he thinks that Nike top management intellectually understands the idea of reduced technology uniqueness and flexibility through standardization, it may be "emotional poison" for them.[21] However, Roland Paanakker, IT program director at Nike, believes strongly that an ES will have a positive effect on Nike's decision making. He believes that managers will be more proactive and reflective in making decisions, and that an ES will enable many changes to be made more easily since Nike will have uniform processes throughout the world.

Unlike Reebok's IT plan-driven adoption, Nike's decision to employ an ES was driven by a company-wide reengineering effort that sought fundamental change in the way it does business. In order to avoid the clean-sheet-of-paper approach (because you might need to throw out that sheet if the ES does not support your vision), Nike selected their ES vendor fairly early in the reengineering process. It identified high-level reengineering strategies, the "what," and then brought in the ES to determine the "how." Although four other ESs were analyzed, SAP was selected because team members felt it was the only ES that truly supported Nike's industry.

Paanakker at Nike maintains that the ES itself isn't what allows for significant value and differentiation, but rather the integrated relationships with customers and suppliers that the ES can help enable. He explains, "We all have the same tools [ESs]. From these tools, we can develop different processes. The relationships that these processes support is what makes a company unique."[22]

Somewhat similar to Reebok, Nike is striving to develop a close relationship with SAP. By having influence with SAP, Nike hopes to contribute to SAP's future upgrades in its package's functionality. If Nike has process changes that do not affect its competitive advantage, Nike can ask the vendor to make changes to the base package. For competitive-advantage processes, Nike hopes to encourage SAP to add an extra feature or two to the base package, thereby reducing modifications to the system that Nike would have to make. A close partnership would also involve trust that the vendor would not reveal competitive secrets it has learned from doing any work that supports customized processes.

For both Reebok and Nike, deciding on an ES and selecting a vendor were viewed as important decisions that had potential effects on competitiveness. Senior executives were heavily involved in both cases. Managers in both companies thought carefully about how an ES would affect key business processes. However, they adopted different approaches to the timing of their ES decisions and their relationship with an industry association.

Other companies in the industry had to make the same decision about which vendor's package to adopt. Adidas, the German competitor to Reebok and Nike, chose SAP. New Balance, a smaller U.S. firm, didn't want to adopt SAP because it felt that the Reebok/VF/SAP partnership would take too long to yield a working system. New Balance was also concerned about the inability of SAP and other packages to handle information about product width; width sizing was a key marketing distinction of New Balance shoes. As a result, New Balance selected an ES from JBA International, which focuses on mid-sized companies.

These brief case studies illustrate a few of the factors involved in deciding whether to implement an enterprise system in a specific company. They portray the interplay between business and technical factors, between current capabilities and future business requirements, and between an individual company perspective and a broad industry view. One somewhat soothing factor in making such a complex decision is that tens of thousands of companies have implemented ES packages from the major vendors. You almost certainly can find some other organization that has faced the same issues and made a decision from which you can learn.

LINKING ENTERPRISE SYSTEMS TO STRATEGY AND ORGANIZATION

ONE OF THE MOST OFTEN OVERLOOKED TOPICS REGARDING ESs is analysis of their implications for business strategy and organizational structure and culture. Companies think they are merely putting in a computer system, and spend little if any time considering the strategic implications of their ES. They also do not realize that their ES can have significant implications for the way the company is organized and the day-to-day culture of the organization. Those who are aware of the organizational implications often make highly simplistic assumptions about how the system will change the culture—as if by magic.

I'll try to shed light on these seemingly esoteric issues. Every company should be thinking about how ESs—whether they have adopted one or not—affect their competitive position and the way the company feels and functions. Although it's still too early to know the long-term strategic and cultural implications of ESs, I'll give examples of companies who did some thinking on the topic and adjusted their ES projects accordingly.

ENTERPRISE SYSTEMS AND COMPETITIVE STRATEGY

It's not a new idea to say that information systems have an impact on business strategy, but anyone seeking a body of knowledge on how ES packages—the most comprehensive and expensive information systems of all—affect strategy will be unfulfilled. Does implementing an ES yield competitive advantage or disadvantage? How does it change industry strategy when every firm in an industry adopts the same ES package? Has an ES simply become a parity move—a cost of doing business? None of the answers to these questions is known for sure by anyone; we'll explore their key dimensions in this section.

What are the possible ways in which an ES could affect business and competitive strategy? First of all, given the high cost of an ES, there could be a significant impact on financial strategy. One might argue that a "low-cost producer" strategy would be made more difficult to realize when a company is spending hundreds of millions on a complex ES project, although it is possible to pursue a low-cost approach to implementing an enterprise system. Ultimately, however, the costs of an ES eventually have to trickle—or flood—into the organization's products and services.

Other aspects of an organization's financial strategy may ultimately be affected positively when there are major changes in key processes. For example, Elf Atochem N.A. expects that because of its ES it will increase net earnings by 20 percent, or $45 million per year. In this case, improvements in the company's financial position will come from reduced inventories and labor costs, better ability to negotiate with suppliers, and lower distribution costs.

But the more obvious areas for an ES's strategic impact involve operational strategy—how a company goes to market, creates its products and services, and works with suppliers, customers, and distribution partners. Enterprise systems can have a huge impact on operational strategy because of their effect on key business processes. Some popular operational strategies might only be achieved through the help of an ES. Take, for example, the idea of lean production. This form of operational strategy, first achieved in the Japanese automobile industry, has become pervasive throughout many manufacturing industries.[1] It is a "sell one, make one, order one" approach in which little inventory is maintained. It also typically involves a global sourcing approach in which suppliers, manufacturing plants, and distribution centers are scattered around the globe. Although such a strategy is possible without the use of an ES (Japanese automobile companies did not have them when they adopted the approach), it is difficult to achieve the cross-functional coordination necessary for lean production without integrated information systems. Ideally, an ES would note that a sale was made, arrange production, ensure that sufficient inventory was available, and make sure that all necessary resources were available.

Compaq Computer's implementation of an ES is the quintessential example of a lean production strategy in the making.[2] Compaq's goal is to move from a build-to-stock production model to a build-to-order approach. This would let it compete successfully with direct sellers of computers such as Dell, which has taken a lower-tech approach to information integration. Compaq managers concluded that a build-to-order strategy— constructing a computer after it was ordered by a customer— would not be possible or at least efficient without a new, highly integrated information system that would tie together ordering, configuration, manufacturing, inventory management, and distribution processes. So in 1994 Compaq began to install SAP's R/3 package. Today it has the system installed in all its manufacturing facilities, and most of its sales offices. Evidence of Compaq's leanness is its ability to order materials from suppliers on a daily basis, and to plan production on the basis of a week's sales. Previously, both processes were done on a 45-day cycle.

Of course, an ES is not the only factor in Compaq's new operational strategy. The firm also is developing new relationships with its distribution channel, outsourcing production, and building some non-SAP applications. In terms of the distribution channel, Compaq has informed its dealers that they will no longer be the exclusive channel for computer sales. Compaq has also worked with some large distributors/resellers (e.g., Merisel and Inacom) to implement new manufacturing processes in which the resellers customize the product to the customer's specifications. Compaq will use SAP in conjunction with the Internet to make exchanges of data with suppliers and customers in real time rather than in a batch-based fashion. Finally, Compaq has developed its own applications in the areas of production forecasting and order scheduling, reasoning that common industry-wide applications would hardly lead to competitive advantage. There's no doubt, however, that an ES is an integral part of Compaq's operational strategy, and that relatively seamless lean production won't be achieved without it.

Compaq's decisions illustrate some of the issues involved in trying to achieve competitive advantage from the use of an ES. Company managers must ask themselves a series of questions before being able to determine how an ES will affect competitive advantage. These questions include the following:

► What are my current sources of competitive advantage? How will the ES affect these current capabilities? If, for example, my primary basis for competing is excellent customer service, will the ES help or hurt that area of the company?

► Will the ES bring about new strategic capabilities that may be useful in the future? For example, will I be able to engage in lean production manufacturing, and will that be necessary to compete?

► How will the costs of an ES affect the cost position of my products and services in the marketplace? If I'm the low-cost producer now, will I still be after paying the bill for an ES?

► What other firms in my industry are implementing an ES? How is it likely to affect their own strengths and weaknesses? What will be the competitive dynamics if everybody gets an ES? Who is likely to implement one particularly well or badly?

▶ If other firms in our industry are implementing ESs, am I likely to need to connect with them electronically in the future? If I already frequently work with competitors, perhaps those relationships will be more electronic and automated in the future.

▶ Are there particular aspects of the business where it would be damaging to have "commodity," or industry-standard, information and processes? Can I separate these from the rest of the ES implementation?

▶ Will an ES project distract me from doing what is really important in my business? If I have to assign hundreds of people to the project or pay a lot of money to a consulting firm, will I be able to accomplish the projects I need to be successful?

What's good for strategy may not be good for ES implementation, unfortunately. When Compaq managers decided to build their own functionality in competitively important business domains, they knew that it would be difficult to build custom applications and interface them with their SAP system (even though they wrote them in SAP's programming language in order to make the link easier). But they decided it was worth the trouble. Similarly, when Intel decided for reasons of competitive advantage that its ES implementation would not include manufacturing systems, managers knew that interfacing proprietary systems with the company's ES package would be difficult. But manufacturing excellence is one of Intel's core strategic capabilities, and a system that could also be adopted by a competitor was inconsistent with their competitive goals.

If the entire industry is adopting ESs, as is the case with such industries as oil, chemicals, consumer products, and computers (with a few companies being exceptions in each industry), the potential basis for competitive advantage shifts. It is no longer just having an ES that counts, but rather implementing it better than anyone else, or in a way that better fits a company. One company may achieve advantage by implementing its ES faster, cheaper, or more effectively than others; it may achieve a closer fit between its system and the way it wants to do business. The risk, however, is that implementing an ES will simply become a parity move, that is, part of the cost of doing business. This situation would not be unparalleled in the history of information technology: Certainly, automated teller machines in the banking industry, and a brochure-type Internet presence in almost all industries, have become noncompetitive investments that most companies must make. But this is not a state to be envied. Careful thought about whether to implement an ES, and which aspects of it to adopt, can prevent implementation from becoming a parity move.

In order to know where your competitive advantage will come from in the future, it's helpful to know where it comes from today. As I've mentioned, it's important to know to what particular value discipline your company aspires. Product innovation–oriented companies aren't likely to develop competitive advantage through the use of an ES, at least with the current state of the software (though this could be possible in the future, since ES vendors are now moving into the domain of product data management). Therefore, product innovation firms should probably seek to minimize the costs of administrative applications; adopting an ES can be a reasonable strategy for doing so. Intel's adoption of an ES is a case in point. The company clearly excels through developing new, more powerful microprocessors faster than anybody else, and its use of an ES is to support commodity processes.

That leaves operational excellence and customer intimacy. Advantage based on operational excellence is a good candidate for being enhanced by an ES. The supply chain benefits I discussed earlier are often critical to operational excellence strategies, for example. Lean inventory management and well-coordinated relationships between demand and supply activities are de rigeur for an operationally focused manufacturing firm. Excellent financial management processes and information might be critical to operational advantage in financial services companies, although ESs have not penetrated the industry yet to a large degree. Elf Atochem falls into this category; its products are largely commodities, and it wants to compete primarily on excellent customer service and supply chain management.

Customer intimacy has not previously been the forte of ES users, although this is beginning to change. Enterprise system vendors and external suppliers such as Siebel Systems have begun to focus heavily on adding customer information features to ESs. If your idea of customer intimacy involves giving customers access to much of your information, putting in an ES can be essential to an intimacy-based strategy. However, I'd argue that ESs are not yet capable of capturing, storing, and distributing the kind of customer knowledge that is involved in close customer relationships. Right now that involves separate applications, which should be integrated with ES customer information. The integrator of all this diverse information is most likely to be a customer-facing human today, not any particular form of information system.

No two ES implementations are exactly alike, so it's also possible to achieve advantage by simply configuring your system to your own business model very effectively or by selecting the right bolt-on packages to interface with your ES. With more than 8,000 different configuration choices in an SAP package, for example, many idiosyncratic ways of doing business can be accommodated. The options increase markedly when bolt-on systems are added.

For example, VF Corporation, the maker of Lee jeans and other forms of apparel, has cobbled together many different packages to create something truly unique.[3] SAP R/3 holds everything together and is the backbone of the overall system (recall that VF joined with Reebok to work with SAP in developing an ES tailored to the apparel industry). Product development processes, which are not strongly supported by ES vendors, are supported by WebPDM, which links a variety of design programs and manages the process. Warehouse control and manufacturing control is done by custom applications developed in-house. Capacity and raw materials planning are done by i2's Rhythm package. Forecasting is done with Logility. Micromarketing is done by Marketmax, Spectra, JDA Software, and custom-built applications. All of these systems interface with the SAP ES (though some do so with much greater ease— and less manual intervention—than others). SAP and other major vendors make it easier to interface other systems by providing *hooks,* or *application program interfaces* (APIs), to their systems. Also, VF isn't using the bolt-on software packages out of the box. Because of the company's large size, it can persuade software suppliers to write new apparel industry standard software to fit its needs.

If you decide that advantage will primarily come from other applications, either separate packages or custom-developed systems, you of course need to figure out the costs of developing them and interfacing them with an ES. If you feel that your ES can be tailored to support your unique advantage, that tailoring will probably cost you substantially more than a plain-vanilla system implementation. Because these costs are high, you should ensure that the organization follows through on actually delivering the proposed benefits and advantages.

All of the sources of competitive advantage I've discussed so far involve differentiating your business from competitors. But as Michael Porter pointed out more than twenty years ago, it's also possible to compete effectively on cost. Your company could gain a cost advantage over competitors by not implementing an ES, or by implementing one more cheaply than competitors. I've already described Air Products and Chemicals' thinking in this regard in the previous chapter. The company's managers haven't put in an ES because, among other factors, they fear that the cost of an ES might force the company to raise its prices, leading to lost sales in some of the commodity gas markets in which it competes.

Certainly some implementations cost more than others. While the concept of competing on cost and implementing a software package that costs multiple millions of dollars may seem oxymoronic, the two ideas can coexist. If you are going for a low-cost implementation, then of course you'll want a plain-vanilla system, and you'll have to be willing to make your processes and information quite generic. As the CEO of one large chemical firm says, "Competitive advantage in this industry might just come from doing the best and cheapest job at implementing SAP." Is it too obvious to point out, however, that simply putting in an ES is not enough to achieve cost-based advantage? You also need a lot of organizational discipline, measurement programs, cost-oriented suppliers, and managers who focus incessantly on cost.

Competitive advantage might also result from being the earliest in your industry to implement an ES, so factor how early you are into your benefit deliberations. If you install the system first, you have a chance to also be the first to implement the business changes that benefit customers, partners, and your own internal processes. Your organization may learn the package and how to use it effectively before competitors. You could also be the first to install new customer-oriented or product-development-related modules that bring advantage in those domains of business value.

Competitive advantage comes not from systems, but from doing something better than competitors. Before signing off on an ES implementation that's being justified on a competitive basis, make sure you know what the "something" is, and how much better it's going to be done. "We'll deliver in three days instead of three weeks, and our survey of key customers tells us that improving by that amount should gain us ten points in market share"—that's the kind of language you want to hear. Also listen for such comments as "Our competitors won't be able to match our improvements because we have proprietary supply chain optimization algorithms," or something similar about how the competition will react to your moves.

In some cases, of course, the smart competitive move may be to avoid packaged ESs altogether. If there is no conceivable strategic advantage from an ES, a company may be better off pulling together a series of best-of-breed systems or even internally developed applications, or continuing to work with its existing systems.

ENTERPRISE SYSTEMS AND ORGANIZATIONAL STRUCTURE AND CULTURE

If matching ESs to competitive strategy represents an opportunity, matching ESs to organizational structure and culture is more likely to represent a problem. Don't misunderstand: There are surely opportunities that arise from ESs in the realm of organization. Companies can implement the systems to support organizational structures that were not previously possible or to change the organization's culture in a desired direction.

One common approach, for example, is to use an ES to support the centralization of certain services within an organization, typically involving finance, accounting, purchasing, or human resources. Such a shared-services approach is not a revolutionary change in organizational structure, but it does typically allow for savings through economies of scale and through having a single common approach, or process, for doing work. At Amoco (now part of BP Amoco), for example, shared services were a major underpinning of the company's SAP implementation.[4] Amoco reorganized fourteen different services staffed by more than 6,000 people into a shared-services mode, and supported almost all of the services with its ES. More than 1,000 finance and accounting employees' jobs alone were eliminated because of this change; before its merger with BP, Amoco expected to save over $350 million annually from ES-enabled shared services.

But such opportunities are not normally how the relationship between an ES and the organization in which it is being installed plays out. Instead, a company's organization typically crops up as an implementation problem. Either the company doesn't realize that organizational factors will come into play, or it doesn't do what is necessary to realize the organizational objectives it wants to accomplish. These objectives, if they exist at all, usually involve integrating the corporation across geographical or business unit boundaries or creating a more disciplined organizational culture in which everyone uses similar processes and information. However, because many companies view an ES project as just a computer system, they neither articulate their organizational objectives clearly nor manage to achieve them.

There are many variations on these common themes, but most organizations can be classified along one (or more) of them. In the next sections I'll describe each theme and give an example of where it took place.

THE "NO ORGANIZATIONAL ASPIRATIONS" PROBLEM

Many organizations fail to specify any organizational objectives at all when they implement an ES. Either consciously or (more likely) unconsciously, they separate the domain of information technology from that of organizational structure and change. In the past, when most systems assumed no specific organizational model, this separation was no problem. Now, however, the integration and breadth of ESs almost force new ways to organize on those who implement the systems. Generally speaking, the ES-enabled organization does business the same way worldwide. Functional boundaries in organizations that employ ESs are deemphasized in favor of cross-functional coordination. Idiosyncratic ways of doing business or reporting about it are made more difficult. Job skill requirements are raised.

If an organization is unaware of these types of changes and does not manage the achievement of them, it is likely to run into trouble. A leading electronics firm, for example, implemented an ES as a technical solution to problems caused by poorly functioning legacy systems. The company is highly decentralized, and it actually ended up implementing the same system in several different versions across the organization—but not across all of it. This was not terribly efficient, but it had the desired effect of preserving the company's decentralized structure.

But where the company did not anticipate or articulate its organizational direction was at the business unit level. For example, several business units were particularly interested in the purchasing and supply chain management functionality of the ES, because they were in markets that were fast-growing and particularly sensitive to availability of the company's products. They had strong hopes that the purchasing function of the company—never noted for its sophistication in the past—would be made more professional as a result of the new system. The company had a strong process orientation and referred to the desired changes as "reengineered" purchasing processes; organization and culture within the function were never mentioned.

As the system began to be implemented, however, some managers within the company realized that a problem had surfaced. The employees of the purchasing function were simply not up to the task. Many were high school graduates; few were certified by the professional purchasing association (APICS). Their skills had been suited to the old "look for it in the warehouse" approach to supply chain management, but with complex, ES-enabled information about available-to-promise inventory, EDI linkages to suppliers, and distribution routing algorithms, they were lost. Fortunately for the workers (but unfortunately for the company in this situation), the company's somewhat patriarchal culture made simply replacing the workers with more skilled ones out of the question. The workers would have to be remade through education, APICS certification, and patience. As a result, the ES project manager in one business unit felt that the project had been set back at least two years.

These organizational issues could have been anticipated if the company had faced them squarely. But it never considered the issue until this lack of skills blocked the critical path for the implementation timeline. If you don't know what your organizational objectives are, it's a good bet that hidden ones will come along and bite you.

THE "LET'S GET INTEGRATED" PROBLEM

Perhaps the most common organizational problem in ES initiatives is the failure to achieve an envisioned higher level of organizational integration. As you know by now, ESs exist to support firms that are, or want to be, integrated across functions and business units. But the system does not bring about the change by itself. Many companies do not take the necessary steps to realize the level of integration they seek.

Let's look at an example. A natural resources company was highly divisionalized. It had one division that sold to consumers through retailers, one that sold to industrial customers, and one that produced raw materials for other divisions. For its entire history the divisions had been largely autonomous, both with regard to information systems and in many other respects.

In 1994 the company's CEO began to talk about achieving greater integration across the divisions. Some of its retailers were also beginning to distribute to industrial customers, and the retailers were demanding more divisional coordination. The company's chief information officer, who had been aware that several divisions were out of gas with regard to their legacy systems, heard the talk of business unit integration and went to the CEO with a proposal. If we get one of these ESs, he said, we'd be able to have common information and processes across all of our business units, and the integration would occur naturally. The CEO, of course, knew little about information systems, and took the CIO at his word.

A large ES project was initiated late in 1994. All three business units were encouraged to replace their old systems with the new ES. From the beginning, however, the integration was compromised because each business unit was allowed to replace its systems separately. They had successfully argued to the CEO that their manufacturing, order management, inventory management, and other operational processes were too different from the other divisions to allow full commonality. The only systems that would be common throughout the corporation were financial and human resources (HR) applications.

The level of integration deteriorated from there. One division, whose existing systems were hopelessly inadequate to its needs, implemented the ES with vigor. The head of that unit convinced second-level managers that the change was necessary, and once they committed to the ES he held them accountable for the process, information, and organizational changes necessary to complete the implementation successfully. The other two business units, however, were in much less of a hurry to put in the systems and did only what was necessary to placate the CEO and CIO.

Other than occasionally mentioning the goal of integration at staff meetings (and approving the ES project in the first place), the CEO did nothing to bring about a higher level of integration. No steps were undertaken to bring about greater commonality or similarity of key processes or information. No managers who resisted the ES were punished or even scolded. No education was offered on why the integration or the system that supported it was desirable, or how integration might be achieved.

In early 1997 the CEO realized that despite expenditures of over $300 million on the ES, little progress was being made toward the goal of integration. He cancelled the corporate-wide initiative and backed away publicly from the goal of integration. The one division that had made progress with the ES—not coincidentally, the one division with a high level of executive support for the project—was allowed to continue, but the other two divisions killed their projects. The human resources module, which replaced an HR system with severe Year 2000 problems, was also allowed to continue, and it became partially functional in early 1998. In short, the project was not a total loss, but its achievements bore little resemblance to the original integration goals.

This is actually a fairly common story. Because ESs are associated with the idea of integration, company managers often assume that the integration will happen automatically. But achieving process and information integration requires a high level of organizational change. Some parts of the organization will undoubtedly have to adopt ways of doing business that are suboptimal for their purposes. Managers won't see the benefits of making the change, or will wonder why they have to change to fit a computer system. Particular functions or units will resist or drag their feet.

It's perhaps inevitable that organizations based in the United States would have difficulty with the level of integration many are trying to achieve with ES projects. Most American firms have allowed functions and business units considerable latitude in how they perform day-to-day business processes, define their information requirements, and embody them in computer systems. With the advent of minicomputers, and later PCs and small client/server systems, thousands of computer applications were allowed to bloom like flowers (some might say weeds) around the organization. To switch to a centrally defined and controlled ES in which everything must be common is a bracing change, to say the least. It is perhaps easier in some parts of Europe (Germany comes to mind) and in Japan, where the corporate center is often stronger and divisional autonomy less pronounced. Even in German firms, however, I've seen highly decentralized approaches to implementing an ES.

Now that we know that problems with ES-enabled organizational integration are somewhat expected, how can they be addressed? The answer should be fairly obvious from the case study just presented. Here are a few suggestions:

▶ Education is the greatest single need in this area. Managers must know (preferably before adopting an ES) what they are getting into. They should be told what the implications of the system are in terms of key processes, organizational structure, the information they use, and the systems they have today.

▶ Consensus on the need for and pace of integration is an important step after education. If managers agree that the integration is necessary, they can be held responsible for the changes involved in carrying it out. If they don't agree or aren't asked, they probably won't be enthusiastic about the changes and may actively resist them.

▶ A strong sense of "who we are" is necessary. As I discussed in chapter 2, it's critical for organizations pursuing the goal of integration to know just how much of it they want and what the organization will look and feel like when it's achieved. Many of the problems in ES projects have arisen from companies thinking they wanted to be an integrated firm, but backing away from it when the real implications became clear.

▶ Another requirement is a bit obvious, but often violated anyway: high-level executive support. Organizational integration is only achievable when there is strong commitment from those whose commitment counts. As one Intel manager put it, using Arthurian language, "Senior management must have purity of heart" on these issues. A senior management team may not feel like King Arthur and the knights of the Round Table when contemplating ES projects, but similar levels of commitment and sincerity are necessary.

THE "LET'S WIPE OUT RENEGADES" PROBLEM

A related organizational problem with ES implementations involves the objective of creating a more disciplined culture around information, processes, or systems. The firms that adopt this objective have usually had a laissez-faire approach to the domain in question in the past, and renegades have been allowed to take whatever approach they preferred. The result has usually been a proliferation of systems and ways of doing work, each with its own information. Companies find that some systems users and managers are happy with this approach, but it makes integration across business functions and units very difficult to accomplish. It can also be quite expensive to build and maintain this kind of IT environment, since basic functions are replicated across multiple parts of the business.

A typical off-the-record remark for ES project managers in this environment would be, "We've had lots of renegades in the past, but we're going to put them out of business with our ES." The expectation is that when an encompassing, technically up-to-date system is available (or, in some cases, when its impending arrival is merely announced), the renegades will be forced, or at least strongly encouraged, to abandon their renegade systems. Centralized control over information and processes will finally be restored.

This sort of environment is most commonly encountered in companies where there are many knowledge workers, where the overall corporate culture is both loose and entrepreneurial, and where the company has had considerable early success. It is also more commonly found in information technology companies, in which many employees and managers feel that they have expertise in information systems (though a little knowledge can be dangerous). Two examples are Apple Computer and Intel. Both implemented ESs in part because they wanted to get control over renegade computer systems that had proliferated around the organization. Intel was concerned that integration across such systems was difficult, and IT costs were rising even faster than the successful company's revenues. Apple had the extra incentive of declining business performance: Systems costs had to be brought into line. In both companies, project managers hoped that the prospect or the actuality of an ES would bring renegades into line.

Managers of both companies found, however, that the ES alone did not change the culture to a more disciplined model. Neither firm is finished with its ES project, and it is safe to say that neither firm has yet brought all renegades under control. Both firms have discovered that there are several other explicit steps that must be taken to corral the renegades in addition to announcing the ES project. In short, the cultural and organizational aspects of the project must themselves be viewed as a program of change. Some of the specific elements involved in the change include the following:

▶ There must be a close accounting of what systems exist within the company, and which have functionality that will be replaced by an ES (though this may be a matter of opinion and debate!). Simply finding all the renegade systems will be more difficult and time-consuming than you think.

▶ The managers who "own" the renegade system should be given some chance to argue their case. The higher the manager playing the "judge" role is in the organizational hierarchy, the more apparent the value of integration. At Nova Pharmaceuticals, a Canadian drug firm, anyone can continue to use a renegade system—as long as they meet with the CEO and get his approval. Of course, he gives it quite sparingly. In most companies, there are at least some valid reasons why a manager or user would resist the transition to an ES. Listen to them and provide for exceptions to the policy of moving all renegades to the corporate ES.

▶ Those who currently use renegade systems and will have to change over should be educated not only on the functions of the new ES, but also on the rationale for converting and the benefits to them and the company from using the new system.

▶ Managers of renegade systems should be offered some benefit in exchange for what they will lose in terms of processes and information tailored to their specific needs. For example, funds saved from no longer having to support and maintain the renegade system could be redeployed to other purposes within the same department.

▶ The schedule for converting from the renegade system must be agreed upon by the ES project team and the manager and users of the renegade system, and if the ES schedule slips, don't be surprised if the renegade system transition schedule slips as well.

THE FEDERALIST ALTERNATIVE

There is an alternative to the idea that all parts of a company need to have fully common information and processes and a single corporate ES. I call it *information federalism,* and it's perhaps a better fit to most American firms than the full-integration model.[5] In this nation of rugged individualism, it's usually extremely difficult to get everyone to do the same thing. Federalism in politics, of course, is pretty well institutionalized in the United States. It means that the federal government controls some aspects of governing, and the rest are left up to the states or even smaller governmental bodies to handle as they please.

The analogy to corporate governance is obvious.[6] The corporate center controls some policies and processes, and remote units have discretion over the remainder. Of course, federalism represents a continuum of approaches. If the corporate center specifies most (but not all) approaches to business and leaves local units with only a bit of discretion, the arrangement might be called a monarchy with a slight degree of federalism. If, as at one European company I studied, the corporate organization specifies only that a particular ES vendor's package be used but then allows more than 400 different versions of the ES to be installed around the organization, we're really talking about information anarchy with a slight degree of federalism. Not surprisingly, this company has spent well over $1.5 billion on its various ES implementations thus far.

Although the idea of federalism isn't new even in the information systems context (though it has never really been described using that term), how federalism works in the context of an ES is an unfinished story. Not all vendors support this approach, and virtually no one is really finished with establishing ES-enabled federalism. There also exist an "automated" version of federalism, in which common information is aggregated by a corporate-level ES, and a "manual" federalism, in which the mostly common information is made fully comparable and aggregated via significant human intervention. With these caveats, here's a description of how federalism works.

The first and most difficult aspect of instituting ES federalism is for the organization to decide which information and processes need to be common worldwide. It might decide that the term *revenues* has to mean the same thing everywhere, for example, because they have to be aggregated for financial reporting. However, the same organization might decide that because different divisions have different supplier relationships, supplier information could be allowed to vary across divisions. Since information is closely aligned to business processes, flexibility in one area usually implies flexibility in another.

After the extent of common information has been determined, a company seeking automated ES federalism installs one instance of, say, SAP R/3 (one of the packages for which federalism is possible, but only in the more recent versions of the package) in corporate headquarters. This is the system on which corporate financials are kept, along with any other information that needs to be rolled up to the corporate level. Then each business unit can have its own system, supporting its own information needs. Only those data elements agreed to be common need match those in the corporate system. It is even possible for the noncorporate systems to be from a different ES vendor than the corporate system, although the resulting interface issues are obviously trickier than when all software is from one vendor.

If different business units have different customer or supplier types, basic business processes, and management approaches, they can also have different information under the federalist approach. This is the situation in many large firms, and the ability to accommodate it is the primary advantage of ES-enabled federalism. Previous approaches to federalism in which each business unit had its own unique systems made it difficult to aggregate information that needed to be common.

Federalism also has its disadvantages, however. The process of deciding what information should be common can be difficult, time-consuming, and contentious. Some managers will argue that their preferred version of federalism involves supplying headquarters with the information it wants, but using their own system. They may also advocate simply integrating diverse sources of information at the data warehouse level. Unfortunately, if the company desires real integration and information transparency across the organization, these faux federalist approaches don't really work. Further, the rebellious managers may well be treating enterprise-level information requirements as an extra task for today that will be abandoned tomorrow. It's not really worth doing an ES in the first place unless the entire organization takes the enterprise-level information requirement seriously.

ES-enabled federalism also involves a higher degree of technical and implementation difficulty than merely installing an ES. Instead of implementing one system for an entire company, federalism means putting multiple systems in place and getting them to talk to each other. Instead of fitting one large organization—with its processes, organizational structure, and preferred information environment—to one system, federalism means going through the fitting process several times. In short, federalism means more business flexibility at the cost of greater technical complexity. It's only feasible and desirable if it's truly important to maintain specific ways of doing business in different parts of a company. Most firms shouldn't even mention the possibility of ES-enabled federalism unless they have already determined that one ES size doesn't fit all.

At Hewlett-Packard (HP), for example, a company with a strong tradition of business unit autonomy, there has been little advocacy for commonality across the company's several large divisions that are implementing SAP. Not all business units are even implementing the system; there is no corporate mandate. Except for a small amount of common financial data across all divisions that are implementing the system (necessary to roll up

results for financial reporting at the corporate level), HP's federalist approach gives all the power to the divisions as far as ES
decisions are concerned. This approach fits the HP culture well,
but because implementation resources aren't shared and the system architecture is complex, it is very expensive: Managers estimate that well over a billion dollars will be spent across the
corporation before the various projects are completed. HP's
approach qualifies as federalism, but it's a limited version of the
concept.

ENTERPRISE SYSTEMS AND EMPOWERMENT

It may seem incongruous to speak of ESs and empowerment in
the same breath. These systems are often discussed in terms of
standard ways of doing business, hierarchical organizations, and
forced marches to commonality. How can they allow any sort of
empowerment?

The space for free action is admittedly limited. It doesn't
work very well, for example, if individual workers or even
departments have a say as to how key information elements
should be defined, or even how the system should be used to
support a particular business function. That kind of empowerment would place severe restrictions on the function of a system
across disparate parts of an organization.

For this reason, it's important to make clear from the beginning of an ES implementation that workers and individual
departments won't be able to design their own systems. At one
manufacturing company, for example, workers were excited
about the new ES their company was installing. Memos from
the CEO had been sent out to the entire firm, basically promising that the expensive new system would be all things to all people. Plant workers, who had suffered greatly from inflexible and
obsolete manufacturing systems, were particularly enthusiastic
because they believed that they would finally get better information at the plant level. Each plant had previously controlled its
own information environment (including its own part number-
ing system), but the plants' systems were mainframe based and

difficult to change. Looking forward to the new system, several plant groups put together lists of their information preferences and of employees who volunteered to work with the new system. Unfortunately, managers had to inform the plant workers that their inputs were not particularly helpful, and that no such local empowerment was possible with the new system. It's not hard to imagine how the plant workers felt: disappointed, misled, and generally unhappy with their employer.[7]

However, there is, as you might suspect from the title of this section, some opening for individual and small-group empowerment with ESs, although it's small. It involves flexibility not in the creation of information or processes, but in the use of them. The widespread availability of information in an ES environment means that workers and departments can be offered more information than they've ever received in the past. They no longer need an intermediary to get whatever information they need out of the system, and the information they can get is likely to be broader, more accurate, and more timely than any they've gotten in the past.

At Union Carbide, for example, the managers of the ES initiative took a typically structured approach to defining processes and information. The demands of global connectivity dictated common data elements and business processes. But the company's culture lauds empowerment and individual initiative, and managers didn't want the ES to run counter to that cultural dimension. The project leaders, therefore, focused on "information empowerment," making unparalleled amounts of information available throughout the organization (and even outside it, to customers and suppliers). Workers at relatively low levels of the organization no longer had restrictions on what information they could access (other than obvious ones, such as the salary database). While it's too early to tell at Union Carbide whether this type of empowerment is sufficient to fit the broader culture, it's at least a step in the right direction.

Workers can also be somewhat empowered through the sharing and use of ES- and process-oriented knowledge. A new ES generates a variety of new work processes and information transactions for workers to perform. In the beginning, and perhaps forever, some workers will know more than others about how the system works and how it relates to their jobs. If workers can share their knowledge with each other, and build a knowledge base about process and information transactions out of their own experiences, they will be empowered to perform their own jobs more effectively.

One software company, Ventix Systems, has developed a capability for users of ESs to capture, share, and access job, process, and transaction knowledge. The knowledge is organized along the lines of the key processes of the organization. If workers can access a knowledge base of ES-related insights, their work can obviously be more efficient and effective, as well as empowering. Another key benefit of managing this type of knowledge is that internal help desk personnel or "super users" will not be bothered as much by questions if users can consult a knowledge base. Enterprise system package vendors are working on similar capabilities, and I believe it's likely that all ES packages will ultimately include the capability to manage knowledge during implementation and use.

ENTERPRISE SYSTEMS AND MANAGEMENT CULTURE

I've described ESs as primarily affecting culture from the perspective of workers within a company. But an ES also has important implications for the management cultures of firms that adopt one. Unfortunately, the changes are not empowering, but rather involve a higher level of managerial discipline and accountability. Most managers—at least senior ones—can already get the information they need to do their jobs, even if it takes a horde of analysts to pull it together. The big change with an ES is that other managers can get information about them.

When I talk to managers of ES projects and of organizations in which ESs are being implemented, a common theme emerges. They say that too often managers have been able to hide poor performance of their functions or business units behind poor, unintegrated computer systems. One executive described an "electronic white-out" culture, in which results could be easily manipulated if they weren't flattering. When processes and information practices vary widely from one part of the company to another, it's often true that the only comparable performance measures are financial—and any sophisticated manager knows how to tinker with accounting figures to make them look more impressive.

After an ES has been implemented, "there is no place to hide," as another manager I interviewed put it. Performance figures mean the same thing across the company and are reported without human intervention. Anyone can find out at any moment how a particular manager's unit is performing. It's easy to see how a culture of greater management accountability could develop. Although it's too early to say how quickly or how easily this trend will take place, or how managers will react to it, companies embarking on ES projects should be aware of this dimension of cultural change, and prepare managers to deal with it.

ORGANIZATIONAL CHANGE DURING IMPLEMENTATION

If there's one thing that managers of ES projects say they regret, it's not devoting enough attention to people and organizational change during the implementation. Setting up the right organizational structure for the project, as I'll describe in chapter 6, is part of the organizational change process. As with any other major business change, the leaders of an ES project must also identify the key change roles in the effort: the change leaders, the agents, the targets, the resistors. It's a good idea to clearly identify the types of behaviors and attitudes needed by the various involved parties in an ES initiative and to assess their readiness to adopt those new attributes. These principles are "Change Management 101" ideas, but they are particularly relevant to ES projects because of the size and scale of the change involved. An

ES project sponsor and leader should regularly consult key texts on change management in an information systems context.[8]

But the most important organizational change issues in any ES initiative have to do with education and training. It's fashionable, almost hackneyed, to point out that most organizations underestimate the amount of training and education needed by both the technical staff and business users of a new ES. It's still true, however. A few firms have not underestimated the issue, and it's worth noting that they spend high percentages—between 25 and 50 percent—of their overall project budgets on educational and skills development issues.

On what kinds of subjects do people need training? Just for example:

▶ Technical people need to learn the nature of the package, the hardware and networking requirements needed to run it, and the overall system's performance characteristics.

▶ Process designers need to learn what process designs the system is capable of supporting, and what the implications would be of seeking a change in the configuration.

▶ Each business user needs to learn the day-to-day use of the system, how the system supports the process that he or she performs, and how it affects the broader organization each time he or she presses a key.

▶ Senior executives need to learn the implications of the system for strategy, organization, and business processes, and how an ES-enabled organization can compete more effectively.

Even if a company uses a consultant to help implement an ES, it needs to be sure that the consultant trains the necessary internal people on how the system works in the context of the business and on how to maintain and modify it. This should be specified in the consulting contract, and not left to goodwill. Even if you decide that you want to largely eschew consultants to help you implement the system, you may find that they can be very useful as trainers of your own people.

Training often starts too late, but it can start too early as well. It has to be given just in time, shortly before the learning is needed. This typically means that most training must take place after the system has been installed, so that users can actually use it. Training that takes place before the system is really available often doesn't stick.

It's worth thinking about building or buying a technology-based *performance support system* that will give users training on the system at their desks when they need it. These systems can be very technology focused, as with traditional help functions. However, they can also be quite sophisticated on business issues, helping users learn about the technology, the process, and the business objective all at the same time.

At Intel, for example, a group of advanced learning technologists is preparing a set of performance support tools while an ES is being implemented at the company. Because both the system and the processes it supports are highly complex, the training challenges are quite difficult. The Intel learning experts sometimes suggest to the implementers of the system that a change to the process or system would considerably ease the training problem. Intel is wise to begin developing these training tools while changes in the system can still be made. Perhaps the most frequent error I've seen in training and education—other than not devoting sufficient resources to them—is starting too late in the game.

One last word about the human side of implementation. I've mentioned that ES projects often mean that companies don't need as many people to work in an ES-enabled environment, but they have to be considerably more skilled and educated about the business: the "half as many, twice as smart" phenomenon. The employees have to figure out how to do their existing jobs with a new system. They have to know the implications of their actions with the ES for the rest of the organization, which entails having a broad, cross-functional perspective. They have to learn new analytical and reporting approaches. In short, they have to learn to live in a different, more complex world. Do I need to say that it's difficult to make or find people who are twice as smart and who can deal with all of these issues? If you are committed to upgrading the skills of the people you have—and I strongly advocate this—you need to start very early in the ES process.

ENTERPRISE SYSTEMS AS A WAY OF LIFE

Most organizations feel that although ESs are difficult to implement and the organizational changes are substantial during implementation, there is a light at the end of the tunnel. That is, the difficult period will come to an end and the organization can relax again in terms of strategic, organizational, and technical change. In other words, a little pain now will be rewarded by peace later on.

But while it is likely that the types of changes found in ES projects will slow down to some degree, I'd argue that almost all firms will never be finished with ES-related changes. Companies are embarking upon not a project, but rather a way of life. The major changes during implementation will subside, but other changes will continue:

► Adaptation of the system to changes in the structure and function of the business (e.g., mergers or acquisitions, development of new products and services)

► Installation of new releases of the software, which may include new software modules and capabilities

► Training new users on the system, or old users on new functions and capabilities

► Bringing new business units into the use of the ES

► Dealing with new managers' opinions about how the system should fit the business, or vice versa

To adapt to these ongoing changes, companies will have to ensure that resources are available to staff and support what is essentially a permanent function. Intel managers claim that twelve people are necessary on an ongoing basis just to make changes in the system corresponding to the creation of new business and financial units; many more people will be necessary to install new versions and modules. Day-to-day support of the system is also a never-ending task; early evidence suggests that many "power users," who expected to return to their jobs in business functions, may be needed indefinitely in ES support roles. Firms may also need to keep project managers and an entire project office in business to deal with ongoing ES change issues.

Even without changes in the system or the business, ongoing resources are necessary to maintain and enforce new organizational structures and behaviors. For example, a company may decide that all customer information will be common worldwide with its ES, and that the customer master data will be maintained centrally. In order for this wish to be realized, however, a strong central function must be established to create, modify, prune, and maintain the customer data. Moreover, some sort of "information police force" must be present to ensure that remote functions and units don't establish their own customer databases. Commonality of either functions or processes is a virtue that must be invested in over time.

It's often said that "the only constant is change," but company managers often fail to realize that the maxim extends to ES projects. Before starting an ES project, they should realize that they are embarking upon an irrevocably different way of life. The need for organizational resources, attention, and change management will never go away.

5

LINKING ENTERPRISE SYSTEMS TO BUSINESS PROCESSES AND INFORMATION

ENTERPRISE SYSTEMS ARE PROBABLY MOST DISTINCTIVE FOR their orientation to broad, cross-functional business processes and common information. Unlike previous information systems, ESs are able to pass information freely across an organization's key business functions. No functional stovepipes need apply. For decades firms have wanted to integrate their information systems across broad processes; for just as many decades they have built or installed systems that address only a single part of the organization's needs. Salespeople have been unable to find out what inventory is available for sale because that information resided inaccessibly in a manufacturing system. Manufacturing could not build only what the salesperson had sold because there was no linkage between the manufacturing function and the systems used by the sales force. In overcoming this segregation, ESs have been the single most important factor responsible for advancing a process view of the business.

There's a catch, however. Or rather several catches. This chapter will primarily be devoted to the catches and what to do about them. As a preview, one catch is that it's quite difficult to start working as if the organization were process oriented just because an information system makes it possible. Another is that the complexity and integration of ESs make it infeasible to modify them substantially; therefore, it is not generally possible to support highly idiosyncratic process designs. A third problem is that it's hard to determine just what the design possibilities and constraints are for your business processes. A fourth catch involves the difficulty of achieving common information across an entire organization. I'll discuss each of these problems in greater detail and describe solutions, or at least compromises, to help deal with them.

The great overall compromise in using ES-enabled business processes relates to the set of implementation choices I described in the first chapter. It lies between the twin goals of getting a system in place that supports or enables the company's strategy, and getting a system with basic technical functionality in place quickly. It takes considerable time—in a large company, several years—to achieve the best possible fit between the system's parameters and the strategic "to be" designs of the many business processes that an ES supports. This sort of work also usually involves either expensive consultants or highly expert internal employees. Consequently, most companies will face considerable pressure to go with only an approximate fit between process and system. I'll talk later about how best to address this issue, but compromise is almost inevitable.

In addition to creating change in process designs, ESs also involve substantial changes in information. As I noted in the last chapter, it's common for firms to want common information— to have the terms *customer, product,* and *6.5-inch diameter flanged pipe* mean the same thing across an organization. In the latter part of the chapter I'll address some of the issues involved in creating common information.

ENTERPRISE SYSTEMS AS PROCESSWARE

Since process thinking is still somewhat unfamiliar to many business people, it may be useful to review basic process concepts and their relationship to ESs. What is it that makes ESs process oriented? Which business processes are supported by the typical ES, and which are not? Is it possible to use an ES and not really be managing business processes?

In 1993 I published a book—for what it's worth, the first book—on "process innovation," or reengineering.[1] I'm not pleased with how reengineering turned out in many firms, but I am still happy with the definition of *processes* in that book: "A process is thus a specific ordering of work activities across time and place, with a beginning, an end, and clearly-defined inputs and outputs: a structure for action."[2] Less formally, I'd call processes the way that work is supposed to be done in an organization. This second definition of processes makes it clear that processes are an abstraction; no one actually does their work all the time exactly as the process design specifies. Some researchers have called the way work actually gets done *practice;* whatever it's called, the distinction between the abstraction and the reality of how work is done is important, and I'll refer to it later.[3]

There is process design and then there is the implementation of those designs. Implementation can be viewed as the attempt to turn process into practice. There is plenty of anecdotal evidence, and some empirical research, suggesting that there has been a big gap between design and implementation in many corporate reengineering projects.[4] Many projects involved very ambitious change goals in the design phase, but during implementation these goals were abandoned or watered down considerably. One major problem that many organizations encountered was the difficulty of supporting new process designs with process-oriented information systems. Building their own new systems was impractical, and available packages were not widely explored because they did not support clean-sheet-of-paper designs.

In the early days of reengineering, ESs were not widely known; only a few companies (Dow Chemical, for example) in the early 1990s made explicit linkages between their reengineering projects and an ES. I referred to ESs only briefly, for example, in my 1993 book on reengineering (pp. 63–65 if you're highly motivated), and I know of no other mentions in the reengineering literature of the time. In the mid-1990s, when ESs were more common, they came to be viewed as the savior of reengineering. Since then, ESs have increasingly been viewed (by their creators and by their users) as processware.

What attributes of ESs make them supportive of a process orientation? There are several:

► Enterprise systems provide a structure for work similar to that in process thinking; the flow of activity and information across the organization is orchestrated by the system.

► Enterprise systems are integrated and link different business functions or subprocesses together.

► The modules of ESs more or less correspond to how organizations divide up their work into major processes.

► Enterprise systems allow the performance of processes to be measured (primarily in the metrics of time and cost) as they are carried out.

► Enterprise systems link process design and implementation through design aids (*templates*), that guide an organization in best-practice process designs, for which information systems support is available when the resulting system is implemented.

► The documentation of ESs and of the specific configurations of the systems selected by a company force a certain level of awareness of that company's business processes; this level of discipline is not often found in companies prior to the implementation of an ES.[5]

What processes do ESs support? Not support? Most major operational processes are supported by the larger and more sophisticated ESs, including those from SAP, PeopleSoft, and Oracle. Although there is some variation across vendor packages, the processes typically supported by an ES include the following:

▶ All financial and accounting processes, including treasury, controllership, accounts payable and receivable, investment management, and financial reporting

▶ All supply chain processes, including sourcing, procurement, shipping, billing, and payment, as well as planning and optimization in the most sophisticated ES systems

▶ All manufacturing processes (although many companies have separate shop-floor systems that are interfaced with their ES)

▶ Customer and order fulfillment processes

▶ Customer service processes (either integrated within a vendor's ES or in interfaced but separate systems)

▶ Sales force management (again, integrated or interfaced)

▶ Human resources management

▶ Maintenance of plant and equipment

▶ Construction and project management

▶ Some management processes (reporting, ad hoc analysis, etc.)

As you might guess, this list includes the great majority of processes that companies aspire to improve or reengineer and support with information systems (as well as some that are rarely improved in Western firms, such as management processes). Some processes, such as sales force management and customer service, have been added only fairly recently to ESs, so these modules are not yet in wide use.

The only major process that has generally been untouched by most ESs is new product development. To the degree that that process is supported by technology at all, the computer-aided design (CAD) systems employed are almost always separate from, and do not communicate with, ES packages. However, even in this latter area, ES vendors have started to announce support for so-called product data management systems, which keep track of product design specifications and components and are often a link between product development and engineering departments and manufacturing groups.

Thus, adopting an ES definitely predisposes a company to manage itself along business processes. Is the process orientation encouraged by ESs achieved automatically upon implementation of the system? The answer is no. Can a company that has implemented one still do business by functions, geographies, products, and all the other nonprocess dimensions of organizational structure? To a large degree, yes. Process management is much more than process-oriented information systems, as Michael Hammer argues in a post-reengineering book.[6] It includes process-oriented management and leadership styles, process-oriented compensation and evaluation structures, organizational structures that reflect process ownership and management, and many other facets. Putting in an SAP, PeopleSoft, Oracle, or other ES system does not bring about any of these other types of changes. In fact, only a few organizations of the thousands that are implementing ESs have also adopted many of these other process-oriented steps. All that an ES really does in the context of process management is to remove a major barrier to it. If the organization wants to manage and measure itself along process lines, it will have to undertake a broad change effort in addition to implementing an ES.

One company that has is Owens Corning. The maker of fiberglass insulation and other building materials made multiple changes at once when it installed its SAP system, including adopting a process orientation. Key processes were identified, including sourcing, finance, and customer fulfillment, and then reengineering projects were started for each of these three. "Process executives" were appointed to own the processes and lead the change projects (though some of these managers also held functional titles—the finance process executive was also the CFO, for example). An Owens Corning manager noted, however, that determining exactly what the responsibilities of the process executives were, particularly in relation to existing functional, product-based, and geography-based roles, was one of the most difficult aspects of the company's process management journey. One responsibility of the process executives was determining how the SAP system would support their respective processes. The executive for the customer fulfillment process, for example, noted:

> *The key to our new process organization is the ability of Advantage 2000 systems to deliver data. With the data it provides across our businesses, the opportunities for process improvement are tremendous. Our customer fulfillment process, which spans all of our business units and business regions, will deliver more than $30 million in cost savings over the next two years through gains in productivity in each part of our process.*[7]

In addition to reengineering the three key processes just mentioned (I'll have more to say about these later in the chapter) and establishing process ownership, Owens Corning managers undertook such process-oriented steps as changing their headquarters building to allow more cross-functional communications, creating a new process measurement system, and even developing a new product strategy. Advantage 2000, as the project was called, involved radical changes in virtually every part of the business, and was supposed to take place in an ambitious time frame of two years (the project has already taken considerably longer; five years is more accurate). The information systems changes alone at the firm have cost roughly $200 million; reengineering and reorganization costs add considerably to that total. There is no question that these changes were valuable and necessary at Owens Corning.

Another example of a firm that has moved to a more process-oriented organization in conjunction with an ES project is NEC Technologies, the division of the Japanese electronics giant. Once NEC's SAP system was substantially in place, the organization began to organize around business processes, rather than traditional business functions. For example, one set of teams was established based on serving particular customer groups—retailers, systems integrators, and so forth. Each team managed the entire process of customer relationships, from credit approvals to shipment schedules to receivables. NEC Technologies executives point out that two years of educating and persuading different members of the organization were necessary to make the shift. Some managers lost activities; others gained new ones. The company's senior executives, however, are now confident that the organizational change management efforts were worth the trouble in terms of increased customer satisfaction and more efficient processes.

PROCESS-ORIENTED IMPLEMENTATION OF ENTERPRISE SYSTEMS

The key to creating process-oriented information systems—and information-oriented processes, for that matter—is an effective implementation. Implementation, in turn, has several key aspects, which I'll discuss in this section. One is the new conception of ES-enabled reengineering that incorporates what many organizations have learned by experience with these concepts. I'll discuss the role of clean-sheet-of-paper reengineering and the reasons why it is almost obsolete in this context. I'll describe the critical nature of the configuration process—the point at which ESs are aligned with the processes and organizational structures of the companies that implement them. I'll also discuss the issue of process commonality, and just how much of it is necessary. This chapter's analysis of processes will end with a discussion of how to narrow the gap between process and practice after an ES has been installed.

WHAT DOES REENGINEERING MEAN IN THE ES CONTEXT?

In the early 1990s, when reengineering was a new idea, the concept of having an information system constrain design choices was not well understood at all. The rhetoric of process design involved no constraints at all, but rather a "clean sheet of paper." Companies were encouraged to start from scratch, to think out of the box, and to throw away all existing systems and other constraints. Reengineering, according to Hammer and Champy, entailed "breakthroughs, not by enhancing existing processes, but by discarding them and replacing them with entirely new ones. . . . Reengineering is about beginning again with a clean sheet of paper. It is about rejecting the conventional wisdom and received assumptions of the past. Reengineering is about inventing new approaches to process structure that bear little or no resemblance to those of previous eras."[8] Obviously, with such a revolutionary approach, there was little room for thinking about the limits that ESs would place on process designs; they would only get in the way.

PROBLEMS AT PAPERCO AND UNKNOWN COMPUTER

But what happened when companies took their revolutionary new process designs and tried to build information systems to support them? Let's just say they discovered the importance of good systems, and the difficulty of reconciling clean-sheet-of-paper thinking with the need to build and use systems. One example took place at a paper company, and Unknown Computer Company also had difficulty with reengineering and ESs. The difficulties of both companies are symptomatic of those faced by many other firms.

PaperCo (company executives I interviewed requested anonymity) went through a full-fledged, clean-sheet, think-out-of-the-box reengineering engagement with little thought about the information systems it would eventually have to use (there were no representatives of the IT function on the team). A PaperCo team worked with a hot reengineering consulting firm to identify and reengineer key processes.

The project took more than a year to focus on and redesign the supply chain and customer order management processes.

The goals for that part of the project involved order-of-magnitude time and cost reductions and vast improvements in customer service. Specific new process designs were painstakingly drawn on brown butcher paper on conference room walls. In addition to redesigning the processes themselves, several other organizational activities were addressed, such as the following:

► Redesigning the compensation and reward system to stop rewarding long production runs

► Stratifying the customer base to focus on more profitable customers

► Improving the measurement of customer service

All of these activities were designed to create an entirely new organization and to change the basic identity of the firm from being a paper company to being a true consumer products firm. Another overall goal was to make the company much more responsive to customers. Obviously, such broad changes required a broad program of change.

Of course, after the ambitious new process designs had been created, managers figured out that they needed much better information systems in order to tie manufacturing capacity to sales processes and to respond quickly to customer requests. In fairly short order it was determined that the right type of system was an ES, and the company selected SAP R/3.

All of this work had been with the oversight and approval of the consultant, at least until serious consideration of software was undertaken; the consultant was not technically oriented. In fact, a different firm was brought in to manage the selection and implementation of SAP. And when the process design work was completed, it fell to yet another team to discover how best to support the processes with information and technology.

Predictably, the business change goals from the reengineering project began to fall by the wayside. The only goal became to put in the system; the only process changes actually implemented were those necessary to make the system work successfully. The only customer-oriented change was that PaperCo's largest, most important customer was transferred over to the new system early in the process. Amazingly, the customer was not informed about the changeover until a few weeks before the system went live, when a low-level PaperCo employee asked the customer to initiate some changes in its ordering process in order to accommodate the new system. Needless to say, the customer was not amused, and PaperCo lost some of its business for a year.

According to one manager who participated in the reengineering project, "Our BPR [business process reengineering] project was a complete failure. None of the things we discussed ever happened and none of the changes were ever implemented." Members of the process design team felt betrayed; more important, no real business changes were realized.

What went wrong at PaperCo? The problem was the separation between the reengineering project and the ES implementation work, and the use of a clean-sheet approach to reengineering that had nothing to do with information systems. The use of two different consulting organizations—one of which knew lots about strategy and reengineering but nothing about IT, and the other just the opposite—didn't help the project any. The effort to install the system was successful, with the first phase of the SAP installation up and running within only nine months. The effort to change the company in a more strategic sense was not successful. As a postscript, PaperCo ran into even more problems a couple of years later when it merged with another large company. Now the ES project is on hold until after the combined company addresses its Year 2000 problems.

Unknown had a different problem with reengineering. I mentioned earlier that the great compromise in matching ES and processes is between time and a close fit with process designs and objectives. Unknown erred on the side of too close a fit with processes; it took too much time and money to determine what it wanted to do. It was an admirable stance, but it ultimately led to the demise of the ES project.

Unknown's managers and its consultants decided that it would take three different passes at analyzing its key processes. The first analysis was an "as is" cut. The goal in this phase was to identify the key processes, determine the current flow of work, and measure the existing processes in terms of cost and time.

The second cut at Unknown's processes, done after the first was complete, was a "could be" analysis, focused on determining the best possible way of performing key processes. Unknown managers believed that because of the constraints imposed by its ES, which it already knew it wanted to use, it could not start out with the ideal process design. However, the managers wanted to know what the ideal was in the hope that the company could evolve toward it over time.

Finally, the Unknown project team also carried out a "to be" analysis of what process designs were possible given the constraints of the SAP software it planned to install. This step was viewed as the real reconciliation between what Unknown wanted to do and what it could do with SAP as the supporting ES. As a simple example, Unknown inventory managers might want to be able to reallocate scarce components when a new order came in, but the SAP system commits inventory to customers and completed products as orders come in, limiting the ability to reallocate it. Thus the "to be" process design could not include reallocation of inventory.

What was wrong with this extensive, multilevel process analysis? Nothing—except for the time and resources it consumed. The completion of all three process analyses took about a year and a half and consumed a significant chunk of the total $225 million that Unknown spent on its project. In retrospect, the project manager felt that all three levels were "overkill." And the time and expense of the process analysis work certainly contributed to Unknown's eventual cancellation of most of the project, as discussed in chapter 2.

In the PaperCo case, the company paid too little attention to the relationship between processes and systems, at least at first. At Unknown, it might be argued that managers paid too much attention to the topic. There has to be a happy medium!

THE NEW REENGINEERING

It doesn't have to be the way it was at PaperCo and Unknown. Companies are increasingly using a new approach to process change that deals with both the opportunities for significant process improvement and the constraints of a packaged information system at the same time, and relatively quickly. Let's call it *ES-enabled reengineering;* although the approach is becoming widespread, it has no commonly accepted name to my knowledge. Owens Corning called its approach "good-enough reengineering"; that company, and many others as well, simply wanted to get a system in place quickly without having to modify its ES to suit custom-tailored process designs. But the term "good enough" implies a rather slipshod approach, with little thought given to maximizing the fit between system and organization. There is a way, however, to achieve most of the process designs an organization wants, while still taking a reasonable amount of time. It's described in some detail in this section, and at an overview level in figure 5-1.

ES-enabled reengineering involves a decision early in the change process about whether an ES package is likely to be used as the primary vehicle for process information support. Unknown actually employed this aspect of the approach. Let's face it: If your company wants cross-functional systems and you don't have any today, and if you don't want to be on the bleeding edge of technology, chances are very good that you're going to need an ES. You may also be predisposed to using an ES if other companies in your industry have already adopted one. In many cases, not only can a company decide early on whether it's likely to need an ES or not, but it can also decide which vendor's package is the most obvious fit. Again, one package may be

FIGURE 5-1

GRAPHIC OVERVIEW OF ES-ENABLED REENGINEERING

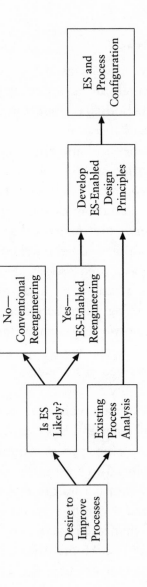

prevalent in an industry, or there may be a likely match between a package and the size and structure of the company. In any case, if a company can decide not only that it needs an ES early on, but also which one it's likely to use, then it's ahead of the game in the new reengineering.

Simultaneously with thinking about whether an ES makes sense, a company should in most cases do a quick analysis of its existing business processes. This has been a somewhat controversial issue since the beginning of reengineering. Why spend considerable time understanding existing processes when they're obviously going to change? I've always argued that it's worth some time and effort to map and measure existing processes, for several reasons:

1. It gives you a baseline for knowing how much you have improved.

2. You may uncover process problems and constraints that will affect the ultimate process design.

3. You build a "case for action" that the existing process simply won't meet the business needs of the future.

4. You can start to identify issues affecting whether the work will actually be done in the way you specify—the "process vs. practice" issues I described earlier in this chapter.

Thus, the analysis is worth doing, but even in a large company it's only worth doing for a few months.

The next key step is to start reconciling the process you want with what the ES package will allow you to do. This step can be accomplished through a variety of ways, and however you do it the task is difficult. One important starting point is to have in mind some key process objectives or design principles—the way in which your company would like to do business if possible. Perhaps you've uncovered some of these in the earlier steps, or maybe these principles are what motivated your company to begin this sort of thinking in the first place. If not, you'll have to do some research and brainstorming. Some sample design principles that your company might articulate are the following:

▶ We'd like to be able to answer a customer call and take an order for any of our products or services during the call—including pricing it, promising delivery, checking the customer's credit, and arranging shipping.

▶ We'd like to close our financial books in half the time we do it today.

▶ We'd like to have our suppliers be able to determine when shipment of their products is necessary, and have them manage our inventory of their product.

▶ When we buy from suppliers, we'd like to commit at that time how and when the product we purchase will be used in our own products or services.

▶ Anytime we do an acquisition, we'd like the acquired company to take customer orders in exactly the way the rest of the company does within three months.

These examples of process design principles will provide some high-level guidelines for how the process should work when you're finished. You may have to compromise on some of them, but at least you didn't spend a lot of time creating the principles. You'll rarely get what you want if you're not sure what it was you wanted in the first place. The activity of creating these design principles is a good way to engage the senior business executives of the firm. They may not understand all the intricacies of an ES, but they should know what they want out of it.

THE CRITICAL CONFIGURATION PROCESS

The actual configuration of the system to the desired process is difficult and at the core of getting the ES-enabled business processes you want, but it used to be much more difficult than it is today. *Configuration* is the step in the new reengineering process in which the details of the system are mapped and fitted to the details of the process, and vice versa. In the early days of ESs, configuring a system meant that companies had to painstakingly decide how each of thousands of switches within the system should be set. This process is still necessary today, although typically much easier and quicker.

Configuration is an issue that is larger than process design in that it starts with what processes the organization wants to support in the first place. In ES terms, this means deciding which of a vendor's application modules the organization wants to install. For example, a service company may not actually have any manufacturing processes, so installing manufacturing and plant maintenance modules wouldn't make much sense. A more difficult decision might involve whether to go with the vendor's capabilities in the human resources area, or instead to use a best-of-breed HR package that has more features desired by the company.

In many cases, the decision about whether to implement an ES application module is based on how important it is to have that application integrated with the rest of the organization. Other factors in the decision may be the state of existing application functionality in the area, the ability of the company to make the needed business changes in a particular process domain, and of course whether the vendor offers reasonable functionality in that process.

Configuration may also involve decisions about when to implement a particular module. A company may determine, for example, that it does want HR functionality eventually, but that it doesn't want to implement it right away. As I argue in chapter 6, however, it's usually not a good idea to postpone integration of multiple applications and information in an ES project, simply because that integration is usually a major reason for undertaking the project in the first place.

After a company has decided what processes it's concerned with in the first place, it must begin the much more detailed work of determining how each process will work with the new system in place. This may mean a broad array of types of decisions—from the organizational and reporting structure of the company to the tax treatment of certain assets. As one manager of an ES project at an oil company once said to me, "You feel a certain sense of vertigo on these projects. One minute you're talking about the high-level strategy and structure of the company, and the next it's some tiny little bit of informational detail."

In the early days of ESs, a company might have to make literally thousands of configuration decisions. Each little detail of a process had to be specified. Do we want FIFO (first-in-first-out) or LIFO (last-in-first-out) treatment of inventory? Do we want an alias for this product name, and if so, what is it? To whom does this particular report go? In many cases, it took years to make all of these decisions. In some situations, it wasn't clear whether a particular process design was possible or not. Process approaches that are somewhat idiosyncratic may be difficult to achieve with an ES. Even discovering what can and can't be done with ES-enabled business processes can be a struggle.

Visio, a relatively small software company with revenues of less than $100 million, had two idiosyncratic processes that proved difficult to accommodate in its ES project.[9] One involved the company's revenue recognition process; the company had previously recognized revenues when product was shipped to distributors, but then adjusted them based on actual sales to end customers. Another involved ownership of inventory. Visio outsourced manufacturing and handled product that it didn't technically own in the pre-ES process. The ES process model required the company to either own all its inventory or send two different invoices to cover changes in ownership through the process. Neither option was viewed as palatable. After months of study and analysis, it was determined that both idiosyncrasies could be accommodated, but only with substantial extra programming.

At Compaq Computer, managers had always double-counted revenues along two separate dimensions of organizational structure: product group and geography. But when they were implementing their ES, they couldn't figure out whether such double counting was possible. After six months of investigation, including work with the system itself, all available documentation, and experts within the vendor organization, they had concluded that it just wasn't possible. However, just as they were about to go live with single counting, someone discovered a combination of system parameters that would make the double-counting approach possible.

TEMPLATES

Configuration is much easier today in part because of the availability of process and industry templates. These constitute a predefined set of answers to the many questions that used to bedevil a company when configuring a system to its processes. The templates are often structured by industry, so that if I work for an oil company, I can start with a set of configuration decisions that are typical for an oil company. If there are certain aspects of the template that don't fit, then the company can perform a detailed analysis and change particular aspects of the template.

Of course, the risk with such templates is that companies will settle for a poor fit between their enterprise system and the way they would like to do business. Adhering to an industry template may mean that the company loses a better, perhaps even more competitive, way of performing a key business process. As with most standard solutions, what the company gains in expediency may be outweighed by turning parts of the organization into commodities. Some companies say that they will put in a template first and then later, after the system is installed, go back and create a better set of processes and a better system configuration. But I'm afraid that the exhaustion many companies feel after "successfully" implementing an ES will prevent a lot of ex post facto customization.

PROCESS MODELING

Another way to enhance the fit between an organization and its ES is through the use of process modeling and modeling tools. These are not, to be honest, quite as well developed as the templates I've just described, and overall it will probably take more time and effort to configure a system using modeling tools than templates. But it may be worth the trouble, since the use of modeling can lead to a more tailored business process.

The idea behind modeling is that process designs can be created and manipulated at a high, overview level using graphic models and point-and-click software interfaces. You design the process by illustrating how you want the work and information to flow through the organization. Most of the worthwhile modeling tools are linked to particular ES packages, so that you can quickly realize if you've violated a system constraint. Some modeling tools even provide guidelines as to best practices in the area of particular processes. Once you have designed the process to your satisfaction, the modeling software will tell you the implications for particular configuration switches and options.

The appeal of these tools is perhaps obvious: It's far easier to design processes at this graphic overview level than to have to descend into the detailed muck of systems choices. And actually specifying the process design that best suits the organization and seeing it transformed, within some limits anyway, into a fully functional system is quite appealing. But the strength of such tools is also their weakness. Companies have to give considerable thought to how they want to do business, and that's always difficult. The process analyst will still need to be somewhat expert in the ES, the modeling tool, and the process itself—and you can imagine how few people there are with such expertise. Furthermore, compared with a process template, these modeling tools may not be as well integrated with ES packages. They are usually supplied by third-party firms rather than ES vendors. But if you want the absolute best match between your process and your system, these modeling tools are well worth investigating.

Process models can also be viewed as a vehicle for *process knowledge management*. The idea is that the flow of the process, and the fit between the process design and the ES, represents a form of knowledge that should be captured, saved, and reused. One company that has made this concept a reality is Dow Corning, where modeling was used to capture process flows, good or "interesting" practices, and different views of processes.[10] Since Dow Corning was implementing an SAP system at this time, the models also displayed the relationships between processes and system support. The Dow Corning models showed, for example, which activities in the process were performed using SAP functions, which were performed with other legacy systems, and which were performed manually.

Dow Corning began recording process models using a graphic display tool (Visio), but later switched to process modeling and repository software based on research done at MIT and marketed by a company called Phios.[11] After the Visio models were loaded into the Phios repository, they were more easily maintained, updated, and viewed in new contexts. For example, when Dow Corning managers wanted to view their SAP-related processes in the context of an integrated supply chain using the Supply Chain Council's Supply Chain Operations Reference (SCOR) model, the Phios-based processes were modified to create a Dow Corning–specific version of the Council's "plan, source, make, and deliver" model.

Dow Corning followed several accepted principles of knowledge management in relation to its process knowledge. It established a "Process Network" of process owners and managers, whose job it was to keep the process models current. Two "process knowledge managers" were made available to the network to help modify the process model content. Dow Corning managers believe that the primary value of the models in the repository will come when the company modifies its processes in the future. The company is investigating using the repository and models for ISO 9000 modeling and for regulated processes such as those for handling hazardous materials.

How Common Is Common?

One of the key issues in configuring ESs and business processes is determining just how "common" a system or process needs to be in an organization. In small, single-business companies, there's normally no decision to be made. Every major process that's covered by the system, and every piece of information that's used within the system, should be the same around the organization. But in larger, more complex organizations, commonality is also a more complex decision. When products, customers, government regulations, and employee motivations vary widely around the world, it may not be reasonable to expect that every process and bit of information can be common world- and organization-wide.

As I discussed in chapter 4, the idea of federalism assumes that some processes and information can vary across the organization. The good news is that this provides flexibility for the company; the bad news is that you have to make decisions about what's local and what's global. The other bad news is that letting some things vary means that your organization will probably need multiple different instances of the ES package. This will complement your complex process and information environment with a very complex technical environment!

If you want to undertake a federalist configuration, you must have an approach for determining which processes will be common and which will be variable. Because local variability has a cost as well as a benefit, it's best to start with an assumption that unless there is a compelling argument that something should be different, it stays common. The method for commonality analysis comes down to reviewing the way work is done in the key parts of the organization. When variability is discovered, the analysts should push back and question whether the common solution would be workable. The part of the organization that desires an "uncommon" approach should have to document its rationale and the benefits it will achieve from its uniqueness.

Another, simpler means of assessing the need for unique solutions is to declare at the beginning of implementation that the overall system and related processes will be common unless a business unit, function, or department successfully petitions otherwise. In this approach, the reason for doing something different should be quite compelling. Recall the case of Nova

Pharmaceutical, which required the petitioning to be done before the firm's CEO. Not surprisingly, a highly common solution prevailed.

Perhaps obviously, common processes and common information are closely related, but not perfectly so. It's possible for two parts of a firm to have similar processes but to define the information differently, and vice versa. Since they aren't always the same, it's important to think about commonality in both contexts. Later in this chapter I describe some issues concerning information commonality and give several examples of how companies addressed the issue.

PROTOTYPING, PILOTING, AND ALL THAT

The last step in configuring a new ES system is to test it in practice. Whether it's called a pilot, a prototype, a probe, or some other word beginning with the letter *p*, it's extremely important to test in a realistic environment the system, the process, and most importantly, the people who are going to use both. No company, no manager is sufficiently brilliant to think about all of the complexities and complications inherent in a cross-functional ES project.

It's desirable to do this prototyping as early in your ES project as possible. If the system isn't going to be ready for a while, then prototype the entire process using paper printouts of the computer screens with which users will be working (this is sometimes called a *conference room prototype* or pilot). If you encounter serious problems—which are particularly likely to occur at the intersection of system and humans—you may still have time to modify either the system or process, or to train users to develop necessary new skills. It's therefore important to use human beings who will be the actual eventual users of the system as your ES project guinea pigs.

Ideally, you'll first prototype each key ES module with its accompanying process, and later the fit between the different modules and processes. Even the test of a single major activity will probably reveal some problems and issues to resolve. For example, I know of at least three companies (Unknown, Owens Corning, and an industrial distributor who'd rather not be named) that had significant early (and in Unknown's case, late) problems with their order processing module and process. Each of these companies takes most of its orders over the telephone. Imagine the concern of these companies' managers when they discovered that their new order processing module and system was not faster and more efficient than their old one, but actually much slower. In fact, for order-takers to negotiate their way through the several (as many as twelve) screens required to complete an order took anywhere between three and eight times the amount of time needed previously.

Owens Corning and the distributor discovered this problem fairly early in their ES projects, and were able to simplify their process and information requirements and speed up their systems (though at last report they're still a bit slower than their old systems). Unknown, as you probably remember, cancelled its ES project and wrote off a couple hundred million bucks. The order processing problem was one of the final nails in the project's coffin.

LIFE AFTER CONFIGURATION

Unfortunately, there is no life after configuration. By the time they finish configuring their ES and installing it, most companies are quite willing to wash their hands of the whole thing. But configuration is really something that is never finished. First, there is the fine (or in some cases, gross) tuning of the system over time to fit the way an organization works. The organization itself may change through mergers, acquisitions, or divestitures; external events (customers, regulation, etc.) may force a change; or maybe the system never really fit the organization's processes in the first place. Maybe it jammed the system in quickly, and it doesn't want to live with the result forever.

The system you've put in will also change over time. Enterprise system vendors are always announcing new releases or bringing forth new modules, and ES-related software will come out continually. You may add new bolt-on functionality. Each new program, release, or module will require some level of configuration or reconfiguration.

To avoid changing everything all the time, the wise organization will have a specified time for reexamining process requirements and system changes. You don't have to install every new release or new module; the analysis of system and process changes should include an assessment of what kinds of business benefits would accompany a new round of configuration.

In short, fitting your systems to your processes is a matter of business-driven continuous improvement. But then that's what process management is all about. In addition to creating better information support for your processes at all times, you should also be continually reevaluating and readjusting the other factors that lead to good process management. Your reporting structure, evaluation and compensation systems, people skills, and other aspects of the organization also need continual refinement and should themselves be modified to fit with your new processes and information systems.

ACHIEVING COMMON, HIGH-QUALITY INFORMATION

In addition to having a dramatic effect on business processes, ESs have a radical impact on a company's information. One key goal in organizations since the beginning of information systems has been to achieve common definitions and meanings of key information entities across a diverse organization. In the past, many companies would strive for common information by undertaking detailed data modeling or "information engineering" across multiple diverse systems. It usually didn't work, however, and consumed lots of time of highly paid employees and expensive consultants. Since ESs became available, companies have found that having one big integrated system is a much more feasible way to accomplish common information.

As with processes, it's usually necessary for companies to think carefully about the type of information they want, and how a specific information environment will fit with corporate strategy and structure. The most efficient information situation will be one in which all information is common throughout the company. That way, it will be easy to aggregate or compare information from one part of the company with another, and two reports about the same information won't have different results.

However, the most efficient situation may not be the most effective. Companies' information environments should reflect their business environments. If one division's markets, products, suppliers, employees, customers, and so forth differ markedly from those in another, it may not work to use the same information units to describe the diverse elements. Or, if some executive decrees that everyone must use common information, it may be lowest common denominator information—so generically defined that it meets no one's needs. The term *customer* may have to be defined as anyone who buys or might buy anything from the company, which includes customers, prospects, distributors, retailers, consumers, competitors, and sometimes even salespeople (if they are forced to buy inventory before selling it). A company that collapses all of these different types of customers into one category will not be able to learn much about any of them.

The first task, then, is to decide whether your organization wants everything to be in common or whether some information can be allowed to vary across business units, departments, and functions. Generally, every part of the organization with a different information environment is going to need its own instance of the ES software. The more instances you have, the more complex your installation and support process will be, so you don't want to make the decision lightly. You need to be sure that information variations are really necessary before allowing them.

To illustrate the process of deciding on information commonality, I'll give three examples. The first company, Millipore, decided that everything should be common. The second, Monsanto, decided that most information should be common. The third, Conoco, concluded that at least at first, not very much information would be common across the organization. I'll try to explain both the process and the context that each of these organizations followed. Making information common, however, isn't the only objective in managing ES information. After discussing commonality, I'll discuss issues about improving data quality and integrity—a difficult problem in ES implementation.

COMMON INFORMATION AT MILLIPORE

In the early 1990s, Millipore, a filtering systems company, wanted to achieve a higher level of organizational flexibility.[12] The company's executives—particularly its CEO, John Gilmartin—concluded that the best way to achieve flexibility was through common business processes, information, and information systems. Thus the company was one of the earliest to adopt Oracle's ES application suite, and engaged with the vendor in a development partnership.

Gilmartin felt that to achieve the commonality would require strong, hands-on management. He therefore appointed a series of common-systems czars in such areas as order entry, manufacturing, field service, and finance. The role of the czars was to solicit input about business processes and information, but to ultimately decide on a firmwide approach. The czars encountered substantial organizational resistance to commonality. In the financial area, for example, "everyone had detailed and complex explanations about why their financial measuring process was absolutely essential for them." In the task force to design the new system, "the level of debate generated by the choice of codes for products or processes was so heated you would think we were asking people to change their own names."[13] However, I believe that the presence of the czar role made it much more likely that the resistance could be overcome.

Common information and business processes did lead to business improvements at Millipore. The logistics function, for example, reduced its costs while improving on-time shipments. Customer service levels improved dramatically after a brief period of problems with the new system and process. In finance and administration, common systems and practices led to a 21 percent downsizing in personnel, saving over $2 million per year. Millipore also found it easier to reorganize the structure of the manufacturing organization, to restructure sales force territories, and to combine previously separate divisions, thus achieving its goal of flexibility. However, managers found it difficult to measure the value of this newfound flexibility.

ALMOST COMMON INFORMATION AT MONSANTO

Monsanto decided early on in its ES implementation that data and processes across its chemical, biotechnology, and pharmaceuticals businesses could not be entirely common. Each business had different customers, markets, and business processes. During the course of its ES project, the company even divested its chemical business into a new company, Solutia.

To determine just how common information should be throughout Monsanto, the chief financial officer formed an "enterprise reference data" team to study the problem and to try to maximize common data. The team asked business unit managers what absolutely had to be unique. The team concluded that over 85 percent of the ES data could be common across the corporation. Data on suppliers, for example, was reduced from twenty-four separate coding schemes across the organization to one. All financial data was held common throughout the organization. All materials data was made common using a new set of substance identification codes.

Some customer data remained unique simply because different business units have different types of customers. Selling to dairy farmers, Monsanto's customer for its milk production hormones, requires different information to be recorded in databases than selling to food companies who buy from the Nutrasweet division. Some plant data will also be local because of idiosyncratic manufacturing processes (although plant maintenance processes and data are common). Ordering data—for example, codes used for credit terms—could vary across businesses. But even most locally managed data had to adhere to certain naming and management conventions. In short, Monsanto managers strongly encouraged commonality, but allowed exceptions where necessary.

Ultimately Monsanto managers created five different levels of commonality for all of its ES-based information. Ranging from most common to least, the levels were as follows:

1. Fixed by corporate headquarters (e.g., the corporate Chart of Accounts)

2. Chosen from a list of options (e.g., purchasing terms codes)

3. Open, but of a specified format (e.g., product hierarchy)

4. Open format, but mandatory usage (e.g., descriptions)

5. Optional (e.g., contact name)

In some cases, Monsanto business unit managers imposed further rules on the data stewardship function. In no case, however, could the local rules contradict the enterprise rules.

COMMON INFORMATION IN GOOD TIME AT CONOCO

Conoco, a $23 billion (in 1998) oil company that was recently spun out of DuPont, has a typical culture for an oil company. Conoco was born in Oklahoma and nurtured in Texas, and the company's leaders often managed oil field sites in the rural Southwest in a necessarily autonomous manner. The strong sense of independence persists among managers who now lead geographical, functional (exploration and production, or refining and marketing), or product-based (chemicals, lubricants) business units. Culturally and historically, no one at the top of the organization has told them how to run their businesses.

In the early 1990s, Conoco managers from business units around the organization were beginning to identify a need for more capable and more integrated information systems. Their information systems managers, who were distributed throughout the company, started to talk with vendors of various ESs about employing their software in the different Conoco units they represented. Some units even began to write their own applications, on their own or with consultants, to meet specific business functional requirements.

Conoco's corporate information systems function, which had a small group of people devoted to looking across the company and developing standards where feasible, noticed this move toward new software and decided to see if one vendor's system could meet the needs of the entire company. Analysts mapped the processes of the different business units, and the functions of existing and new systems, onto the capabilities of SAP's R/3 system and concluded that the great majority of information and process requirements across Conoco (at least, that is, those that were being considered with regard to any ES) could be met with the package. With relatively little difficulty, Conoco's business unit managers were persuaded that the SAP package should be adopted.

However, there was no intent to have information be common across the units. Instead, every unit that wanted its own information environment would get its own version of R/3. It was clear that managers felt that their businesses differed so their information should as well. Various Conoco units, particularly those in Europe, began to implement the ES, with different versions by country. Not all units implemented the same SAP modules. Some countries that were earlier adopters of the package configured it to meet their needs, and then offered it to another country unit to use as they desired. Most modified the systems slightly to meet their own needs. The United Kingdom unit, one of the earliest implementers, gave its system away and then later adopted a version that another unit had modified from the original U.K. version.

By 1999 Conoco had at least eight different versions of SAP in place across the company. Some business units were working on getting common definitions of information within the unit. For example, within the U.S. Refining and Marketing unit, analysts were working with managers at the four different refineries to get common definitions of materials and supplies.

By that time European units were beginning to think about whether a more common solution would work, even though they had insisted on their uniqueness at the beginning. Part of their interest in commonality was driven by a corporate demand to save $50 million in procurement costs. If everyone defined procurement information in the same way in one system, managers reasoned, it would be possible to achieve economies of scale and better vendor management and thus meet the cost reduction targets. It seems likely that at least a common procurement system will eventually come to pass in Europe.

Conoco's corporate information managers believe that more commonality across the corporation will eventually be achieved as managers strive for efficiencies. But the process of "commonization" can't be forced or rushed, they believe. The company's independent culture forces them to let business unit managers come to their own realization that common information is desirable. A big, top-down battle for commonality at the beginning of the ES initiative would never have worked, they believe.

INFORMATION OBJECTIVES OTHER THAN COMMONALITY

The most popular information objective other than common information is information quality. Since ESs almost always involve integration across multiple previously employed systems in an organization, the process of putting in an ES involves efforts to combine and integrate different databases. Populating an ES with high-quality data may not seem a strategic or value-adding activity, but it is absolutely essential if the system is ultimately to provide useful information.

The task of data hygiene can't be put off until later. The various activities that are necessary—harvesting, cleaning, matching, converting, loading, testing, and maintaining data—can take up to an entire year. Most of these tasks can, and should, be done concurrently with other ES implementation activities so that the data environment is in good shape when it's needed.

Enterprise system data management and stewardship are ongoing, not finished when the system goes live. Sophisticated organizations will already have a data stewardship function in place prior to adopting an ES; they may be able to shrink it a bit with a rationalized data environment, but it can't be eliminated. At Monsanto, the post-ES data stewardship function had only three people at the corporate level (who reported to the controller, not the IT function), several experts in particular subject matter areas (e.g., purchasing or manufacturing data), and many data administrators dispersed throughout the company's functional and business units.

As with business processes, it's possible to design an information environment to achieve objectives other than quality and commonality, although firms are not yet particularly skilled in designing information environments.[14] The state of the art is simply to let individual business units or functions decide what information they want; this was the case at Conoco. Such an approach might be viewed as addressing the objective of a good fit between the information environment and the business.

I would also argue that some firms are trying to maximize the efficiency with which information is delivered to managers for analysis and decision making. When firms put in an ES for purposes of information analysis and reporting, they often do not think in depth about exactly what information they want. As I describe in chapter 7, they often use the same information they used before their ES, simply producing the information more quickly and with less manual intervention. There is nothing wrong with such efficiency, but firms should also try for greater information effectiveness.

One way to achieve that effectiveness would be to articulate what type of information is most important to the organization. Firms implementing ESs usually think about the entire range of information, not about any single type. But just as business strategy is about making choices, good information strategy involves choosing what type of information best fits the business. An organization implementing an ES might decide, for example, that better customer information was the most important information objective. That might dictate, for example, that individual business units have their own customer information, rather than a fully common approach. It might also suggest specific add-on applications for customer information management. The company might take more care in building a customer information repository using ES and other data. And if there is a choice among the types of data that might be addressed first—in terms of developing clear definitions, cleaning data, and integrating diverse sources—the company could then start with customer data.

For both processes and information, the key is to design the environment that you want, rather than to simply stumble into something. Achieving a good fit between an ES and the organization means making explicit choices about these two key aspects of the business, in addition to those described in other chapters. Never before in the history of information systems have the quality and design of processes and information been so bound up with a system. If you fail to explicitly consider process and information issues as you implement an ES, it's very unlikely that you'll get the process and information environments that you want.

ACHIEVING VALUE DURING ENTERPRISE SYSTEM IMPLEMENTATION

IMPLEMENTATION OF AN ENTERPRISE SYSTEM IS THE MOST difficult part of the project. It is such hard, slogging work that many organizations lose sight of their business and financial goals for the project during it. By the time many companies reach the middle of implementation, concerns about benefits, budgets, and ROI calculations seem to have little relevance. But, as I hope you all believe by now, ES implementation is not a goal in itself. Companies put in these systems because of the business changes they enable and because of the financial benefits they will (eventually, anyway) make possible. Steps taken during implementation are critical foundations for the ultimate value an organization receives from the entire project. If you lose sight of the goal during implementation, you may never achieve it.

In this chapter I'll talk about a number of different issues that an organization needs to consider while implementing an ES. There are a large number of topics involved in this discussion, none of which I have the space to address in great detail. If it's any comfort, there are books focusing on ES implementation, which usually address the specifics of installing particular types of ES software. My focus in this chapter will be on the processes and approaches that help to ensure that value is achieved. Of course, as I've argued throughout this book, companies need to be thinking about value before and after implementation as well. Because of the many distractions during implementation, however, I'll stress the topic even more in this chapter.

I'll admit here that some aspects of a high-quality ES implementation are simply good project management. Others are chestnuts of business and organizational change of any type. In the interest of completeness, I'll have to mention some implementation tactics and project management approaches that seem like common sense. However, I'll try to focus on the ES-specific aspects of such strategies.

THE MODEL FOR IMPLEMENTATION THINKING

To succeed with implementation, a company needs a model for how the implementation will work at a high level. Since ES projects are more extensive than other systems projects and involve higher levels of technical and business risk than most systems, it's not really a good idea to view ES projects in the same light as other IT initiatives. One alternative, for example, is to view ES projects as if they were new business ventures. Another is to view an ES project in the context of a much broader business change program. These are not mutually exclusive perspectives, although I will discuss each separately here.

In a recent working paper, Rob Austin and Dick Nolan, professors at Harvard Business School, argued that it's a mistake to view an ES implementation as just another systems or capital expenditure project. The nature of ES activity, they argue, is not well suited to traditional project management techniques. "IT systems management, with its emphasis on exhaustive requirements definition and detailed planning, has never worked that well on the large IT projects it was designed for and is simply not a realistic basis for managing the high and multidimensional uncertainty involved in ERP."[1] (ERP is, as you will know if you were paying attention in chapter 1, another acronym for ESs.)

As an alternative to traditional project management, Austin and Nolan argue that the appropriate style of management for ES projects is similar to that in managing new business ventures. Taking a venture-oriented approach to an ES project, for example, would involve dividing the implementation into stages so that the necessary capital can be committed piecemeal over time. Venture arrangements involve giving participants substantial incentives to be successful, and sharing the financial risk and rewards broadly. Austin and Nolan also argue that any venture capitalist places a very strong emphasis on the people involved in the company; a venture-oriented ES project would do the same.

I agree in most respects with Austin and Nolan's idea. They are undoubtedly correct in any case about the shortcomings of traditional systems project management, and the uncertainties about risk and benefit in ES projects do seem conducive to venture-style management. My only concern is with the issue of staging. As I discuss later in this chapter, staging is appropriate as long as it doesn't hinder the development of cross-functional integration.

Another overall model for implementation involves viewing an ES project in the context of a broad business change involving not only implementation of an ES, but also changes in organizational structure, business processes, and culture and behaviors. As I've noted, any company implementing an ES faces a choice between maximizing either systems or overall business change. Focusing solely on getting the system installed will yield a more rapid, controllable implementation, but you'll be leaving a lot of potential business change on the table. Although the jury is still out on the feasibility of these large-scale changes, most of the research in this area suggests that companies that combine business and systems changes simultaneously do better than those that put systems in without changing anything else.[2]

172 ◀ *Mission Critical*

An implementation involving major business change will feel remarkably different from one focusing on installing systems alone. The number of people and business functions involved, the amount of organizational communications, and the roles of senior executives are all substantially increased over a systems-only effort. Ideally, the changes will involve not only internal activities, but also improvements in product and service strategies. Most of the organization will need to be aware of what's going on, because you'll be looking for changes in behavior and work processes. It's probably a good idea to roll out the usual communications apparatus for such changes, including a catchy project name, vision statements, slogans, memos, videotapes, CEO broadcasts, and so forth. Senior executives of many functions need to be on board in regard to the changes, since they'll have to sponsor and direct the business change aspects of the initiative. Business changes of this magnitude should certainly be reviewed with the company's board of directors, and may even be discussed with external analysts. After all, the goal is to improve performance, which analysts are supposed to care about.

Owens Corning's Advantage 2000 program is one example of such a broad business initiative. The internal changes I've described in previous chapters were tied to an external strategy involving buying building materials not individually, but as a coherent system ("System Thinking"). The new product strategy took advantage of the ES-enabled ability to configure building material solutions across products and company functions. Coca-Cola's Project Infinity is another example, involving not only putting in a new ES, but also creating tighter organizational and informational linkages with bottling companies.

These broad change programs usually require several years to come to fruition, and are rarely successful in every respect. Like any other broad change program, you're lucky if you accomplish a good chunk of the objectives. Some of the most important success factors for these programs are expectation management and long-term journey management. These races are not won by the swiftest or most boastful. Although I've just endorsed a broad pattern of communications for these broad programs in which ES initiatives are embedded, it's useful not to say too much about these programs to people who won't actually be affected by them.

THE IMPLEMENTATION PLAN

You won't be surprised to hear that for an effort typically costing tens or hundreds of millions of dollars (or pounds, euros, yen, or whatever) and thousands of person-months of effort, an organization needs a good plan to implement the project well. One of the most important issues in planning is the decision about how much of the corporation to take on at once with your ES implementation (figure 6-1). The two extremes in this regard are the *incremental* and *big-bang* approaches, with a phased rollout in the middle. As you might guess, an incremental approach implements the system and associated business

FIGURE 6-I

IMPLEMENTATION OPTIONS

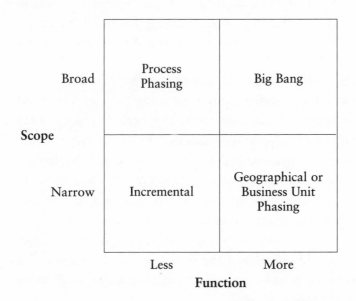

change in small pieces; a big-bang approach involves implementing everything at once. A phased rollout implements either some functionality on a broad scope, or full functionality on a narrow scope. If you have the capacity to handle lots of simultaneous change, the phases can be undertaken in parallel, with design and coordination at the enterprise level.

I don't recommend fully incremental implementations. They take a very long time and tend to be very expensive. Unless there is a strong need to examine each part of the business with extreme care before implementation, the incremental approach involves too much analysis of differences between geographical and business units. At a large chemical company, for example, an ES was implemented differently for each combination of geography, business function, and product-based business unit. The project manager called the process "battling cube by cube," referring to the three-dimensional nature of the three factors involved. The implementation took over ten years to complete (although the firm was admittedly an early adopter of the software, which added time) and cost hundreds of millions of dollars.

Phasing in larger, more concurrent chunks is a more reasonable approach—a better compromise between speed of implementation and the difficulty of undertaking ES-enabled change. Phasing may be undertaken along several different dimensions:

▶ *Geographical phasing.* The assumption here is that not all geographical locations within a company need to have their ES implemented at the same time. The logic of phasing may be to implement the most important locations first, or the least important if the company is worried about implementation risks. Conoco, for example, started its ES implementation in Europe, where processes were simpler and the business in general much smaller than in the United States. Home Depot, the building materials retail chain, is implementing its ES in out-of-the-way places (Argentina, for example) first in order to get the bugs out of the implementation and change process.

▶ *Process phasing.* Some business processes are more important than others to the success of the business. One ES phasing strategy is to implement core processes first and ancillary ones later. It does not normally make much sense, however, to implement some core processes and not others, since a primary reason to employ an ES in the first place is to achieve integration across business processes and functions. Few organizations, for example, should implement an enterprise system's financial module without its manufacturing and order processing modules. Such phasing can be done, but it defeats the overall purpose and value of the technology.

▶ *Business unit phasing.* Some business units are more central or isolated than others. It may be useful to begin an implementation in a unit that is relatively small or noncore to the main business. One large pharmaceutical firm, for example, decided to implement a new ES first in a small medical diagnostic equipment business unit, rather than starting the ES work in the core drug business. If for business reasons an organization decides to start in a core unit, it might benefit from focusing all efforts there and leaving ancillary units for later on.

Big-bang implementations involve high risk and high reward. A rapid big bang gets the system in place quickly, thus delivering its benefits quickly. Perhaps the rapid implementation is needed to meet business or system deadlines, for example, a Year 2000 problem. Big-bang implementations may cost less because consultants or internal systems people spend less time on the project; however, the costs are incurred in a short time. Business changes may be minimized simply because there isn't time to make them (although this isn't necessarily a benefit, it can be under some circumstances). Thus, if your primary goal with an ES is ensuring that business changes are achieved, be aware that a fast big-bang approach can sometimes lead to focusing on getting the system in and working, with other objectives being forgotten.

Big-bang projects are also the most likely to lead to problems when the system is turned on. A recent study of ES implementations noted, for example, that many firms suffer some sort of "performance dip" shortly after implementing their system.[3] The study doesn't comment on the implementation approaches of these companies, but I would guess that they were disproportionately likely to use a big-bang approach. It's simply too difficult to anticipate all of the problems and changes involved in an implementation when everything is changing at once.

For example, at A-Dec, an Oregon manufacturer of dental equipment, a big-bang cutover to a Baan system in 1997 led to more than a year of performance problems.[4] The company couldn't process its orders, manufacture products, or ship to customers. "We lost a lot of business," said the company's chief information officer. Workers had to work around the system because they didn't understand it, and the initial performance didn't meet the company's requirements. After a long adjustment period, the company is now getting substantial benefits from its system.

A phased rollout gives the organization time to adjust to the system and the changes it brings—time for configuring the system to fit the organization, time for testing, time for training, and so forth. It allows later adopters to learn from earlier ones. It doesn't risk the ability to take orders, issue payroll checks, or finish the annual report on time. It allows for plenty of business change—perhaps too much in some organizations. As noted previously, a phased rollout allows the organization to stage the investment and risk over time, which is almost always preferable.

The overall message here is that phasing is desirable if your company or organization can afford the increased time it may take to achieve full implementation. Of course, there are some drop-dead issues that may make big-bang approaches necessary; the Year 2000 problem was such an issue for many companies. Even in such cases, however, it's usually important and beneficial to limit scope or system changes as much as possible and to focus on making decisions rapidly.

I've argued that implementations can be incremental, phased, or big bang. In actual ES projects, however, the choices are seldom as definitive as these terms imply; there are many intermediate positions between the extremes. A company may choose a relatively slow rollout of some functionality, and a big-bang implementation of other features. Different parts of the company may have different implementation schedules. Hardly any firm's implementation can be characterized as totally in one category or another.

At Bay Networks, for example, the implementation team consciously took a hybrid approach in order to combine a rapid implementation with relatively low risk. They mixed business unit phasing in some units with process phasing in others. Because the company's California manufacturing plant was growing rapidly and already had some sophisticated systems, it wasn't included at all in Phase 1 of the implementation project. Order management in relatively standalone subsidiaries was also put off until Phase 2. The project manager described the process as follows: "We implemented financials worldwide. We did a global deployment on some (but not all) modules. In addition, at some sites, we implemented all the modules."[5]

TIMING OF IMPLEMENTATION

The overall issue of how long an ES takes to install is among the most controversial topics in the field. I argued in chapter 1 that the time dimension is one of the two most critical factors in planning your approach to implementation. In the mid-1990s, many firms found that their implementations were stretching out for several years, and complained to their ES vendors and consultants. In response, the vendors introduced marketing and implementation approaches emphasizing speed of installation (e.g., SAP ASAP, Oracle Express). Consulting organizations developed industry templates for process designs and systems settings that made system configuration much easier.

As a result of these "improvements," vendors have argued with some credibility that implementation cycles have been shortened. Press releases abound with stories of full ES implementation in six to nine months. It's true that going live can happen in a matter of months, but the system is typically not complete or cross-functional. It's also true that a rapid implementation precludes the possibility of a system that's closely configured to a company's idiosyncratic ways of doing business. Perhaps most important, an extremely fast implementation limits the ability to achieve substantial business change.

I worked with many companies during the reengineering era of the mid-1990s, and I know it's impossible to redesign and fully implement new cross-functional processes in a few months. The design of processes takes even longer when they have to be synchronized with an ES. New organizational structures have to be developed. In addition, workers have to be trained on new processes, and new roles and responsibilities have to be clearly established before you're ready to do business in the new way. In short, for major business change across multiple processes and ES modules, we're talking years, not months. In my view, it's important not to settle for systems change just because it's available quickly. The key value of ESs is the business changes they enable. That said, a sense of urgency is also important. It's easy to spend years investigating all the possibilities that ESs enable, and only some of the investigations really add business value.

There are ways to speed up an ES project without sacrificing business change. For example, a major factor in project length is how quickly decisions are made. Much time in ES projects is spent deciding on various things (big and little issues), and a longer decision cycle is not always associated with a better decision. Companies can set a policy that decisions about configuration or any other matter will be resolved in a specified time—a day or two, perhaps. Managers can also decide on an escalation path for a decision: If a front-line group can't decide, who gets the issue next?

At Bay Networks, project managers resolved all issues by the end of each week. They dealt with the scope issue by issuing "IOUs" to managers and departments who were discovered during the project to have valid needs for functionality, but whose requests were turned down because adding such functionality would delay the project unacceptably. Some obligations were repaid in the first phase of the project, but most were delayed until the second.

It's particularly important to make decisions quickly up front, at the beginning of a project. On decisions such as selecting a package vendor or a consultant, the time scale is often much more leisurely than later on in the project. The time for the whole project is what matters, though it's often just the time actually spent installing software that companies try to accelerate.

It is important to instill a sense of urgency among members of ES implementation teams and senior executives. Compensation and other rewards should be tied to finishing the project on time, along with the accomplishment of business change objectives. Scope changes should be limited whenever possible. When a new task is added, an old one should be taken away. With no sense of urgency and limits, the project could drag on for a decade.

Cisco Systems provides a good example of a company that excelled at putting its ES in quickly, although it was in the context of a technical, rather than strategic, implementation approach.[6] The company's managers accomplished a nine-month implementation. Cisco faced substantial time pressure in the form of a legacy system that was already giving it trouble (in fact, it conveniently died on the day that the ES proposal was presented to the board). A factor in emphasizing systems change over business change was that Cisco needed the underlying transaction systems in place before being able to offer customers direct Web access to ordering and supply chain processes.

The project was a big-bang approach, with all systems and processes being implemented at once. The project manager noted:

I knew we wanted to do this quickly. We were not going to do a phased implementation, we would do it all at once. We were not going to allow a lot of customization either. There is a tendency in MRP systems [the predecessor to ESs] for people to want the system to mirror their method of operation instead of retraining people to do things the way the system intended them. This takes a lot longer.[7]

The Cisco team spent seventy-five days choosing a package in the first place (fast compared with many firms, but slow compared with the length of the overall project), and only two days developing an initial configuration of its chosen Oracle system. The implementation time frame was driven largely by the need to implement before the fourth quarter of Cisco's financial year, when financial results were reported and substantial amounts of product shipped.

The implementation team used a series of *conference room pilots,* in which the system and processes were discussed and prototyped on paper. Each pilot refined the prototypes further to create a better fit with Cisco's requirements. Even when the early pilots revealed that the system would have to be modified to meet some of the company's business requirements, the schedule was preserved. Modifications were limited as much as possible; they had to go to the project's steering committee for approval.

The rapid schedule also led to a problematic cutover to the new system. As the company's chief information officer put it:

[After cutover] I wouldn't say that the company hit the wall, but I would say we had major day-to-day challenges that needed to be solved quickly to avoid significant impact to the company. For example, our on-time ship [percentage], shipping on the date we commit to the customer, fell from 95% to about 75%[;] it was still not miserable but it was not good.[8]

This is an example of how a big-bang approach can be more likely to lead to problems after implementation. In this case, a number of things went wrong; for example, the hardware chosen for the system could not initially handle the transaction volume. Cisco eventually recovered from these problems, but a bit more time during implementation might have avoided the problems altogether.

PREIMPLEMENTATION: CREATING AN ORGANIZATIONAL STRUCTURE

The implementation of an ES is so significant an event that it requires the establishment of its own organizational structure. A cadre of specialized roles must be created to ensure not only that the project is completed successfully, but also that it achieves significant business value. Each of the key roles is described in the following subsections. Of course, it's not a matter of filling the slots with just anyone. Successful implementers of ES systems always point to particularly talented individuals and their personal contributions to the project as factors in their success.

EXECUTIVE SPONSOR

Enterprise system projects almost always require a senior business executive to be the executive sponsor for the project. The sweeping nature of the business changes, the high costs of the system implementation, and the importance of the projects to the long-term success of the organization all justify the active leadership of a senior manager. Placing a senior business executive in the role of sponsor rather than a chief information officer or other senior IT manager conveys the message that an ES project is a business initiative, not merely a technology project.

The executive sponsor should be drawn from the primary part of the organization in which the system will be implemented, that is, from the same division or business unit. Sponsors are most frequently, in my experience, chief executives (who, according to survey results, are most likely to feel that they're in charge), chief financial or operations officers, and occasionally such other roles as vice presidents of logistics, customer service, and sales. The choice of a sponsor should be based not only on which functional area is most affected, but also on which executives are most comfortable with information technology and which (if any) have a history of effectively managing large, systems-oriented projects to successful completion.

The roles of the executive sponsor include the following (illustrated by quotes or examples from the chief financial officer of In Focus Systems, who sponsored an Oracle ES project at the manufacturer of video projectors):[9]

► Relate the system to the overall strategy of the company. ("[B]eing able to learn faster than anybody else.")

► Communicate the value and importance of the project to the rest of the organization. ("We closely managed the project with a lot of help, a lot of banner waving, and monthly meetings of the senior staff.")

► Develop and advertise performance improvement objectives. (Reduction in operating expenses from 30 percent of revenue to 18 percent; gain market share.)

► Enforce the inevitability of the system and related processes. ("This tool is coming; you will use it or you can go somewhere else.")

► Create necessary organizational changes. (A new "super user" position.)

► Ensure that the implementation proceeds on schedule. (Emphasized completed implementation over adding more functionality.)

The executive sponsor should also take the lead in educating other senior executives about the ES project and their roles in bringing about the desired business change. Some firms have organized such executive participation in a formal steering committee; others use more informal means of participation. What successful projects do have in common, however, is a high level of participation and understanding by the senior management team.

At Union Carbide, for example, the project sponsor and leader convened a series of meetings of the firm's top twenty managers over the life of the company's SAP project. The goal of the meetings was to acquaint executives with the kinds of organizational and business changes that would accompany implementation of the company's ES. Some members of the group visited other companies that were already achieving success in their ES projects. For each major business process of the firm, the executives considered what kinds of high-level models were possible and most feasible. They also addressed how much global commonality was necessary in each process and how decisions about process and information flows would be made. The emphasis throughout these meetings, and in the project more broadly, was that the effective implementation of the system was the responsibility of the entire management team, not just the IT function or the executive sponsor.

PROJECT LEADER OR MANAGER

Because of their size and complexity, ESs are redefining the nature of project management. In no other domain of business are there so many difficult, intertwined issues with regard to business, technological, and organizational change. Enterprise system project leaders at one moment will have to deal with highly complex and detailed issues of transaction volumes, and at the next will have to address high-level changes in organizational structure and culture.

Some organizations feel that no one person can deal with such variety, and therefore name several project leaders. At Monsanto, for example, the company's ES project has a business and process change leader, a technology leader, and an overall project manager. It's particularly important that all leaders have a familiarity and comfort with information technology, even though the overall goals are business related. To achieve those business goals, they also need to have a strong business background and credibility with the firm's business leaders.

One article described the ideal ES project manager as a combination technologist, business expert, drill sergeant, motivational speaker, politician, and psychologist. The first several roles may be self-evident; some of the latter ones may need explaining. The politician is necessary because of the need to mediate among the many different groups who are affected by an ES. Just as politicians need to make a series of deals to get a road or a school built, ES project leaders will also have to construct many back-room deals to get the system in successfully ("I'll configure the system the way you want if you'll give me three of your best people to help with the implementation"). They will also, however, have to work the "front room" and articulate—as would a motivational speaker—the overall principles or maxims by which the system is being justified and put in place. At any moment there may be a tension between up-front principles and back-room deal making.

The psychologist aspect of the project leader role is necessary to manage the expectations of the organization concerning the system and business changes being implemented. Expectations are inevitably high for what an ES project will accomplish because of the cost and time involved. The project leader should "underpromise and overdeliver," according to several organizations I interviewed.[10] This is true in many projects, but particularly important in ESs. The project leader should also attempt to communicate the linkages and the differences between the business changes and the systems changes in the project, as that will undoubtedly be a source of confusion.

PROCESS OWNERS

As I argue in chapter 5, ESs are process oriented, but by themselves they don't make an entire organization process oriented. A key change that an organization must go through, and a key aspect of the organizational structure for ES implementation, is to establish process ownership roles. Several organizations have told me that this was one of the most difficult changes they went through in their entire ES journeys. The difficulty is related to the entrenched nature of existing organizational arrangements based on business functions and departments. Although a full discussion of process ownership is beyond the scope of this book (I recommend Michael Hammer's book *Beyond Reengineering*,[11] which has a chapter on the topic), I will discuss it here in the context of ES implementation.

Why are process owners necessary during ES implementation? Somebody has to take responsibility for how the process fits with the system. Should revenue be credited to product groups or geographies? Ask the financial process owner. How about inventory: When will it be counted as officially belonging to the customer—when it's shipped, or when it arrives? A good question for the supply chain process owner. The design of business processes by process owners in an ES environment isn't exactly a clean-sheet-of-paper exercise, but there are clearly decisions to be made. If there are no process owners to make them, a company will spend a lot of time hashing out decisions that cut across functional lines; no particular functional manager will be well positioned to make them.

What kind of person makes a good ES-enabled process owner? During implementation, it doesn't have to be someone with experience in managing a large group of people. Unless an organization has adopted process management well before implementing its ES, process ownership is a relatively solitary activity. During implementation, what matters more than people skills is business design skills—the ability to gather data, analyze alternatives, and see the big picture. At this stage, process owners should be open to all possibilities in process design. If they own an existing set of people and activities, they may be less likely to support radical changes in the process.

After implementation, of course, it makes sense for the people who perform a process to report to the process owner (though there are many contrary examples), and then people management skills matter a lot more. It's not unreasonable to think about changing process owners after the system has been implemented. Process ownership can be a part-time role during implementation, but the process owners should have at least half of their time to perform it. One pitfall to avoid involves ensuring that process ownership doesn't conflict with management of a business function (e.g., the manufacturing manager being put in charge of the order management process). First, running a function should be a full-time job; second, a functional manager may find it difficult to make objective decisions about how a cross-functional process should work.

SUPER USERS

One ES implementation role that is not widely known in other contexts is that of *super users*. These are typically middle-level employees or managers from the business functions or departments that will be affected by the ES project. Their role during implementation is to determine how the system will affect their particular part of the organization, recommend system configuration and design details, serve as "typical" users during testing and piloting of the system, and train others who have jobs similar to their own. When the system is actually turned on in the organization and usage begins, super users will be perhaps the most critical employees in the firm for making the new systems and processes work.

With such an important responsibility, these super users need to be really super, that is, the best performers in the functions and departments they represent. High performers will not only do a better job of getting the system implemented effectively, but can also help sell the system and its business impacts to their co-workers. By definition, the high-performing super users are in very short supply and are important to their organizations in performing their existing jobs. This is often a source of strain in organizations: One reason managers resent ES projects is that they lose their best people to them. *C'est la vie.*

There are no industry guidelines as to how many super users a project needs; I've seen from four or five to more than a hundred on a single project. The number should be driven by the diversity of business functions and organizations that will be affected by the system. If a department isn't represented by a super user on the project, chances are good that something in the implementation will go awry. This set should include, as I argue in chapter 7, representatives of the management function—those who will help figure out how to use the ES to manage the business better.

What happens to super users after implementation? You probably realize by now that there is no such thing as "after" implementation. Super users may not be able to go back to their non-ES roles quite as early as you or they would hope. They'll still be needed to reconfigure the system and process over time, to answer difficult system/process questions in their areas of expertise, and to optimize the performance of the new business processes. Still, they're even more critical to the company in their new roles. They know how to get at all the information in an ES, and they understand in detail how work flows through the organization. Who could be more valuable? Companies may have to develop new fast-track career paths for these individuals over time; you can bet that headhunters and other firms will appreciate them.

THE VISION AND PLANNING TEAM

The implementation effort is divided into two categories: a vision and planning team, and one or more implementation teams. The vision and planning team, which should include individuals with high-level business and technology skills, determines the overall fit between the ES and the organization. The team's deliberations may determine the way the company will work in the future. It's an important responsibility, and hence requires very high-quality people.

The team will be busy. It should be primarily responsible for generating insights about such things as the following:

► The overall time frame for the project

► The primary categories of benefit and value

► How the firm wants to be organized relative to the system

► How key processes are supposed to be structured and flow

► How common key processes and information are across the organization

► How the ES-enabled organization will lead to a better competitive strategy and position

► How the changes from the ES should be phased over time and over business units and processes

► How much the system will be modified to fit idiosyncratic processes

If this team has sufficient technical skills, it can also select the ES package that the organization will install. And it is even more reasonable for the vision and planning team to decide which implementation partner or consultant the company will work with. After the consultant is chosen, some high-level consultants may become members of the vision and planning team. It's best if the vision and planning team is full-time, but it's possible to do otherwise. Unless it's a really huge implementation, ten or so members should be sufficient.

THE IMPLEMENTATION TEAMS

The people who actually do the work in ES implementation projects are on the implementation teams. Well, creating visions and plans is work too, but not detailed work, which is what the implementation teams will have to address. Detailed process designs, detailed system configuration switches, detailed training plans—all of these are the province of implementation teams.

Implementation teams need to be full-time, and they need to be substantially larger than the vision team. Some very large implementations involve several hundred members spread over tens of teams. I have heard complaints that teams with more than twenty members become unwieldy. The alternative is to create separate teams for each business unit or major process involved in the implementation.

Some members of the vision team should cross over to the implementation teams so that the fundamental principles of process and system design are preserved and monitored. Otherwise, it's common for the emphasis within the vision team to be on business objectives, whereas within the implementation teams it is exclusively on getting the system in.

THE ROLE OF THE IT ORGANIZATION

A company's in-house IT organization can play several different roles during implementation. Perhaps the least desirable option is for it to play no role at all. Some companies turn over all the ES work to outsiders, presuming that internal IT people are busy with supporting existing systems, or that they don't have ES expertise. Both of these suppositions may be correct, but they can be remedied. Training in ES skills is widely available. And it's possible to outsource support of the existing IT environment, as I'll describe later in this chapter. Relying totally on outsiders to implement an ES condemns an organization to a lifetime of dependence and is arguably unfair to current IT employees.

Most organizations employ a mix of their own IT people, internal people from non-IT business functions, and external consultants. Information technology people may play configuration roles, in which they move close to the business functions they're configuring and may even join those functions after implementation. They may be technical specialists, designing the IT architecture on which the ES will run and tuning the

performance of the system. This role is also needed after implementation. In either case, the IT people will have to be able and
willing to acquire new skills quickly.

Theoretically, adoption of an ES means that companies will
eventually need fewer IT people. I emphasize "theoretically"
and "eventually." One semiconductor firm, for example, estimated that 60 percent of its IT people were performing tasks
that would be replaced by the functionality in its ES. All of the
60 percent —and more—are still there, either working on the ES
implementation or on other systems. In only one organization
have I found actual reductions in IT personnel after an ES project. Not only do ES projects require long-term support, but
companies are also continually expanding non-ES applications,
such as Web pages, sales force and customer service systems,
and personal computing tools. Be careful before you justify your
ES investment on the basis of savings in IT personnel.

Getting Good People

Regardless of how you structure your various teams, you're
going to have difficulty finding enough really good people to
staff your project. I don't have any good answers to this problem; I just want you to expect difficulty. The only solution is sacrifice: moving your best people onto the project team, paying a
lot to get and keep the best, hiring expensive consultants. The
skills to change everything at once and succeed don't come
cheaply.

Enterprise Systems Technology Choices

Even after an ES vendor has been selected, an organization is not
finished with regard to technology choices. One key choice is
whether to employ a single ES package or a variety of systems
linked together in an enterprise solution. Enterprise system projects often—one might even say "usually"—involve a range of
software programs in addition to the ES package. In fact, a com-

mon term for the future of ES software is *portfolio assembly*, in which firms will pull together a wide variety of programs with ES modules as the core or backbone.

Every firm implementing an ES has to think about how to meet the entire organization's needs, and what percentage of those needs will be encompassed by the basic ES package (figure 6-2). Some necessary systems functionality won't be covered at all by an available package or application (the white space at the top of the figure), forcing firms to either develop the capability themselves or do without. Obviously, basic ES packages will include a large chunk of functionality from which the organization can benefit. However, it may not choose to adopt all of the available functions. Some perfectly good legacy systems within the organization may already do the job (the blocks of functionality at the bottom of the figure). In such cases it may be easier to interface the existing system with the ES package than to make users go through the change of a new system (though building such interfaces isn't easy either). In other cases, an organization may feel that a third-party vendor's solution is better than anything offered by the primary ES vendor. There may be considerable overlap between the third vendor's offering and that of the ES vendor, or there may be little or none. As suggested by the

FIGURE 6-2

MAP OF SOFTWARE FUNCTIONALITY OPTIONS

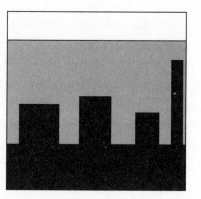

Functionality necessary but not available from any existing system

Functionality available from a basic ES package

Functionality available from other vendors, legacy systems, etc.

blocks in figure 6-2, the overlap may be deep or shallow, narrow or broad.

What the organization must do during implementation is to decide among these options—basic ES package alone, or supplemented with legacy applications and third-party bolt-ons. As you may have guessed by now if you've paid attention, the choice should be driven by business factors, not technological ones. If you're putting in an ES primarily to take care of commodity applications, you should generally go with a straightforward ES package installation and avoid the supplemental systems whenever possible. The goal in such circumstances is not to optimize functionality, but rather to meet basic needs as quickly and inexpensively as possible.

If, however, the goal is to use an ES to support a key business objective and achieve competitive advantage, a hybrid mix of an ES package, bolt-on third-party systems, and your best legacy systems is likely to be a good bet. Let's assume that you're interested in winning with excellence in supply chain design and execution. Perhaps you have a configuration system that's already better than anything an ES vendor can provide. Furthermore, some of the supply chain planning and optimization systems available from third-party vendors seem like just the ticket. A vanilla implementation of a basic package isn't going to give you the advanced functionality you need to effectively compete on this basis. Similarly, if your goal is to use an ES to be better at financial risk management than any other firm in your industry, it stands to reason that you'll be dissatisfied with a standard system. There are financial analysis and reporting systems from third-party vendors that you'll just have to have.

Of course, working with third-party and legacy systems raises the ante a bit on your ES project. It means that you have to spend time and energy deciding what to keep and what to throw away, as well as evaluating the strengths and weaknesses of a variety of third-party applications. In addition, building interfaces between your ES and third-party or legacy systems is not going to be easy, regardless of what your IT people or vendor expert tells you. But then, being the best at anything has never been easy.

BUILDING THE IT INFRASTRUCTURE

There are many other facets of the IT infrastructure that have to be bulked up before an ES can be installed. This can take place throughout the process of implementation, but it should all be ready before going live, and even substantially before that for purposes of testing. For most firms, an ES will be the largest and most complex client/server application they have ever had. Some of the technical components to consider are as follows:

▶ Somewhat obviously, beefy servers and client PCs will be needed for the entire user population (for a large organization, we're talking many millions of dollars for these).

▶ Communications networks will probably have to be improved so that on-line access will be available to the ES from around the globe.

▶ The human side of technical capabilities will require substantial improvement, including operations, maintenance, and technical support and help desk offerings.

A key technical issue involves how many different instances, or separate versions, of the system to install. The decision has both technical and business implications. Technically, the more instances installed, the greater the complexity and cost. Although ES vendors are making it increasingly feasible to integrate information across several different instances of the same package—and even different packages—it's still more complex than a single system.

From a business perspective, multiple system instances make it much easier to let individual business or geographical units have their own information environments. If it's determined that a business unit doesn't need to be tightly integrated with the rest of the business (perhaps it has substantially different customers and business processes, or maybe it's going to be divested soon), it's often a good idea to give it its own instance of the system. Even with a separate instance in some units, it's still possible to exchange information that's common—for example, financial information for the general ledger—across separate instances. As I described in chapter 4, this ES-enabled information environment can be called *federalist,* and is, in my view, well suited to many large Western corporations despite its technical complexity.

From a business value standpoint, however, the only purpose of most technical capabilities is to support the software, so they should never become the primary focus of the project. Servers, PCs, and communications networks are rapidly becoming commodity products and services, so it's not necessary to spend substantial amounts of time selecting them. It's not uncommon, and often a good idea in my view, for companies to outsource aspects of the technical environment to free up human and financial resources for other, more business-related concerns.

Owens Corning, for example, outsourced not its new ES environment, but rather its old legacy systems and data center operations to Hewlett-Packard. The idea was to allow all of the firm's technical resources to be focused on getting the new system in. Dow Corning (which has nothing in common with Owens Corning now other than part of its name) decided to outsource the installation and maintenance of all the desktop workstations involved in its ES effort.[12]

FINANCIAL MANAGEMENT AND BUSINESS CHANGE TARGETS

As you know by now, a lot of financial decision making is necessary to determine whether an ES makes sense for your organization. At the point of implementation, you've already decided to do this thing, so agonizing over the cost doesn't help much. However, during implementation an organization needs another layer of financial analysis that will monitor the spending levels and lay the groundwork for the type and amounts of business value it receives from the ES project. This is where ongoing costs and benefits are calculated, and actual benefits begin to be realized. The types of activities during implementation include putting a financial and benefit infrastructure in place, determining how the benefits will be achieved over time and how to measure them, and thinking about how to structure and motivate actual achievement of the benefits.

Putting an infrastructure in place for financial analysis and benefit management is primarily about roles and disciplines. For a large implementation (say, one costing $50 million or more, or greater than 2 percent of a year's revenues for a small or midsize firm), it's worth dedicating someone full-time to financial and value management throughout the project. The role of this individual includes monitoring expenditures for software, hardware, and consulting (perhaps including negotiating contracts for these); continually rebudgeting costs; and, most important, calculating benefits and ensuring that they are realized.

Financial discipline in the organization drives this latter issue of benefit realization. It's easy to enumerate benefits on a cost vs. benefit analysis, but actually achieving them is another matter altogether. As noted earlier in the section on managing an ES as a new business venture, it helps if all parties involved have some stake in the game. The entire senior executive team should have bonuses tied to the achievement of ES benefits (and this should not end when the system goes live, but continue as ongoing benefits are achieved). At Fujitsu Microelectronics, for example, 25 percent of the executive team's compensation was tied to accomplishing ES process and financial performance goals. It is also usually a good idea to create performance incentives for ES-affected middle managers, project team members, and even consultants. Of course, if performance improvements are to be measured, someone must gather baseline performance metrics before the system is implemented, or no before vs. after comparisons can be made. Even consultants can be motivated through bonuses based on the achievement of benefits, although care should be taken not to evaluate them on factors they can't control.

The business case should not be shelfware, but should be reviewed and revised (if necessary) on a frequent—perhaps monthly—basis. Costs will change as the scope varies, as problems arise, and as business changes lead to systems changes. Perhaps more important, the benefits will change regularly. New aspects of the system and the processes it supports will come on line. Promised benefits will not actually materialize; unexpected sources of value will emerge. Frequent monitoring of costs and benefits, and broad communications about the results, will spur the organization and its employees to achieve its goals.

The inability to fully specify benefits in advance is a primary reason for employing a real options approach to financing the project. I discussed this approach briefly in chapter 3, but it's worth another mention here because of its relationship to benefit management during implementation. The real options approach assumes that benefit will be evaluated at regular intervals for funding of the next stage of the project. Each stage is viewed as buying an option to learn more about the system and its fit with the business. Although detailed discussion of real options is beyond the scope of the book (and beyond the scope of my finance knowledge), I believe it is likely that many firms will eventually adopt this as their approach to financing an ES project.

IMPLEMENTATION COMPONENTS

A detailed description of the entire implementation process would have to vary by the type of ES being installed. However, it may be useful to describe some of the key steps in the process, particularly those that have an important relationship to achieving business value. In the following discussion, I'm assuming that the package and related system components have been adopted, the IT infrastructure is being built, and the organizational and financial infrastructure is being created.

CONFIGURATION

The process of configuring the ES is at the heart of the implementation process. It's where the system is configured to fit the business, and the business is simultaneously configured to fit the system. It's the point in an ES project at which some very difficult decisions need to be made about how the business wants to structure itself and use the system to advance its business objectives. I talk about the configuration process in some detail in chapter 5 regarding business processes and information issues.

The key point to make here is that it just doesn't make sense to shortchange the process of configuration if you want to get any business value out of your system. Unless your organization is hugely pressed for time, it's a bad idea to simply assume, for example, that all processes should be supported by an out-of-the-box system. No differentiation in ESs, no differentiation in (key aspects of) business strategy. Getting the system installed quickly is important, but a fully implemented system with no business value has . . . well, no business value.

INTERFACE DEVELOPMENT

A substantial portion of implementation time is going to be occupied with building interfaces between the ES and existing systems of various types. The details of this activity are not that germane to this book. What is important to emphasize is that certain interfaces provide more business value than others and should be the focus of early efforts to build. For example, interfaces to the outside world—customers, suppliers, and channel partners—whether they are Internet based or use some other means of access, allow the organization to begin using its ES to make money and build the top line through increased sales. Too many organizations put off external interfaces until after all the more prosaic internal ones are completed.

The same point can be made about interfaces to reporting and analysis systems. Many firms feel that they have to get all their basic transaction information in perfect shape before addressing interfaces to analytical capabilities. Yet managing the business better is a key reason for putting in an ES in the first place. So interfaces to data warehouses, decision-support systems, and query and reporting tools should not wait until the end of a project.

At Bay Networks (now Nortel Networks), for example, the idea of external and analytical interfaces was included in the early design and work of its ES project. Letting users be able to generate their own queries against SAP data was viewed as a key component of the new system's value. Nortel developed an "Information Warehouse" with such information as bookings, unshipped order backlogs, and shipment status. Soon after the ES was installed, managers could analyze sales by product line or geography, and could understand the effects of promotions or alternative channels.

Similarly, Nortel managers felt from the beginning that it was important to allow customer and partner access to the system from the Internet. The implementation project included development of an electronic commerce database that could be accessed through the Web. According to the company's chief information officer at the time:

> *Electronic commerce is a big piece of our long-term strategy. Customers can check order status, download their backlog into spreadsheets, see who signed for a delivered product. The data is never more than a day old, and we're working toward real-time transactions.*[13]

Partners can access Nortel's SAP data whether or not they have SAP themselves; all they need is a browser.

DATA STANDARDIZATION AND CONVERSION

The data to populate a new ES comes primarily from old systems. It's rarely the case that information can be easily moved from the formats and definitions of one system to another; considerable cleaning, matching, reformatting, and updating is generally required. Many companies underestimate the time and effort this requires; numerous ES projects have been slowed because the organization didn't devote sufficient resources or advance planning to data conversion. Fortunately, there are external contractors that can help with the task.

As in other areas, however, it's important not to sacrifice business value for expediency in data conversion. There may be valid reasons why the information cannot be rationalized as much as a technologist might desire. For example, suppose that a diligent data converter finds that one particularly fussy business unit has two address fields for each customer. "Strike one down," the rationalist cries. But wait—perhaps the customer that pays the bill for this unit's products and services is not the one that receives the shipment. Perhaps the company has its vendors ship directly to its distributors. Before moving quickly to delete seemingly irrational data, it's worth asking those who created it in the first place.

TESTING AND PERFORMANCE MANAGEMENT

You need a lot of testing and performance management. Enterprise systems involve unfamiliar software and hardware technology, and it's impossible to anticipate all wrinkles and problems. Most important, you're testing not just a system, but a way of doing business. If insufficient testing meant that your company can't take orders or deal with its suppliers, somebody important will probably notice. So how do you do the requisite testing and performance management? What, I'm supposed to know everything? This is what technical people are for.

PROTOTYPING

It's been said that the best way to fully understand an ES is to actually implement one. Doing a small-scale prototype is an incredibly useful way to learn about the system in the context of your business. Lessons learned in a prototype are useful in pursuing broader implementations, and because mistakes are made on a small scale they're likely to be less costly. Doing a prototype first is also a good means of increasing the accuracy of budgets and plans for a large-scale project. In most cases, you'll want to pick a part of the business for prototyping that's relatively small, simple, and self-contained. It shouldn't be so far removed from the mainstream of the business that people will have difficulty learning from it (i.e., forget that subsidiary in the Bahamas).

Dow Corning did its prototype implementation in its rubber supply chain process in the United Kingdom. Twenty-five members of the global implementation team went there to educate managers and explain new process flows. Focusing carefully on some of the old processes (which hadn't been the team's plan, but they found out about them in meetings with staff members) acquainted the team with some key issues to take into account in the new processes, according to the project's "customer focus" team leader:

> We didn't know that the person carrying the title of production supervisor was doing procurement, planning, and scheduling. We had no clue what else this person was doing. We didn't know their roles in their previous environment and we were not prepared to tell management that these are the jobs that these people are doing, this is how these jobs are evolving with the new work flows. And that has been a bottleneck.[14]

This quote illustrates the importance of a firsthand look at existing processes (and firsthand discussions with those who perform them) before implementing new ones. The best way to acquire this firsthand knowledge is often in a prototype.

IMPLEMENTATION KNOWLEDGE MANAGEMENT

You'll learn a lot about ESs and how to install them in the course of a project. The question is, will you remember what you learned, and apply the knowledge later? Most large organizations will install an ES more than once. As I recommended earlier, for example, they might do a prototype project and then a larger effort. They may also have a phasing approach that implements the same ES package multiple times across different business units and geographies. The point of managing implementation knowledge is to capture the lessons learned from early installations and apply them to later ones. Even if you think you'll never do this again, you may be wrong—your company may acquire another company, for example—so it's a good idea to capture the knowledge from your project anyway.

I'm not going to go into the details of knowledge management here.[15] Suffice it to say that all the general principles of knowledge management apply. You need knowledge managers, a knowledge-oriented culture, processes for capturing, maintaining, and distributing the knowledge, and knowledge-oriented technology. Your consulting firm may be willing to give you some of their own knowledge regarding ES implementation that they've captured in a repository, but that shouldn't prevent you from capturing and applying knowledge that's specific to your own firm.

The first organization I observed that was managing ES implementation knowledge was Hewlett-Packard. The company's Tests and Measurements Organization (now moving to becoming a separate company) was installing SAP and had established people, processes, and technologies for an SAP Implementation Knowledge Base. I commended the manager of the effort, noting that many other business units at HP planned to implement the same software, and that they would surely benefit from the Knowledge Base. She replied, however, that the purpose of this initiative was to use the knowledge within her division, and not share it elsewhere. I shouldn't have been surprised, since I knew that HP had a strong orientation to divisional autonomy. Still, I believe that the more widely knowledge can be shared within a company (on ES implementation or any other topic), the better.

7

TRANSFORMING THE PRACTICE OF MANAGEMENT WITH ENTERPRISE SYSTEMS

WHEN COMPANIES VIEW ENTERPRISE SYSTEM PROJECTS AS technology projects rather than business change initiatives, they make several key mistakes. One error, as I've mentioned, is that they don't focus sufficiently on the process, organizational, and strategic changes that should accompany the system implementation. Second, they view the project as ending when the system is turned on, which greatly limits their ability to achieve benefit. Third, they view the output of the system as a set of information transactions, and do not take advantage of the information to manage the business differently. Correcting this third mistake is my primary aim in this chapter, though I will also discuss the second problem.

Enterprise systems do a good job of automating many business transactions, from taking orders to paying suppliers to changing human resources benefits status. There is, however, another set of potential benefits from ESs that have not been as fully exploited. Enterprise system software and, more important, information also make possible the improvement and even the transformation of management and reporting processes. The information supplied by ES is global in scope, delivered in real time, and structured around cross-functional business processes. For most organizations it is undoubtedly the most comprehensive, high-quality information on what is happening in their businesses that they have ever possessed. The question is, What do they do with it?

I asked this question of more than fifty firms in a 1998 research study of how companies use SAP information.[1] Most respondents, however, had little or nothing to say on the issue; either they hadn't thought about the topic at all or they were not far enough along in implementation to feel that they really had a new source of information. This convinced me that the overall frequency of addressing the issue is low, and that when companies do think about the issue, they are likely to do so late in the process of implementation.

Still, I was able to find fourteen companies that had made some effort to use ES information as a tool to better manage their businesses, and I've discovered a few more since the completion of this survey. The companies were all relatively far along in their SAP implementations (with at least a substantial part of the business live with one or more ES modules) and agreed to describe them with regard to information use and management processes. The fourteen firms are generally relatively advanced and sophisticated with regard to information use issues compared with the average company implementing an ES. The companies included in the study are listed in table 7-1.[2]

TABLE 7-I

COMPANIES INCLUDED IN THE SAP SURVEY

Allegiance Healthcare	Georgia-Pacific
Amerada Hess	Intel
Autodesk	Microsoft
DEKALB Genetics	Monsanto
Dow Chemical	Owens Corning
Elf Atochem	Rockwell International
Fujitsu Microelectronics	Union Carbide

KEY RESEARCH FINDINGS

The key findings of the research study are described in brief in the following list, and then in greater detail throughout the chapter. At the end of the chapter, I present a model that embodies these findings in an overall approach for transforming management with ES information.

▶ Although many organizations justified their implementation of an ES on the basis of better decision-making and management processes, few have yet taken full advantage of the information provided by the system.

▶ Improvement of management and decision making with an ES may be a second or later phase of work with the system, after basic transactional processes have been put in place and substantially common information has been achieved.

▶ Those who are making progress have done so from the bottom up, with improvement of day-to-day operational decision making.

▶ The primary information benefits from an ES realized thus far have generally involved producing similar information content with less time and human effort.

▶ A few companies have designed new measurement and reporting systems around data from their ES.

▶ Some firms have begun to achieve measurable business improvements from better use of ES information, notably by reducing management personnel levels.

▶ As is true of other key functions of ESs, a key divide in implementing new managerial capabilities is whether to take the ES package's reporting approaches into account when designing new management processes or to start with a clean slate.

▶ Effective use of ES information to manage the business requires a set of organizational factors to be present in addition to the technological capabilities that most firms acknowledge.

▶ Even after ES information is used to make a decision, other factors must be present to ensure that the organization actually takes action and gets results.

▶ Management education and managerial super users may be very helpful in the effective implementation of ES information use, though they have been rarely deployed thus far.

▶ If you would like to take advantage of the managerial benefits that can be derived from an ES, view use of these systems not as a project with a defined end but rather as an ongoing way of life.

THE IMPORTANCE OF ES-ENABLED INFORMATION TRANSFORMATION

We know that many companies are already getting substantial benefits from the transactional information in an ES. For reasons of opportunity and management pressure, it is important that firms take advantage of the information potential of ESs for management purposes. Almost every respondent in my initial study, for example, indicated that they justified their adoption of SAP partially on the basis of improved management information. Sooner or later, managers will ask whether that promise has been fulfilled. Two firms reported that senior executives were beginning to ask about the advertised improvements in information; one respondent whose company had not yet adopted major changes in management information noted that his CEO had commented, "We're spending all this money for the same information?"

There is no reason why the potential from ESs for changes in management processes—performance reporting and monitoring, stakeholder communications, managing relationships with customers—should not be taken just as seriously as the opportunities for operational process improvements. ES-supplied information can lead to faster and better decision making, lower management head counts, and lower costs for information reporting. To use an ES to generate the same reports as those provided by legacy systems, as several companies reported was their case—"And try to get them to look the same too, would you?"—is a waste of business capability.

THE CURRENT STATE

As the previous discussion suggests, the current state of ES-enabled information transformation in most firms surveyed is not a pretty sight. Many of the firms I contacted, some of which were relatively advanced in their implementations, had not yet begun substantial transformations of information reporting and measurement processes. Some argued that they could not begin changes in these areas until other building blocks were put in place first—getting the system fully installed, making changes in basic operational processes, and getting common master data, for example. One manager colorfully stated that to address reporting issues before transactions would be like "buying wine and turning on soft music before you have a date."

Therefore, using ES data for purposes other than completing basic business transactions is often seen as a second or even later stage in the effective implementation of the package. Certainly it is unlikely that changes in reporting and decision making would be possible before the system is installed. And because in the late 1990s many companies were attempting to implement ESs quickly because of Year 2000 problems, reporting and better information for decision making wouldn't have been first on their minds. Indeed, one of the most advanced companies in this study was just going live in its last geographical region; the company's overall implementation process took almost a decade, and they didn't seriously address reporting and measurement with SAP data until about the seventh year of the project. Time, then, is an important factor in managing better with ES information.

Those firms that had begun transformations in their use of information were doing so from the bottom, or at least the middle, up. Employees within particular functional areas, such as production planning, customer service, and accounting and finance, were the most likely group to be using the ES information to make daily operational decisions. Managers who were closest to a particular process or transaction type—for example, available-to-promise inventory—were the most likely to have, and be using, reports about that area of the business.

Senior general managers were least likely to have extensive information from ES packages. This could present a problem in that it is these managers who may be most conscious of the cost and resource consumption of an ES project. If they are among the last to see information benefits, their patience could wear thin. I have to admit that thus far, however, there has been little demand from senior managers for better information or new ES-enabled management processes. At Dow Chemical, where sophisticated reporting systems and new performance measures have been developed, senior executives still rely largely on middle managers for ad hoc analyses and reports, though many have been trained in the use of the system themselves.

A few companies are redesigning their operational and financial measurement systems around the capabilities of SAP or other ES packages, but most of the companies interviewed were apparently content with their existing measures and measurement processes. Most of the companies were using the same information content in their reports as they did before implementing an ES, either by design or by default. Most respondents also reported that there is relatively poor awareness of what information is available through their ES and of how to get it. Although the concept of best practices is clearly understood with regard to a package's support of transactional business processes, the companies surveyed did not seem aware of best practices in ES-enabled reporting and information use.

There is some good news, however. The low rate of changes in measurement systems design does not mean that these companies received no benefit from their ESs with regard to reporting and information use. The content and the process design for measurement and reporting may not have changed, but the process performance did. That is, the primary information benefits from ESs thus far involve efficiency in information access and production. The same information is now more easily available, is delivered through a more automated process, and is furnished more quickly. Most companies reported that heretofore management reporting was a haphazard, labor-intensive process with many handoffs; now it functions much more smoothly and efficiently. Maybe that's worth the price of admission.

One common example of this type of change was improvements in financial closing processes; closings at two companies that previously took ten days, for example, are now done in four. At Cisco Systems, enterprise financial systems can be used to do a "virtual close" every day if desired. A financial closing is on the cusp between a transactional process and a managerial process. These changes and benefits are somewhat evolutionary thus far and could lead to major transformations over time.

The Benefits of ES-Enabled Management Transformation

Why would a company be motivated to adopt changes in how it manages the business with an ES? The benefits from transforming or improving management processes can be difficult to document, since most organizations do not have measures or even structured processes for management activity. In some cases, however, the benefits are obvious and measurable.

Perhaps the most measurable of all types of benefits are those involving reductions in management personnel. Several organizations are envisioning such reductions; some have already accomplished them. Most of the reports of these benefits are anecdotal rather than systematic. For example, at one Monsanto plant, nine of fifteen accountants were no longer needed when accounting processes were made common and moved to the corporate level. Overall, the company eliminated about 40 percent of its accounting staff by implementing an ES-enabled shared-services organization. Amerada Hess and Elf Atochem also reported measurable benefits from personnel reductions or redeployments; these savings were among the benefits used to justify the adoption of their SAP systems in the first place, and were closely measured and reported internally.

Other benefits are measurable in principle, but the companies I studied were less likely to measure them in practice. This category of benefits includes the rationalization of reporting processes. Smoother data flows, less data complexity, and fewer handoffs of management data could lead to savings of time and cost, but none of the companies in this study that reported such improvements had measured the savings thus far. Microsoft financial managers did report that the easy availability of good data from its SAP ES system has eased considerably the *ad hoc* reporting burden for their finance organization; users can now get their own reports. While it's difficult to know how much time and money were devoted to centralized reporting, it's undoubtedly a benefit for the finance group. The decentralized costs, however, are even more difficult to measure.

Another important but difficult-to-measure benefit involves taking a process-oriented view of the organization, or a broad global view. Owens Corning, for example, is relying on its ES to supply information about its business processes. A manager there cited the example of global sourcing as a new process that would be impossible to administer without better data from its ES. The new global sourcing organization can save money by monitoring worldwide inventory levels more closely, negotiating more favorable worldwide contracts, and avoiding disposal costs for overpurchased commodities. Of course, just putting the ES in doesn't ensure a process orientation, but it does make it possible.

Perhaps the most difficult benefits to measure involve better decision making. Most companies today do not rigorously assess the economic impacts of even major decisions, and it is unlikely that they will start when ES data is used in decision-making processes. But there can be little doubt that the more comprehensive and timely data available from an ES can lead to better decisions across all sorts of business processes. In fact, several companies in this study reported examples of improved decision making. Fujitsu Microelectronics, for example, discovered through analysis of its SAP data that its distributor channels were more profitable than its direct channels, and decided to put additional resources and attention into distributor sales. Amerada Hess found that because data on the value of particular oil wells could be obtained much more quickly, its managers could make better decisions about investments in them. These are only two examples of what will presumably be many instances of improved decision making due to ESs.

THE PROCESS FOR REPORTING AND MEASUREMENT CHANGE

Perhaps the most important aspect of the process used by organizations in getting value from ES information is that for the most part there was no conscious process. "Using ES information more effectively" was rarely the focus of a specific project, task force, or implementation step. Further, no executive was generally in charge of achieving such objectives. The two most prominent exceptions, at Owens Corning and Dow Chemical, were led by a process management organization and a strategic planning group, respectively. Microsoft, which was also something of an exception, had an initiative led by the controller's organization. In most other cases, the idea of managing differently with ES information was unplanned and occurred only from the bottom up. Perhaps other organizations will create formal projects as they approach completion of their implementations, particularly now that the Year 2000 issue has come and gone.

I've argued throughout this book that a fundamental question for organizations is whether to envision their basic business processes as a clean sheet of paper or rather to start with the capabilities of an ES as a design constraint. The same question presents itself with regard to reporting and measurement processes with ESs. Although none of the companies in this study called their analysis of reporting processes "reengineering," it is clear that new information processes and structures are necessary. Should companies then design their measurement systems and processes with regard to what is easy to do with an ES, or should they design measures, reports, and information flows without any constraints, reconciling their desired approach with an ES only later?

The companies researched were roughly evenly split on this issue. Union Carbide, for example, is starting its thinking about the issue with SAP's reporting and measurement capabilities in mind; Monsanto, on the other hand, began its focus on the issue by thinking about the best possible measurement and reporting system. One means of ensuring that a fresh approach will be taken to the problem is to eliminate all previously existing reports; this approach was taken by Fujitsu Microelectronics managers. If reporting structures are not changed, companies may find themselves seeking old information in legacy systems that they had hoped to abandon, as two companies reported. Because most major ES vendors are currently enhancing their reporting and analysis capabilities, it may be more reasonable in the future to start with what the system makes easy to do.

Another key issue in reporting and measurement change involves the creation and timing of related organizational changes. In two different respects organizations pointed out the need for organizational changes before ES-based reporting and measurement processes could become effective. One aspect of the problem deals with the elimination of managers and professionals involved in the reporting process. Several firms had adopted an ES with the goal of reducing head count in measurement and reporting processes. Two of these firms, Monsanto and Amerada Hess, pointed out the need to make head-count reductions in advance of knowing the details of reporting changes. This early action provides motivation for business units and departments to actually change their processes and activities to reduce steps and needed labor. Monsanto and Amerada Hess reduced the budgets of units and departments where head-count reductions were planned, which ensured that the reductions would be carried out. Dow Chemical reduced not only the number of managers but also the number of management layers: The managerial hierarchy was shrunk from twelve layers before SAP to four or five. This reduction was a management objective that Dow's ES helped to enable.

Several companies also described the need to add new organizational units and personnel when new information-based activities are envisioned. At Elf Atochem and Fujitsu, for example, new groups were created whose roles involved matching manufacturing demand and supply. Rockwell International, now primarily an electronics manufacturer, combined aspects of such functions as operations, finance, marketing, production planning and control, warehousing and distribution, and billing and collection to form a new "front to back" supply chain organization. At Owens Corning, a new global procurement group was created where one had not previously existed. Without these new organizational units, managers felt that the information provided by the ES to perform those functions would not have been used. Indeed, at one company where the ES was supposed to support a global purchasing function, the purchasing process has not really changed—largely, one manager reported, because there is no organizational unit with global corporate purchasing authority.

In addition to new organizational units, those who are interested in reporting and measurement issues should think carefully about the basic business processes of the organization. Each new process design creates a new information need. For example, when Microsoft implemented new financial and purchasing processes, the process design teams were also charged with defining new "key performance indicators" to measure the process. Union Carbide is redesigning not only operational business processes, but also management processes. The company's ES implementation team is mapping out new managerial work flows and how existing management roles fit into them. The goal is to understand what percentage of management jobs involves doing things that are no longer necessary when ES information is widely available, and to eliminate or redeploy managers in unnecessary positions.

Another means of determining what information an organization needs is to plan the structure of a data repository. While this might seem like putting the cart before the horse, Monsanto managers inadvertently discovered that it was a very useful means of configuring the information to be delivered by an ES. Because Monsanto needed a financial data warehouse in advance of finishing its ES implementation, the company spent considerable time assessing what information managers wanted in the warehouse. Creating the design of the warehouse first made apparent what information the financial modules of ES needed to output.

Given the complexity of the ES information environment and the changes in business processes most organizations go through during an ES implementation, it may not be possible to predict changes in management processes in advance. Familiarity with the system and with new ways of working may lead to new uses for information. At Georgia-Pacific, for example, before the advent of an ES in the Packaged Products Division, both production planning and customer service functions spent much of their time juggling inventory and reallocating it from one insistent customer to another. Because there was little visibility of inventory information, the planning group could do very little actual planning. With the implementation of SAP, however, there was all the inventory information these functions needed. Users in these functions initially reacted negatively because they could no longer shuffle inventory around. However, they were able to commit inventory to customers much more effectively. Service personnel could tell customers where their order was even after it had been turned over to shippers. Planners found that they had the time and information to plan. Their initial reservations about the system turned into enthusiasm as they realized they could finally do their jobs as logically defined.

A final issue to be considered with regard to measurement system processes is who is the customer for the new measures. Companies may want to identify particular internal customers for the change effort—for example, a particular management level, business unit, or business function. More important, firms should think about the relative importance and sequencing of internal versus external customers. Several of the firms in this study, including Union Carbide and DEKALB, had objectives of eventually supplying customers, suppliers, and other stakeholders with reports. Microsoft already makes available ES-derived information on its corporate Web page that is up-to-date and produced without human intervention.

THE CONTENT OF ES-ENABLED MEASUREMENT SYSTEMS

Some of the companies I studied have begun to think in detail about the content of measurement systems in a post-ES world. As mentioned previously, for example, Microsoft is focusing on the key performance indicators that it needs to gather and analyze. Dow Chemical implemented a new set of measures around value-based management. Amerada Hess's financial measures are changing from a focus on the balance sheet to a stronger orientation to the income statement. It is obviously important to determine the strategic direction for financial measurements before beginning to implement the measures in an ES.

Several firms, both users and vendors of ESs, are beginning to develop a direct relationship between their ES information and the *balanced scorecard* approach to performance measurement and reporting.[3] The balanced scorecard features a set of measures with equal (according to the official approach) or unequal weights for the areas of financial performance, internal operations, customer measurements, and "learning and growth." Despite the fact that some of the measures in the scorecard are not now, and will probably never be, included in an ES (e.g., customer satisfaction, and many of the measures in the learning and growth category), companies would like to populate the scorecard automatically with ES data when possible.

Managers at Owens Corning, one firm that is building ties between its ES and a scorecard, report that one of the most difficult tasks in applying the balanced scorecard concept in an ES context is the translation of high-level financial targets (e.g., a certain level of return on invested capital) into the operational and process-oriented measures captured in an enterprise system. J.D. Edwards is working on direct input from its internal ES (which is, of course, its own ES product) into a balanced scorecard, and is planning to incorporate these features into products for all customers. PeopleSoft is working with the creators of the balanced scorecard to translate output from its package into a scorecard format; SAP has also announced functionality of this type.

Few of the companies in this study had yet explored, however, the specific details of reporting processes. One issue given little attention thus far, for example, is how often to do reporting, or how often to encourage managers to monitor certain types of information. Cisco may be able to do a virtual close every day, but is it worth doing? Some firms reported that they are trying to get away from regular report frequencies, moving, as an Amerada Hess manager put it, "from just-in-case reporting to just-in-time." Microsoft produces a series of daily on-line reports in key business areas using data extracted from its ES. A largely unexplored topic, however, is the issue of what level of reporting detail is appropriate for what circumstances. Which measures should be rolled up to the corporate level, and which are not appropriate to be aggregated? As firms gain experience with ES-enabled reporting they will be better able to make generalizations about reporting frequencies.

Another issue on which there is not yet a clear best practice is how to determine the specific content of measures. Managers I interviewed in several firms stated that simply asking managers what information they want is not very effective; they typically do not know and have not devoted much thought to the issue. Otherwise, no firms reported any particularly useful techniques or tricks for eliciting information needs. One company representative stated that it would be helpful if consultants who were familiar with both the potential information in ESs and the business environments of specific industries could specify the types of reports that should be adopted and monitored by a company.

Dow Chemical is probably the furthest along of the surveyed companies in the process of specifying new management systems. A cross-functional steering team led by the head of Strategic Planning developed a set of measures and reports for the business derived from SAP data (Dow uses the R/2 mainframe package). Standard information deliverables were defined by process experts in different areas of the company, such as expense management, inventory management, and sales. A data mart, or small warehouse, was developed for each type of data. There are more than twenty marts, but they are all part of an integrated system for the company, so that numbers in the "business results" mart balance to numbers in the expenses and sales marts. Standard queries and views were built using a third-party reporting tool. Up to 10,000 concurrent users can access the reporting system; almost 5,000 users have already been trained, ranging from Dow's CEO to plant floor workers.

Dow has also implemented a new set of performance measures centered on shareholder value and activity-based costing called *value-based management*. SAP data is used to compute these measures. Instead of reporting in terms of product and income, the emphasis is on contribution margins and customer accounts. The company has data and reports that allow calculation of current and lifetime account value.

BEHAVIORAL AND ORGANIZATIONAL CHANGE ISSUES

Companies participating in the study generally reported that they would have to undergo considerable organizational and behavioral change before they could make full use of the information provided by their ES. In some cases, the software and the information it provides lead to a different culture by themselves; in other respects an organization and its employees must change to take advantage of the new information environment.

In terms of cultural changes due to the information from an ES, several companies' representatives argued that a new information culture was beginning to evolve. It is a more open and visible information environment in which managers and employees at multiple levels of the company can see instantaneously what is happening around the world. There is no more hiding when performance is poor, and no more ex post facto revisions or "electronic white-outs." Bad news travels quickly; all operations are transparent. All of the respondents who reported this effect felt that it would be good for the company overall, but that a period of adjustment would be required and new information behaviors would be necessary. One company reported that it may eventually impose limits on how far down or up in the organization an employee can find data.

Several managers also reported that their firms would need a more data-based and analytical culture. "We will need to start making decisions based on facts, not rumors and gut feel," one reported. Another stated that because his company is already highly analytical ("we're a left-brain organization"), it would thrive on the better data provided by its ES. One firm's ES project manager also reported that employees will have to take more decision-making risk in the future. Another reported a somewhat paradoxical set of changes in information culture: It is tightening up on the kinds of basic information transactions it allows for reasons of commonality and efficiency; at the same time it is loosening up and empowering all levels of employees on information analysis issues. Of course, no one in this study argued that a change to a different information culture would happen just because new software was installed; other managerial changes are necessary, though they have not been started in these firms.

Similar to the cultural changes described previously, several firms believe that individual workers will need a higher level of analytical skills. Even the overall level of intelligence of workers might have to change, according to one manager. He repeated the often-heard comment, "We'll need half as many, twice as smart." Some organizations say that a small cadre of employees will specialize in data mining and analysis. Others plan to educate a large group of employees and managers to use the information. However, one company manager's comment was typical with regard to the current level of expertise about ES information and its use: "They don't know what's there and they wouldn't know what to do with it if they did."

There are also two implementation issues with regard to the use of ES information. One involves the employment of so-called super users (a role defined in chapter 6) in implementation who are managers, not line workers. The deployment of super user managers would seem to be an effective technique for understanding the information implications of ES implementation. Their role could be to help system implementers determine the reporting and management process needs of the organization. However, in the firms studied, even when managers were employed as super users, their focus was typically on representing their departments for basic process and transaction information, rather than designing reports and management processes. Firms should consider using managerial super users when they do begin to think about reporting issues.

A potentially difficult issue regarding ES implementation and culture involves personnel reductions, particularly at middle-management levels. As noted earlier, several firms are planning to use the better information from their ES as a rationale for eliminating some administrative and managerial positions; some have already done so. However, it is probably important to avoid the perception that the implementation of an ES is an excuse for widespread reductions in managerial or analytical staff. In that case at-risk managers or employees might withhold cooperation in using the software. Thus far, however, no firm in this study has reported this type of problem.

TECHNOLOGY AND SYSTEMS ISSUES

There is no typical technology architecture for ES-enabled reporting and information distribution. Other than an ES itself, no single platform predominates. As I mentioned earlier, ES vendors are beginning to offer substantially improved capabilities in the areas of performance measurement and reporting. These capabilities were not available when I talked to managers about reporting and management process issues. Since then, informal discussions suggest that these functions are being greeted with high levels of interest. This software collects many of the reporting and management process functions companies previously had to develop themselves into a packaged application.

At the time of the study, companies were using either the limited query and reporting capabilities from major ES vendors, or third-party query and reporting software. Several firms reported that they wanted an open query and reporting system, as well as an open data warehouse, because they wanted to interface with several different transaction data sources, not just their ES. Microsoft, as might be expected, used its own software for querying and reporting.

Most companies had some type of data warehousing approach for ES data; their objective was to avoid both performance problems with, and potential corruption of, the ES transaction system. However, three of the fourteen companies interviewed were actually going directly into the transaction system for data access and reporting, and were not currently concerned about data integrity or transaction volume issues. They felt that another level of data architecture would only confuse users. Among those who used data warehousing, several broke up the ES and legacy system data into several smaller marts specific to functional or process areas; Dow Chemical has well over twenty marts, Microsoft four.

Intranet webs were a popular vehicle for information distribution; half of the companies planned to use that technology for access to common reports. Two firms had adopted the Web in place of previous executive information systems (EISs); one firm, Autodesk, still employed a home-grown EIS and was pleased with its integration with its ES (but even Autodesk has recently adopted Web-based reporting, and it may eventually replace the EIS).

A MODEL FOR TURNING ES DATA INTO ES KNOWLEDGE

It should be clear by now that managing with the information from an ES is not just a matter of installing one, or of developing a data warehouse and populating it with ES data. It's achieved not through technology alone, but through a complex collection of factors that most organizations have never even considered. In a broad research project in which I am participating, we've been trying to identify the factors involved in turning data into knowledge, which our team has concluded are basically the same issues involved in managing effectively with ES information. Therefore, I'll describe the research model for that project in the context of ESs specifically and present a case study from that project, Earthgrains Company. We've found the model to be quite useful in describing environments in which transaction data from systems like ESs is turned into knowledge and results.

The overall process by which organizations turn ES data—or any other type, for that matter—into knowledge and business results has never been articulated, to our knowledge. Based on research in more than a dozen companies that have succeeded at it, we hypothesize that the model in figure 7-1 accurately describes this important process. The model consists of three major steps. *Context* includes the factors that must be present before any specific attempt to transform ES data into knowledge and results. The *transformation* of data into results takes place when the data is actually analyzed and then used to support a business decision. *Outcomes* are the events that change as a result of the analysis and decision making. I'll describe each step and its respective components briefly.

CONTEXT

One important, but perhaps overemphasized, prerequisite to the process is the *technology context*. These are all the technological factors that affect an organization's ability to extract value from data. They might include the capabilities of the ES itself for reporting and analysis, software and hardware for data extraction and analysis, the access that potential users have to the data over networks and infrastructure, and even the ability to distribute the results of analysis.

A desirable *data context* is substantially more difficult to achieve. This refers to the accuracy, availability, currency, and overall quality of the data to be analyzed. Enterprise systems have relatively high data quality compared with most applica-

FIGURE 7-1

A MODEL OF HOW ES DATA IS TRANSFORMED INTO
KNOWLEDGE AND RESULTS

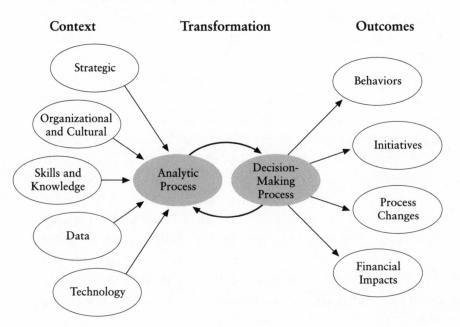

tion programs. However, the data that emerges from them is generally intended to serve business transactions, not analysis and decision making. Further, it's often necessary to combine ES data with other information that comes from different systems or perhaps isn't automated at all. Creating an effective data context is difficult in the beginning and forever after; it's a never-ending, but necessary, struggle.

Skills and knowledge are human attributes that are often overlooked in efforts to use ES data effectively. There are many types of skills and knowledge that are relevant to this objective, including analytical skills, technical skills, and business skills, and general experience with this process. Since ESs are particularly complex systems, knowledge of the structure of available information is particularly critical. Not even the most sophisticated analytical software obviates the need for a high degree of skill and experience in the successful analysis and use of ES data.

The *organizational and cultural context* includes many different facets of the organization that affect how well and how easily it takes advantage of ES data. Fundamental among these facets is the orientation to fact-based decision making: Does the organization prefer data to intuition? There are also political factors involved in whether data is available to be used in decisions and actions. Organizational factors are difficult to measure and change, but without a positive context, successful data transformation is unlikely on a regular basis.

The *strategic context* is the broader business context in which ES data is analyzed and used. If there is no clarity about what strategic objectives the organization is trying to achieve with the transformation of ES data, it will capture and store far too much data to ever be useful. The strategic context specifies what questions are to be answered by the data, the critical business and management processes in which the data is to be applied, and the overall business value to which the data transformation can lead.

TRANSFORMATION

At the center of the overall model are the processes by which ES data actually becomes knowledge and is applied in decisions and actions. The *analytic process* involves the means by which ES data becomes knowledge. These are commonly statistical and numerical analyses, from taking the mean of a distribution to a neural network analysis; alternatively, analysis may involve the combination of simple, straightforward reports with insightful observations and thought by humans.

The *decision-making process* itself may, as I implied previously, be based on high-quality, well-analyzed ES data or a multitude of other factors. Management scholars over the past several decades have documented the sometimes tenuous link between data, decisions, and actions. However, if the results of ES data transformations are not used to inform decisions, then what is the point of the transformations in the first place? Some companies are beginning to tie decisions to the data and knowledge used to assist them, but the linkage isn't a common one, and I know of no instance of doing this in an ES context.

OUTCOMES

In this entire process of converting ES data to knowledge to results, prerequisites and transformation count for little unless something changes in the organization as a result. Changes in *behaviors* of individual managers and employees are perhaps the most basic potential outcome of this process. Just as personal decisions lead to individual behavior change, decisions by executives can lead to broad behavioral change. A data-based decision to focus on cost control, for example, can lead to thousands or millions of individual behaviors to curtail spending. If it doesn't, the point of the analysis and the decision is questionable.

A decision and the aggregation of behavior changes may also result in a new *initiative*—a project to improve the business in some regard, or changes in an existing project. Analysis of customer transaction data may reveal, for example, that a promotion isn't working and that a new marketing initiative is needed.

The results of decisions can also include *process changes*—which are themselves the result of many small initiatives and behavioral changes. A determination that an existing process is not working effectively can lead to a new process design and to its implementation. If ES data transformation suggests that a new product development process takes too long, for example, decisions may be taken to shorten it incrementally or radically.

Of course, the ultimate result of all this activity for profit-seeking businesses should be *financial impacts*. Decisions lead to new behaviors, which lead to new initiatives and processes, which don't matter much unless they improve the bottom line and the return to shareholders. It may be difficult to draw a direct chain of influence from prerequisites to transformation to nonfinancial outcomes to financial results, but establishing that linkage should always be the objective of an organization that invests effort and resources in ES data transformation. Financial impacts shouldn't be sought by themselves (because they won't be found), but only as the end result of a variety of behavioral and organizational changes.

MANAGING WITH ES INFORMATION AT EARTHGRAINS

This case draws on one company's experiences in trying to leverage data from its ES investment.[4] The case illustrates a conceptual framework (see figure 7-1) that managers can use to evaluate their own situation and identify areas that need special attention to make sure their firm's ES investment enables improvement in how the business is managed.

Earthgrains is a $1.9 billion bakery products company that was formerly a subsidiary of Anheuser-Busch. Since being spun off from the beer giant in March 1996, Earthgrains has been a publicly traded company whose stock has appreciated more than 200 percent. Its core businesses are organized in two divisions—bakery products and refrigerated dough.

STRATEGIC CONTEXT

Earthgrains' U.S. refrigerated dough products division is the only manufacturer of private-label refrigerated dough products in the United States. The company makes canned dough products that are sold in the grocery refrigerated section, including biscuits, dinner rolls, crescent rolls, cinnamon rolls, cookie dough, breadsticks, pizza crust, and pie crusts. (I get hungry just reciting them!) Dough products are marketed nationwide under more than 100 store brands. The refrigerated dough division competes primarily with Pillsbury, which, as the only branded manufacturer of refrigerated dough, dominates the category. Earthgrains' strategy is to copy Pillsbury's successful products with private-label offerings and to capture significant volume in the particular product. Sales for the division's refrigerated dough segment, including in Europe, were nearly $300 million, with margins of more than 10 percent, compared with approximately 5 percent in the bakery segment.

Senior managers in the U.S. refrigerated dough products unit had chosen to pursue a strategy of operational excellence, as opposed to taking a customer or product focus. Historically, however, the division had no integration between its order-to-cash, picking, delivery, and accounts receivable processes and systems. There was no visibility into finished goods inventory if a customer had a question. And the company couldn't price an order until it was shipped, which significantly delayed the invoicing process. In addition, product forecasting efforts were hampered. Managers only discovered that they had a shortage of manufacturing capacity when the line ran out. On the sales side, management also had limited visibility of who its most and least profitable customers and products were. In general, then, management lacked the detailed understanding of its business needed to improve operations.

The refrigerated dough division had a clear strategy and was in a competitive position in the industry to achieve it. The management team also recognized what types of decisions had to be made to support the strategy so that there could be a direct connection between daily operations and strategic objectives. But because the division lacked the operational data it needed, there was no way to make the necessary decisions, much less measure their effectiveness in strategic terms. Finally, there were some other organizational capabilities needed to make the decisions necessary to support the strategy, as we will see.

TECHNOLOGY CONTEXT

Earthgrains' lack of operational data to support decision making changed with the implementation of SAP's R/3. Most of the enterprise system's modules had been implemented by early 1999, and the refrigerated dough division now has unprecedented visibility into its operations and customer base, which has dramatically changed its operations. Several modules were also installed in the bakery division, but so far, deployment there has been more limited. In addition to the hardware and software technologies needed to create, capture, and store the transaction data used to support decision making, several other technology elements are present, as discussed in the following subsections.

Data communications. When transaction data crosses organizational boundaries, the communications technology needed to transfer the data between entities becomes an important factor. Earthgrains had invested considerable resources to develop its electronic data interchange (EDI) capabilities for the interorganizational transfer of transaction data.

Data access tools. Earthgrains has given its twenty-eight-member sales force laptops to access highly detailed sales data now available through the enterprise system. This tool enables access to SAP data, but it also constrains the types of questions that analysts and managers can ask. For example, the vice president of customer services says, "SAP is good if you want to look at order X by customer by day, but it's very hard to use if you want to see five customers over three days."

Data access tools are probably the most visible example of software or hardware capabilities that can impede the use of transaction data. But other technical capabilities must also be present to support the data's use. For example, initially Earthgrains' salespeople who worked remotely couldn't print any SAP outputs because they were not part of the company's computer network at headquarters. If not anticipated and resolved, technical barriers can inhibit the use of transaction data.

Data analysis and presentation tools. Earthgrains' business analysts use Microsoft's Access and Excel to analyze the data and put it in a format that managers and salespeople will understand. Experience has taught the customer services VP that how data is formatted and presented to different types of end users means everything in getting it used. In addition, special decision-support software may also be needed for particular applications. Earthgrains loads data files into Manugistics, a supply chain planning and forecasting software package that they use for analysis in a variety of ways.

DATA CONTEXT

Relevant data issues will vary significantly across organizations, but there are certain factors that can impede the use of data for decision making.

Controlling data integrity. The ability to develop and maintain "clean" data is always important, but acceptable error rates may vary between industries. Integrity was less of a problem in Earthgrains' refrigerated dough division, where transaction data captured in the SAP system was created internally based on sales orders and shipping invoices. Whereas management could control these processes, the company's bakery division was trying to use scanner data from grocery stores to transform its distribution processes. Data from many retailers, however, had proved to be of variable quality, limiting its usefulness. Clearly, it is easier to control the quality of transaction data created within an organization than across entities.

Synthesizing data from other sources. Enterprise system transaction data must almost always be integrated with data from other sources, such as third-party vendors, to make it useful for management decision making. Earthgrains used census data combined with scanner data to analyze trends in different product categories and to try to interpret what was happening in the marketplace.

Completeness of data. To be useful, transaction data must include data elements (or fields) that can be usefully compared to provide insights for decision making. For example, if the system captures data on product sales, but the specific item cannot be linked back to the specific promotion under which the retailer purchased it, then the analytic insights from the transaction will be limited. Management must always think through in detail the types of data elements needed to address key decisions.

Complete data also means having adequate history to do analysis. Earthgrains needed a one- to two-year history of a retailer's inventory movement and stock outs before they could help the retailer make inventory management decisions. In many cases, just having transaction data isn't enough. It must exist for the right time period to be useful.

Timely data extracts. Transaction data must also be available in a timely fashion to support decision making. At Earthgrains, sales data is pulled daily from the SAP sales and distribution module. This allows the vice president of sales to identify problems early and take action before the end of the sales period. To be useful, data extracts must be available for analysis on a frequency that matches a useful monitoring and decision-making cycle.

ORGANIZATIONAL AND CULTURAL CONTEXT

There are many potential elements of organization and culture that must be aligned to support a business unit's use of transaction data. Some of those evident in the Earthgrains context are discussed here.

Structure supports collaboration. Organizational boundaries can be barriers to the high levels of collaboration often needed to produce high-quality analytic outputs. At Earthgrains, both the sales and customer service departments in the refrigerated dough division have their own set of dedicated analysts who work closely with management, using SAP data to support decision making. Management needs to consider the complexity and ambiguity of the problems requiring analytic support. More complex issues, requiring sophisticated modeling and data analysis, are better served when analysts and decision makers are closely linked organizationally because of the high levels of communication and collaboration required.

Realigning reward systems. Nothing undermines the use of transaction data faster than reward systems that discourage its use in decision making. Historically, the sales force in Earthgrains' refrigerated dough unit had been rewarded only for the quantity of products sold. After SAP was implemented, the compensation system was changed to reward salespeople 50 percent on sales volume and 50 percent on gross profit. This significantly changed the behavior of the sales force, who became much more interested in understanding the current and potential profitability of their customers. Reward systems that aren't aligned with management's objectives for creating and acting on insights from the data are a serious impediment to leveraging this resource. Several elements of Earthgrains' culture also supported the use of transaction data.

Orientation to change. The refrigerated dough division had a relatively new senior management team, with no emotional investment in the old ways of doing things. Thus, expectations regarding behavior changes were high.

Data-oriented culture. The company's CEO was known by his colleagues as "data hungry." When he observed the information available from the ES, he noted enthusiastically, "It's like getting your head blown off with data." He had pushed hard to develop norms that would encourage employees to behave as members of a data-driven organization. In recent years, the quality of management reviews had improved 100 percent, according to one senior manager, because executives were now much more reliant on numbers in explaining their performance and investments. This behavior had trickled down throughout the organization so that salespeople were pushed to become users of data. Management assumed that if the sales force worked with the numbers themselves, they would be more confident in what they were presenting to customers.

SKILLS AND KNOWLEDGE

A variety of skills and knowledge are needed to leverage transaction data for decision making. At Earthgrains, both the customer service and sales departments have teams of analysts whose combined skills include the following:

▶ Detailed knowledge of the unit's underlying business processes

▶ Strong knowledge of the grocery industry

▶ Extensive skills for interpreting the meaning of the SAP data, which requires understanding definitions of key elements, how they relate, and their limitations for analysis

▶ Thorough working knowledge of several analytic and data presentation software packages

▶ Strong interpersonal skills needed to train and support end users, particularly the salespeople, who were likely to become frustrated when they started working with the data

ANALYTIC PROCESSES

All of the contextual elements described previously—strategy, technology, data, organization, culture, and skills and knowledge—combine to shape an organization's capabilities for data analysis. At Earthgrains, these combined inputs provided the motivation and ability to create five types of analytic outputs.

1. *Standard reports.* The vice president of sales looked at a daily report that showed what products had been sold the previous day, in what volumes, their gross margin, and the total sales for the year to date.

2. *Simple analytic outputs.* Shortly after the sales and distribution module of SAP was installed, Earthgrains' management began doing basic customer and product profitability analysis. This analytical approach is simple, although it does require that the organization have previously adopted a disciplined approach to activity-based costing in order to be successful.

3. *Complex analytic outputs.* Over time, as management's understanding of the system developed, they began posing more complex queries to the analysts; for example, how much do sales actually increase as a result of different types of promotions?

4. *Modeling.* Earthgrains had made limited efforts in this area, but had begun forecasting product demand to better plan their manufacturing capacity.

5. *One-time process analysis.* Integrating SAP data also supported one other different type of analysis. It enabled Earthgrains to evaluate the cash disbursements going through its accounts payable process in its bakery products division. This one-time process analysis provided support for management's decision to centralize all accounts payable activities from its forty-four bakeries.

DECISION-MAKING PROCESSES

Different analytic capabilities support different types of decisions and decision-making processes. Access to transaction data, and the ability to interpret and analyze it, can change the types of decisions being made, the confidence management has in making certain ongoing decisions, and even the location of some decisions within a business process.

New types of decisions. At Earthgrains, SAP data made it possible to identify which customers and products were most and least profitable. It is worth noting that although the data analysis revealed unprofitable customers and products, the more important management decision was what to do with those results and how to do it.

Increasing confidence in decisions. Using transaction data effectively sometimes means making decisions that were not possible before, but in other cases it can change the confidence level in decisions that were already being made. SAP data at Earthgrains provided new levels of confidence and support in making decisions about where to invest in promotions, where to invest in manufacturing capacity given expected product demand, and where sales managers should be focusing their attention.

Changing decision-making processes. Finally, the availability of transaction data also sometimes enables major changes in decision-making processes and, notably, where decisions are being made. At Earthgrains, two processes were changed in distinctly different ways. The accounts payable process was centralized and standardized so that all invoices were paid after twenty-eight days. In this case, payables decisions were not only shifted away from local bakeries, but were also embedded in a series of decision rules that virtually automated the process.

In the refrigerated dough division, on the other hand, an attempt to implement a vendor-managed inventory process meant taking decisions about ordering away from buyers in the retail chains and embedding them in an inventory monitoring system managed by Earthgrains. In both cases, changing the location of decision making was intended to improve the effectiveness of the overall business process.

OUTCOMES

Converting transaction data to knowledge is only effective if it produces business outcomes that improve financial performance, which usually happens as a result of new behaviors, new initiatives, or redesigned processes.

Changing behaviors. Historically, disputed invoices have been a major problem for food manufacturers, since retailers often disagree with the prices they are charged on an invoice. Retailers always pay what they contend was the price agreed to, which is invariably lower than what is on the invoice. Because the cost of resolving disagreements is so high, manufacturers have traditionally lived with the deductions, which cost them millions of dollars each year.

Having easy access to invoice data and a clear transaction history has enabled Earthgrains to improve processes supporting price synchronization before the invoice is printed. The ability to minimize disputed invoices has reduced invoice deductions by more than $4 million annually.

New initiatives. With the ability to analyze customer profitability came a new initiative to change the product mix purchased by those customers identified as unprofitable. About 180 of these low-margin retailers were unwilling to change their purchasing patterns, and after ninety days the sales force in the refrigerated dough division was told to stop servicing them. At the same time, another initiative resulted in the elimination of 20 percent of the division's product line, which analysis had shown to be unprofitable. In the first year, the division's operating profit jumped over 50 percent.

Rethinking important business processes. Earthgrains recognized that transaction data could create opportunities for redesigning fundamental business processes that create entirely new sets of decisions. For example, Earthgrains is using data from grocery retailers' inventory control systems, combined with historical data on stock outs, to set up a vendor-managed inventory process that significantly changes its relationships with retail grocers. Proactive use of transaction data may enable the redesign of core processes or it may simply improve decision making within the existing process.

Finally, SAP data made it practical to redesign the accounts payable process in the bakery products division. The decision to centralize and standardize this process increased the company's working capital by more than $40 million almost immediately and provided resources that could be used to support the division's strategy to acquire additional bakeries.

CONCLUSION

Of course, not every management process supported by the use of ES data provides such significant returns. Many activities will have a much more indirect financial impact on the business. But one common characteristic of all the successful examples of leveraging ES data I have seen is that management demonstrates the political will to act and follow through in applying the new insights and capabilities made possible by better ES data. Business results will follow only in a culture that supports bold, proactive decision makers.

8

USING ENTERPRISE SYSTEMS TO MANAGE THE SUPPLY CHAIN

THE HOTTEST AREA IN ENTERPRISE SYSTEMS TODAY IS THE supply chain—and with good cause. As more and more businesses complete their initial, multiyear implementations of core ESs and reflect on the many millions of dollars it has taken to reach this point, too many are still unclear on how they will leverage all this integrated information into real competitive advantage. The supply chain, with all its transaction and information intensity, offers low-hanging fruit left and right. Cross-enterprise integration really pays off here—in measurable operational efficiencies that have a clear relationship to profitability. Even more significantly, the ES role in supply chain management needn't end at the borders of the enterprise. Even greater benefits become evident when a firm begins to consider how it can extend its ES outside its own walls and use it to achieve tighter integration with vendors, suppliers, manufacturers, distributors, retailers, and other trading partners. Enterprise systems, it's

---

Julia Kirby, a researcher at the Andersen Consulting Institute for Strategic Change, researched this topic and wrote a draft of this chapter.

becoming clear, are just a stone's throw away from being *inter-ESs*—the backbone of the "extended enterprise" that so many strategists have envisioned.

A WORD ABOUT SUPPLY CHAIN MANAGEMENT

What do we mean when we talk about supply chain management? Basically, the term refers to the close linkage of activities involved in buying, making, and moving product. The major goals of supply chain management are to cut costs by taking excess time, redundant effort, and buffer inventory out of the system, and to improve service by giving customers more options, faster delivery, and better visibility into order status. Mostly, this is a challenge of information integration. The idea is to allow everyone involved in the flow of goods to make decisions based on the latest and best information from everyone else both upstream and downstream. The company that manages its supply chain best gets its product from points of origin to points of consumption in the least amount of time at the lowest cost.

Using information systems for supply chain management is not, of course, a new topic. Some of the earliest uses of information technology in business were designed to make operations more efficient by keeping closer track of procurement, manufacturing, and distribution activities within a business. And electronic data interchange (EDI) has existed for a couple of decades to link industrial vendors with their customers. EDI, however, was heavily concentrated among large firms, was restricted to prosaic forms of information like order quantities and bills of lading, and relied on complex relationships with third-party value-added network providers. The connections between firms that it made possible could hardly be called seamless.

Supply chain work isn't even a wholly new topic in ESs. Bolt-on vendors such as Manugistics and i2 were focused on building cross-enterprise supply chain applications at the same time that firms such as SAP and PeopleSoft were primarily focused on financial and human resources systems. What is new, however, is the broadening of interest and investment in supply chain management—by ES vendors and, more importantly, by corporate management. New, more powerful packaged solutions, in many cases running over the Internet, are suddenly putting supply chain excellence within the reach of virtually every company and making it a competitive imperative for businesses of all sizes.

WHY FOCUS ON THE SUPPLY CHAIN?

Managers love to draw the distinction between "doing things right" and "doing the right things." The best job of implementation, in other words, ends up counting for naught if the idea being implemented was misguided to begin with. In the case of ESs, happily, firms are discovering two equally important reasons to go forward with supply chain solutions: first, because they are critical to competitive success, and second, because the tools exist to put them in place competently and cost-effectively. They are, in short, the right things to do and increasingly easy to do right.

COST CUTTING IN INTERNAL OPERATIONS

At the most fundamental level, ESs offer ways to squeeze costs out of internal supply chain operations. They accomplish this mainly by cutting across and linking together the traditional functional silos of the business, in the same way that good business process management does. In fact, it's fair to say that cross-functional process management is not even possible on a large scale without ESs to provide a shared foundation of information. It's easy for top management to declare that Manufacturing should only make what Sales has discovered it can sell, and that Procurement should buy the right quantity of raw materials for what Manufacturing is about to make. But in most firms, these functions are supported by completely separate systems, designed to handle only their own piece of the business and incapable of talking to each other. Manufacturing has no idea what Sales is seeing in the marketplace. Procurement has no visibility into what Marketing plans to promote.

Lack of information integration among supply chain functions, of course, means that handoffs from one part of the business to the next are far from smooth. To avoid lots of dropped balls, managers build ample redundancy and slack into the system—which, in a product business, typically takes the form of inventory. And inventory isn't cheap. To paraphrase Everett Dirksen, a billion units here, a billion units there—pretty soon we're talking about some real money. This is the great motivator for many firms' use of ESs in the supply chain. The theme often sounded is to replace inventory with information.

This is what Dreyer's Grand Ice Cream had in mind, for example, when it undertook to build its supply chain management system. Dreyer's, a $970 million company based in Oakland, California, has all the typical supply chain problems of a food manufacturer, and then some. Its raw materials and finished goods are highly temperature sensitive and perishable— and its product line experiences seasonal sales peaks that would give most planners vertigo. Dreyer's used an ES to link its forecasts to production scheduling and ultimately to procurement. As a result, it dramatically cut inventory levels—a key cost driver. It used to be that Dreyer's entire finished goods inventory turned over twelve times per year. That number is now up to fifteen. Faster turns translate to higher warehouse capacity, and no immediate need to spend capital on a new warehouse as the business grows. It's tempting to say that Dreyer's has its inventory problems, well, licked.

Improving the efficiency of internal operations was also the goal at Eastman Chemical when it linked its SAP R/2 software into a new supply chain planning and forecasting application. The application, made by Logility, pulls sales data from the ES to generate forecasts based on special algorithms and past experience. Those forecasts are then published on the ES's database for the use of managers throughout the organization—including salespeople in the field, who can input revised information via an intranet to reflect what they're learning in customer calls. For Eastman, a business-to-business supplier of plastics, fibers, and chemicals, better supply chain management keeps its resources working in concert to meet customer demand with maximum efficiency.

EFFICIENCY ACROSS THE EXTENDED SUPPLY CHAIN

For most companies, streamlining operations within their own walls presents enough of an immediate challenge. But the firms that are known for supply chain management have understood for a long time that the really big game is external. The inefficiencies in the handoffs between different functions in a firm usually pale in comparison with those between the different firms that make up the broader supply chain. The classic example is that old chestnut case study from the 1980s: the Procter & Gamble/Wal-Mart relationship forged around the sale of disposable diapers. By sharing forecast and sales data, the two firms took a huge amount of inventory out of the total system while at the same time improving in-stock performance—and they shared the financial benefit.

Today, this kind of cooperation across the supply chain is being made easier by the availability of ESs. This is true in part simply because firms are getting their own acts together internally. Once integration has been achieved across the enterprise, it begins to seem possible to attack the larger issues of the extended supply chain. Once you have good information on your own sales, inventory, or production figures, it's much easier to share that with other companies. In keeping with the interests of their customers, major ES vendors are also making it an explicit part of their strategy to support cross-enterprise communications in their package offerings.

Reebok International is an excellent case in point. In its main businesses—footwear, apparel, and sports equipment—the company operates mainly as a marketer, producing and selling goods on a global basis. But with some 150 outlet stores of its own, Reebok is also a retailer in its own right. I described Reebok's decision to implement an ES in chapter 3. Reebok has focused particularly on supply chain capabilities, both internally and externally. To cut inventories across its entire system, it simultaneously implemented two SAP ESs in the marketing and retailing parts of the business, and linked them through electronic commerce (EC) and EDI connections. The combination allows Reebok to integrate everything from new product development to analyzing profits in individual stores. But the connections don't end with Reebok's own retail operations. It's also integrating its manufacturing partners and customers around the globe through EC/EDI links, and ultimately plans to tie its systems directly to theirs. Eventually, Reebok also expects to have direct linkages through its ES with the retailers it doesn't own.

The situation is similar at Boeing, which relies on hundreds of internal and external suppliers for the 5 million to 6 million components needed to build a large twin-aisle airplane. Using Baan ESs in combination with forecasting software from i2 Technologies, Boeing is finally getting a firm grasp on the complexity of getting the right parts to arrive just as they are needed. As at Reebok, the communications connections among internal parties are direct, from database to database—but the connection to external suppliers is almost as seamless through EDI links to the ES. At the same time, Boeing is giving customers access to enterprise information through its PART (Part Analysis and Requirements Tracking) Page, a secure Internet site that its customers can use to order spare parts—or just check on availability and pricing. The Web site is especially popular with the 600 or so airlines that have never adopted EDI for parts ordering from Boeing.

Both the Reebok and the Boeing examples offer a glimmer of the revolution just beginning in cross-enterprise supply chain management—with the main instrument of change being the Internet. In fact, it is safe to say that the Internet's promise of instant, platform-independent communication among systems is the biggest thing spurring today's development boom in supply chain management systems. It offers considerable improvement over EDI in terms of the types of information that can be transmitted, the number of firms that can access information over it, and the widespread availability and ease of use of software (i.e., Web browsers) to access the information.

ENHANCED CUSTOMER SERVICE AND NETWORK RELATIONSHIPS

Usually, the first impetus for supply chain management is the opportunity it offers for cost reduction. Along the way, though, companies generally discover it is also key to growing their business. This is true because excellence in supply chain management can make a profound difference to customer service quality. Some studies have suggested that the typical manufacturer stands to cut the time between a customer's order and the arrival of the shipment by 15 to 40 percent with well-implemented supply chain management software. And total lead time, they find, could be reduced by as much as 75 percent. Better customer service naturally leads to increased sales.

One firm that has proved the studies true is Colgate-Palmolive, which undertook to install ESs largely to achieve supply chain efficiencies. As part of a major turnaround effort, it reworked every link in its global supply chain, and used SAP software to link everything from purchasing to inventory management to manufacturing to delivery. The results? Colgate reports it has cut delivery times to customers by 25 percent. And the results are clear on the bottom line. For the first time in its history, Colgate surpassed Procter & Gamble's U.S. market share in its largest product line, oral care products. Adding icing to the cake, Colgate also put the systems in place in model fashion; it is frequently benchmarked by other companies embarking on ES implementations.[1]

The service advantage goes further still when having a strong ES in place allows a company to offer self-serve capabilities to customers and other supply chain partners. FedEx is famous for creating a package tracking system that allows shippers to see exactly where their package is in the system—en route on schedule, delayed by bad weather, or already signed for by the recipient. Companies of all kinds are following suit by creating extranets—secure Internet sites accessible to selected partners—that provide a view into their operations. Heineken, for instance, launched a system that gives its distributors access, via the Internet, to information housed in its ES about product (i.e., beer) availability and sales patterns. Again, the fact of the ES's already being in place for internal purposes was key. Once the brewer's own house was in order, it was not such a huge step to open the doors to others.

The Earthgrains Company is still another company that saw customer service improvement as a key goal of its ES. I described Earthgrains in the previous chapter as an exemplar of using ES data to manage the business better, but it began its ES work focusing on supply chain improvements. In the past, this Missouri-based wholesale baker too often made deliveries to large grocery chain customers that weren't on time or in accurate quantities, or were invoiced incorrectly. Earthgrains decided to clean up its act with enterprise software that would link together its accounting, reporting, order management, and distribution. In fact, Earthgrains' VP of business systems told *Information Week* magazine that his company pinned its hopes for a turnaround on its ES. The gamble is paying off: On-time delivery reached 99 percent by 1997, and operating margins rose from 2.4 percent to 3.9 percent.[2]

GOOD PICKINGS IN PACKAGED SOFTWARE

I've been reviewing all kinds of good reasons that supply chain management is the right thing to focus on in the quest to derive business value from ESs. It is critical to competitiveness and profitability, and is an area where the integration achieved by ESs has a major impact. It turns out there are even more good reasons. As well as being the right thing to do, supply chain management is getting easier to do right, thanks to the fact that software vendors have made it a development priority.

For the most part, this development has been spearheaded not by the major ES vendors—the SAPs, PeopleSofts, and Oracles of the world—but by smaller, more focused software solution providers. While the major ES vendors worked on providing the backbone systems to support supply chain management—the operational transaction processing systems—it was left to others, usually vendors with deep familiarity and expertise in specific industries, to create the tools that would leverage all that good data into strategic analyses and tactical decisions. Their tools were the ones that helped managers do good supply planning, demand planning, plant scheduling, transportation and warehouse management, and so on, drawing on information pulled from an ES's manufacturing applications and other sources. PeopleSoft found the third-party offerings so compelling that it bought one—a company called Red Pepper—to incorporate the functionality into its own ES.

As a result, there are dozens of good packaged applications on the market to choose from, virtually all of which interface— to greater or lesser degrees of difficulty—with the major ES vendors' applications. Some of these are highly specialized point solutions, which make surgical strikes on bottlenecks or leverage points in the supply chain. Others are suites of applications in themselves. Manugistics, Inc., for example, offers a whole slew of software, including tools for vendor-managed inventory; point-of-sale-driven demand; and collaborative planning, forecasting, and replenishment. Strung together, its products enable companies to analyze and manage the flow of products from demand, distribution, and manufacturing through to purchasing, transportation, and logistics, not only across an enterprise but throughout the supply chain.

Speaking generally, the packaged software currently available for supply chain management falls into four basic categories:[3]

► Supply planning tools, which help to align all the resources and activities required to get goods to market cost-effectively

► Demand planning tools, which help companies anticipate market demand for their products with more precision, thanks to sophisticated modeling and statistical analysis

► Plant scheduling tools, which translate overall supply requirements into day-to-day production plans

► Logistics systems for supporting warehouse management, transportation, and order management

Given the existence of best-of-breed packaged solutions in so many of these areas, the favored approach for most firms has been to go with a major vendor like SAP or PeopleSoft for core ESs and then bolt on supply chain software developed by multiple other vendors. Not to discount the work involved in creating and maintaining interfaces, but in a sense operations managers are confronted with an embarrassment of riches. What was once the exclusive capability of only the best in an industry is now available off the shelf. In supply chain management, as in so many areas touched by ESs, it makes less and less sense to put effort into homegrown systems. With vendors taking over the hard work in system development, user companies can shift their efforts to redesigning supply chain processes to work well with the software, training employees and managers on advanced supply chain techniques, and interfacing supply chain applications to their ES packages.

COMING SOON: THE ONE-STOP SOLUTION

If the prospect of cobbling together software solutions, no matter how good they are, holds little appeal for you, then the last bit of good news compelling you to think about supply chain management is that the major ES vendors are quickly building it into their own integrated offerings. Here, the prospect—and in many cases already, the reality—is that companies will be able to implement a single solution suite, in which advanced supply chain functions (often called *supply chain planning and optimization*) will be seamlessly integrated with manufacturing, financial, and other functions such as customer service.

What's paved the way for the major vendors is the prior existence of supply chain integration software. Other vendors have shown what's possible in areas like manufacturing scheduling and logistics—and demonstrated the potential payback on such improvements. At the same time, those more focused vendors have hardly saturated the market. Given high prices and hard implementations (not simply in technical terms but more importantly in business process and organizational change), the typical supply chain package has made it into only a tiny fraction of the corporations who could benefit from it. Consequently, there is huge opportunity for a big player to grab big market share. And finally, making the business even more irresistible, there is the Internet. As Greg Girard, a supply chain analyst at AMR Research, told CNET: "For the ERP players, e-commerce gives them an avenue to transition from being the enterprise backbone to the supply chain backbone. And that opens up all kinds of very sweet opportunities for them to extend their reach and increase their seat counts."[4]

All these conditions are hardly lost on the market for supply chain solutions—the business and IT executives of corporations. In fact, it's fair to speculate that user demand would compel the major vendors to address the supply chain even if they didn't consider it a good business to be in. It's a version of that old truism about how hard it is to keep folks down on the farm once they've seen Par-ee. Once operations management has a taste of integration, they want everything in the business to be that good. And despite the efforts of major ES vendors and best-of-breed software providers to build good interfaces between their products, integration is still complicated and rarely achieves truly comprehensive information sharing and communications. Existing and prospective customers are putting the heat on the big vendors to supplement their internal functional orientation with process-oriented intra- and intercompany supply chain solutions.

With the skids already greased and a hungry market awaiting, the major ES players are rushing headlong into supply chain solutions—most through acquisitions as well as new development. At the time of this writing, vendors such as J.D. Edwards, Oracle, Baan, PeopleSoft, and SAP are all working furiously on their shortcomings vis-à-vis the niche vendors, which tend to be in areas like decision support, demand and deployment planning, capacity and resource planning, warehouse management, network optimization, and electronic commerce. (According to SAP co-chairman Hasso Plattner, SAP's supply chain offering is the "most ambitious development project since R/3.") And everyone is planning future versions that will incorporate the biggest news in supply chain management—the collaborative planning, forecasting, and replenishment (CPFR) model recently developed and piloted successfully by a consortium of consumer goods manufacturers and retailers. This term refers to software and business processes in which supply chain partners exchange not only orders and shipment notices, but also sales plans and production forecasts with each other, so that they can synchronize their respective processes more fully.

But even in their current suites, all these vendors make a compelling offer: a complete connection of the front office to the back office, with the middle office thrown in along the way. Everything makes it into the pool, from product customization, order fulfillment, inventory, and delivery information to sales, client service, and marketing.

The entry of major vendors raises all kinds of issues for managers who are already using third-party software for supply chain management. It also complicates decision making for new buyers who need more sophistication than the big players' products currently offer. But it's great news for firms who would otherwise have found supply chain software too expensive and onerous to implement. For a company like Jo-Ann Stores, for example—an Ohio-based retailer with 1,100 fabric and craft stores—integration makes everything possible. Its management opted for an integrated suite of R/3 applications from SAP, including SAP's own version of merchandise planning software.[5] Because it could strictly limit the number of bolt-ons required to meet its major business needs, it could justify a systems overhaul that might otherwise be overwhelming in a small-margin business.

The bottom line is that fully integrated supply chain modules in ESs are making supply chain management not only the right thing to do, but a thing that's increasingly easy to do right. It still won't be like falling off a log, but once supply chain solutions become this straightforward, it won't even be a matter of competitive advantage to focus on them. It will be a competitive necessity.

Getting Started in Supply Chain Management

One thing should be stated clearly at this point, on the off-chance that it isn't clear already: If you're in a product business and costs and customer service are important competitive factors in your market (or could be), then you should be accelerating development of supply chain capabilities in your ESs. And here's another piece of advice: Even as you're working on those capabilities within your walls and designing all the internal wiring, you should be anticipating the next step—the bigger challenge of connecting up with external supply chain partners. In this section, we'll explore some key issues to consider and some alternative approaches to getting started.

Bring Supply Chain Solutions into the Mix as Early as Possible

Enterprise systems, clearly, are vast in scope and capability. Given unlimited time and money, a company can at this point lay a foundation of integrated information across its entire business and plumb that source with any number of decision-making tools. Unfortunately, though, no one has unlimited time and money, so the reality is that enterprise solutions are applied selectively, and the last parts tackled will come on line much later than the first. This creates one of the biggest problem areas concerning ESs: the difficulty of deciding which parts of the business to support with them most thoroughly, and which parts to attack first.

It makes sense as a first step toward sorting out priorities to think about balancing technical capabilities in an enterprise solution with strategic capabilities—a key implementation decision that I described in chapter 1. Technical capabilities are all those back-office functions that are essentially the foundation that needs to be laid for cross-enterprise integration. In themselves, however, technical capabilities provide very little in the way of real business value. They are infrastructural—critical, yes, but not the stuff of which competitive advantage is made. Supply chain solutions are another matter; they count as strategic, competitively oriented capabilities. But getting maximum benefit from them relies on their being able to draw on a core of integrated information systems. It's a Catch-22 in some sense: You won't get value from technical systems without strategic applications, and you won't get enough payback on competitive applications without technical systems.

The answer, of course, is to find the right balance—the best combination and the right iterative approach to bringing foundational systems and supply chain management tools on line in tandem. Too many firms have focused exclusively on the technical systems at the outset of their ES initiatives, intending to build on the competitive tools down the road. As costs and time pressures mount, they find they haven't the resources left for applications that will turn all that data into information and, more important, into business results. If anything, the thinking should be reversed. Technical capabilities should be prioritized with an eye to the supply chain and other competitive tools they will support.

Deciding which strategic capabilities to support is no simple task in itself. In the next few sections, I'll explore some ways of cracking that nut. But the larger point here is that supply chain management tools are among the clearest opportunities to convert ESs to competitive advantage. Any product-oriented business looking to maximize the return on an investment in an ES should be making them part of the overall solution and working to get the benefit of them as soon as possible. It would have been insane to have laid out a countrywide interstate highway system before the first automobiles were in use, and no one would string up phone lines if households didn't have phones. Enterprise system initiatives should avoid this same kind of folly.

CHOOSING BETWEEN BEST-OF-BREED APPLICATIONS AND PERFECT INTEGRATION

For companies choosing to make supply chain management a focus of their ESs, one decision looms large: whether to lean toward the best-of-breed solutions or the more thorough integration and relative ease of installation offered by the major vendors.

For the moment at least, doing great things in supply chain management seems to require a multivendor approach—some combination of best-of-breed supply chain applications and a core set of enterprise applications to bolt them onto. And so far, this kind of solution is supported by the major vendors. As Peter Zencke of SAP has said, "We see supply chain management as a colorful tapestry and realize that our customers will be using many different threads to make it."[6]

Still, the decision to go with best-of-breeds is difficult because the ground is shifting so rapidly underfoot. With major vendors entering the fray in full force, a shakeout among the smaller vendors is certain—as are continuing acquisitions. Stock prices of bolt-on supply chain vendors are already suffering. Will smaller companies be able to add capabilities at the rate of much larger ES vendors with huge R&D budgets? Will a particular vendor's product continue to feature up-to-date interfaces with SAP software, for instance, when its creator is now owned outright by Baan?

The upshot is that if you have been using one of the major ES vendors' application suites to run back-office functions like finance and material management and using a variety of supply chain software products from niche vendors, you have a decision to make: stick with the patchwork of applications or go for the fully integrated systems? Motts North America, a $650 million food manufacturer, chose the latter approach when it became one of the first companies to deploy SAP's Advanced Planner and Optimizer (APO) software (SAP's entry into the supply chain planning market). It decided to forego some of the best-of-breed functionality in favor of better integration with R/3 and easier installation. Colgate had the same instincts, actually removing Manugistics software it already had in place and installing SAP's package to perform equivalent tasks. But Australian food manufacturer Goodman Fielder took the opposite tack, choosing to implement Manugistics's supply chain package even though it was in the midst of an SAP R/3 implementation. The ES vendor's version of a supply chain optimization system wasn't yet available.

Clearly, the highest-functioning system at the moment is one made up of a variety of tools and software vendors; no one vendor yet offers a fully integrated supply chain management solution, and performance among comparable products is highly uneven. Major vendors still lack the most dynamic, more strategic planning and forecasting tools and, more significantly, they lack the capability to integrate across enterprises. But even with strong willingness today by all parties to create alliances and integration, combinations of tools present difficulties, particularly in interface design.

One thing is clear: A software solution developed by an ES vendor is more likely to take full advantage of the ES's data. Third-party packages may draw on only 70 or 80 percent of your ES data. And as mainstream ES vendors further develop their own supply chain offerings, they probably won't make it any easier for third-party firms to get at core ES data. Also, with an integrated package, there is none of the difficulty typically involved in third-party interfaces. It will be easier to maintain version control and to be sure the two packages will continue to exchange information without glitches. You won't have to worry about updating your interfaces every time you update either your ES package or your bolt-on supply chain tool. As in all things technological, it's tempting to wait for the next versions, hoping that major vendors' products will match the performance of the best-of-breeds. If only your competitors weren't making it a necessity to act now!

Three different approaches are possible in planning a course of attack on supply chain management with packaged software. I'll describe each choice and mention some strengths and weaknesses of each.

CHERRY PICKING THE BEST AVAILABLE SOLUTIONS

It may make sense simply to be opportunistic, capitalizing on the availability of software that functions extremely well in specific areas. With this strategy, you'll have to undertake a detailed analysis of features and functions in various software offerings, decide which ones you need today and which you can wait on, and follow vendor progress carefully. This, in other words, is the land of low-hanging fruit. The choices are easy, and the payback is safe. The only problem is that, no matter how easy it is to pick, low-hanging fruit does divert resources somewhat from higher-stakes efforts. And the payback, while safe enough, may be nowhere near as high as a firm would realize by making change in areas that truly drive its competitive success.

Despite its challenges, this approach has more to recommend it than might seem obvious. In an environment of uncertainty, it at least offers the comfort of the fastest access to world-class performance. It would be hard, for instance, to top a Manugistics tool for transportation planning, or an i2 Technologies product if what you need is advanced planning that accounts for materials and capacity constraints. These may not be the absolute most pressing problems you have to deal with, or the improvements that will mean the most to your profitability—but surely they will provide some benefit, and whatever benefits they do produce will start flowing soon.

GOING WITH THE FLOW

Alternatively, it may be a wise course to go along with the package selection(s) being made by important supply chain partners, with the idea that standardization will make it an easier proposition to extend the benefit of integrated information across firms. You'll want to have extended discussions with these partners to learn what their strategies are, and whether they plan to stick with their current choices.

For example, if a retailer's major suppliers are on a particular ES, and a retail version of that system is available, the retailer might do best to consider getting that software. Constant communication is everything in the continuous replenishment world of consumer goods, and if retailers and suppliers are both on common systems, communications will be that much easier.

Going with the industry flow will probably be increasingly common as the major ES vendors target middle-sized and smaller companies with their marketing efforts. For firms accustomed to following the technology lead of the 800-pound gorillas in their industry, the argument for going with an emerging industry standard will not be hard to make. If you're primarily a General Motors supplier, it will matter to you with what ES vendor GM has cast its lot.

The point here is not to imply that interenterprise computing will not be possible among diverse ESs. Quite the contrary: There are already impressive "middleware" solutions that facilitate exactly such communication, usually employing the Internet. What is at issue here is only the degree to which that information transfer is seamless and comprehensive.[7] Today it doesn't make a lot of difference if you're on SAP and your supplier is on Oracle, but as linkages between firms become more sophisticated, it may be easier to connect firms that have the same vendor's software.

TARGET SHOOTING

The third approach may be the bravest—and hardest—course to pursue. That would be to attack the parts of the supply chain that offer the greatest payback for your own profitability, regardless of whether the packaged solutions that already exist are terrific at what they do or in common use.

If, for instance, demand forecasting is the area above all others that stands to make an impact on your profitability, then that should be the first done and most well-executed component of the solution. If your warehouses are at capacity, perhaps the highest-impact area is production scheduling, which, done well, would lead to faster inventory turns and avoid the need for capital to be spent on new facilities. All the better, of course, if your critical needs map well to the latest and greatest software tools on the market. Even if they do not, however, this approach would say skip the low-hanging fruit and go for the benefit bonanza. If electronic commerce capabilities are what you need, and no best-of-breed solution has yet emerged that fits the bill, don't accept the delay and move ahead in other areas. Put all your energy into getting that requirement served.

Some brave souls would argue that if the packaged solutions you need are in line for development by major vendors, but still on the drawing board, then you are in a good position: As a beta site, you can influence their direction of development. This was the thinking of the fifteen pilot customers who signed up to test and refine SAP's APO software. For all the pain of operating on the bleeding edge of technology, they were able to have real influence on a package that was important to their future operations. SAP had devoted some 180 full-time developers to the creation of the software, and was listening intently to what these pilot customers thought. None of them, presumably, would have considered it more worthwhile to have opted for in-house development on such a scale.

Finally, even if vendors have no plans to create the packages on your wish list, you can start lobbying them, creating development consortia, and generally agitating for the applications important to you. Take a lesson from Reebok and VF, which formed the apparel consortium I described in chapter 3. Managers at both companies loved the idea of wholly integrated ESs, but found existing packages woefully inadequate to deal with the peculiarities of apparel and footwear supply chains. Reebok's chief technology officer, Peter Burrows, and VF's vice president of reengineering, Leroy Allen, created a consortium with SAP that jointly paid for and managed the development of an R/3 add-on appropriate for their companies—which SAP was then free to market to others in the industry. Burrows says it wasn't easy to get SAP to go along, because its management "looked at our industry and thought it was a mess." But in the end, his persistence paid off—the new systems are now up and running basically as Reebok and VF envisioned them.[8]

THE FUTURE OF ENTERPRISE SYSTEM SUPPLY CHAIN SOLUTIONS

Amidst all the uncertainty of a rapidly shifting landscape, one thing seems clear about the future of supply chain solutions in ESs: They will continue to enjoy explosive development and sales growth. Industry analysts at AMR, which focuses on ES markets, recently projected that total revenues from supply chain software would rise from an estimated $2.9 billion in 1998 to $13.6 billion in 2002. While I'm sure they're wrong on the absolute number prediction, they're no doubt correct that that category will increase markedly. It also seems likely we will see a few major trends in the functionality that vendors add to the systems, in the use of the Internet to achieve extended enterprise integration, and in a growing range of outsourcing options.

NEW FUNCTIONALITY

For those who appreciate the software industry as a spectator sport, the jockeying in the supply chain field should make for good viewing in the next few years. We will certainly see the major ES vendors doing double-time to match the sophistication levels of the niche software vendors. This will mean significant development effort to release higher-functioning versions of tools already in their toolkits, industry-specific variations on those tools, and new tools they haven't yet developed their own versions of. Their ultimate goal is to keep customers from having to look elsewhere for any basic functionality. At the same time, of course, more focused supply chain software vendors will be working hard to maintain the performance lead they now enjoy through continued innovation. For customers, all this will make for confusing purchase decisions—but enjoy it. You're the ultimate beneficiary.

Much of what is on the immediate horizon falls into the category of decision-support tools to help senior executives manage and increase profits. These will include sophisticated applications for activity-based costing, to give management an accurate understanding of exactly what cost is being incurred relative to the value added by specific supply chain activities. Other tools will include "supply chain dashboards" that provide up-to-the-minute readings on operational performance, fueled by data in ESs. Some of these will be designed as balanced scorecard applications, presenting a limited set of key process and outcome metrics based on the business model of a particular company.

Lots of business-to-business solutions are on the drawing board, starting with e-commerce tools for procurement, vendor-managed inventory, and collaborative demand management. At the time of this writing, the race is on to capitalize on the new communications standard developed in the consumer goods industry for collaborative forecasting, planning, and replenishment between manufacturers like Nabisco and sophisticated grocery retailers like Wegman's.[9] Enterprise system vendors will develop products to allow their users to use the Internet and the e-commerce model for all types of communications. Those communications could include collaborative demand management or vendor supply management and forecasting.

Most important, all the vendors will be looking for breakthroughs in what promises to be the next major phase of supply chain initiatives: actual system interoperability among suppliers, customers, and other business partners to create highly leveraged value chains. In this environment, your system will talk directly to mine without manual intervention. All the enterprise application packages are being redefined to support Internet-based customer-to-supplier value chains for electronic commerce. Whether third-party vendors are able to perfect middleware to do the job, or the major vendors make such add-ons unnecessary, the linkages will soon be built for a customer order to communicate seamlessly across the multiple members of that value chain. Expect to see real-time, extended enterprise synchronization become a reality. Which brings us to the next major component in the future of ESs: the Internet.

THE IMPACT OF THE INTERNET

The Internet figures hugely in the future of firms using ESs, as it does in the future of all business. Because it provides global standards and ready accessibility, it's an ideal networking mechanism for orders, status checks, and manufacturing design specifications—just to cite a few types of relevant information—to be passed between customers, distributors, and suppliers. It promises to remove most of the redundant activity now carried out by firms in order placing and order taking, status checking and inventory tracking, invoicing and payment.

Consider that, at this point, many businesses send orders to their suppliers via e-mail in spreadsheet form. At the receiving end, clerks retype those orders into their own manufacturing systems. The software now exists for customers to pipe their orders directly into the supplier's manufacturing system via electronic data interchange. Before long, that communication will happen via the Web. It's tempting to imagine the time coming when a business-to-business supplier will tell its customers: "Have your ES call my ES—and will the last person in Customer Service turn out the lights when you leave?" If anyone had been able to ask EDI 20 years ago what it wanted to be when it grew up, the Internet would have been the answer.

Why is the promise of the Internet so different from EDI? One word—inclusiveness—probably sums it up. First, because EDI required complex systems of local area, wide area, and external value-added networks, not many companies could afford to develop it and use it extensively. Only in situations in which a business had high volumes of structured transactions with a fairly limited number of partners did the economics really make sense. And unfortunately, no uniform standard across industries was ever developed (standards you may have heard of, such as ANSI X12 and EDIFACT, were widely employed in some industries, but others had their own standards and versions of standards), so the knowledge of how to use it didn't transfer easily from firm to firm. Innovation often disseminates with the movement of trained people, but here, technology barriers kept much of that knowledge from being generalized. Some analysts estimate that, at its high point, EDI was being used by less than 1 percent of global companies who could benefit from it. But e-commerce over the Internet, as a relatively cheap and effective alternative, is changing that. Now, any supplier who can afford a Web page can compete for business from such firms as General Electric or Texas Instruments.[10]

There's another side to the inclusiveness of the Internet as compared with EDI. It also allows communications to include much more than strict transaction data. As well as highly structured information, the Web also facilitates the exchange of richer forms of information and knowledge—allowing companies to connect in deeper ways than a mere transaction handshake. Here's an example: Adaptec, Inc. is a California hardware and software company that relies on partners in Asia to manufacture what it designs and markets. Using a piece of middleware to translate, the company transmits information directly from its ESs into its partners' ESs. The solution goes a big step beyond EDI in automating the communications among the firms; it is not, for instance, limited to order placing, but allows complex information to be sent as well, such as CAD drawings to guide assembly. As ESs achieve greater penetration into product development and front-office processes involving customers, we'll see greater use of ES/Internet combinations to ship product design and sales and marketing information back and forth.

One aid to full exchange of information across programs will be new standards for information exchange. Some such standards will emerge within industries and will involve data definitions for commonly employed terms and components. A new generation of Internet markup languages (such as XML, succeeding the popular Web language HTML) will make it possible for one company's term and product number for a 3-D titanium widget to be translated in real time into what another company calls it. Both ES vendors and many user companies are investing in this technology.

As a result of all this new functionality, the Internet will go well beyond even the fondest dreams of EDI to enable the creation of extended enterprises, and even truly virtual companies. Along the way, it will bring a whole new perspective to ESs, which are now viewed as data repositories and analytical tools to be used by individual companies to optimize their performance. Once the Web is integrated into an ES, the whole focus shifts toward communication and work flow among companies in a supply chain.

Of course, the prospect of interenterprise sharing of information raises a whole host of technical and business issues. On the technical side, there is the nontrivial challenge of developing and enabling interfaces from the ESs to the Web. And there is the risk that response time to internal users will suffer from outside users' access bogging down the system. On the business side, managers wonder how they can possibly expose enterprise data to business partners without placing their business and its proprietary information at risk.

Issues like these will continue to arise in particular circumstances, but the overall trend will be toward supply chain management writ large. Companies will still compete with companies, but on a higher (and higher stakes) level: Supply chains will compete with supply chains. And companies that aren't connected with partners, suppliers, customers, and service providers through Web-based services, and only use their ESs for internal management, will find themselves slipping behind.

But if the Internet is important to ESs, ESs are important to the Internet. If companies don't have smoothly functioning and integrated business processes and accurate, real-time data about internal operations, they won't be successful players in electronic commerce. Scratch a highly effective e-commerce company like Cisco Systems, and you'll almost always find an ES underneath.

THE RISE OF NEW MARKET STRUCTURES AND NETWORKS

One final development that may affect the relationships between supply chains and ESs is the rise of new network-based market structures and interorganizational alliances. These are not entirely new phenomena—companies in the past have often formed alliances with members of their supply chains—but they have been given new impetus and shapes by global overcapacity and mega-mergers on the business side, and the growth of the Internet and electronic commerce on the technology side. Enterprise systems and their focus on supply chains will only accelerate this trend, as well as themselves being accelerated by it.

The new network-based structures may take several different forms. In some industries, such as automobiles, one or two dominant firms may act as hubs of a network of smaller suppliers. In other industries, such as industrial components, new online marketplaces are emerging that make it easy for any buyer to reach a much broader range of suppliers, either directly or through an intermediary. All that is clear is that companies will increasingly link their systems and processes electronically with other firms, individually and in groups.

Companies that align into networks now do so on the basis of various criteria, which rarely include information systems. But as ESs and e-commerce become more central and developed within organizations, the ability to share information easily outside the organization may become more critical in deciding with whom to align. Having similar approaches to ES strategy and technology will undoubtedly also be a factor in creating and maintaining relationships.

Enterprise systems, as I've discussed before, have a tendency to "commodify" certain aspects of organizations because many firms in industries adopt the same processes, information, and other organizational arrangements. Because of these ES-driven similarities, it may become easier for organizations to align in the future with companies in their own businesses or in closely related parts of the supply chain. Logistical and supply processes, for example, may become part of a shared-services activity across firms, or may be turned over to third-party organizations that excel at supply chain processes and information management. It's already the case, for example, that several Canadian oil companies have collaborated to build a commonly owned refinery, with shared financial management processes and a shared ES across the consortium. It's not hard to imagine the extension of such arrangements to purchasing, replenishment, delivery, and other supply chain processes.

New ES-enabled demand and supply structures may also be accelerated by a shift toward *netsourcing,* or external hosting of ESs over networks by so-called application service providers. I'll describe this trend more in the next chapter, but its implications for supply chain management are worth mentioning here. While most outsourcing arrangements today are focused on the core back-office applications of ESs, it won't be long till they expand to include supply chain applications—and this may be where the value of outsourcing proves greatest. With the use of an outside party to host applications, one more barrier to extended enterprise cooperation will drop.

An external service, after all, provided over the Web, can equally serve many different users of a system, not just its "internal" customers. Expect to see more companies opting for outsourcing arrangements as time goes on—and more of them using these flexible and scalable arrangements to strengthen their supply chain partnerships.

It's Payback Time

Enterprise systems are already bringing about a revolution in the way supply chain managers think about their work. Supply chain issues will similarly revolutionize what software vendors—and their corporate customers—see as the real work of ESs. Increasingly, it's becoming clear that the greatest impact of, and payback from, ESs is in supply chain management. A quick analogy may help to drive the point home.

In September 1998, surgeons in Lyon, France, did an incredible and unprecedented thing: They were able to give patient Clint Hallam a transplanted hand to replace the one he'd lost to an accident years before. The procedure was unbelievably complex; it involved grafting not just skin, but also muscle, nerve, and bone. And it produced an amazing outcome. Now, when Mr. Hallam thinks to wiggle his fingers, his fingers wiggle. When his hand touches a hot surface, he senses it and pulls back. It's a simple and obvious wish to have such seamless integration between a core being and a newly added part that they cooperate flawlessly—unconsciously, even. But getting there has taken decades of learning and technological evolution.

Think about that surgery: about that difficulty, and about that wonderful outcome. Now think about the ESs you're installing in your business. Over the next five years, the systems you're installing today will allow you to integrate seamlessly with entities outside your firm—your customers, your suppliers, your outsourcers, your alliance partners. When you get an order, your supplier won't need to be told to replenish your raw materials. When your distributor detects a new pattern in sales, your marketers will instantly perceive it, too. The technology involved will be daunting—and it won't even be the hardest part, compared with the process and behavior change required. But the new capabilities you'll have at your fingertips—all the power and reach of an extended enterprise—will be nothing short of amazing.

9

THE FUTURE OF ES-ENABLED ORGANIZATIONS

ENTERPRISE SYSTEMS AS THEY EXIST TODAY REPRESENT JUST A snapshot of one segment of the overall spectrum of information technology at one moment in time. Changes in that field are rapid and constant and include other technology domains such as personal computing and the Internet. Given the speed and unpredictability of technological innovation, it may seem arrogant to predict the future of ESs. Some changes to ESs will have occurred even by the time this book is published. However, the speed and uncertainty of the process make having some idea of the likely direction of development all the more important to those businesses already using ESs, and to those that will use them in the future. Further, as science fiction author William Gibson noted, "The future is already here—it's just unevenly distributed." Some firms are already experimenting with technologies and approaches that will constitute the future for later adopters.

I was greatly aided in this chapter by Jeff Brooks, then a student at Boston University, who researched the topic and wrote a draft of the chapter.

Enterprise systems don't exist in a vacuum: They are products that are developed, sold, and implemented with the hope and belief that they provide value to the companies that use them. Business value is thus what drives the development of ESs, and by looking at the potential for creating value, one can map out areas of probable development for the technology. Most companies that have implemented an ES have done so with a focus on tactical value, and the same focus is likely to prevail into the near future. However, as I've noted, many companies are poised to begin to achieve strategic value from their ESs, and their business environments increasingly demand this kind of change. As this wider context changes, the ways in which value is translated to business processes will likely shift, and these shifts will have their own impacts on ESs.

In this chapter I'll attempt to provide a rough guide to the future. I'll discuss some possible directions for ESs within the context of possible large-scale changes to the business environment within the next several years. Enterprise systems as they currently exist will only partially support companies' attempts to respond to these coming changes; the gaps between what capabilities will be valuable in the future and what capabilities are currently available can be viewed as developmental imperatives for ESs. I'll present a capability development framework suggesting that the ES industry will address these capability gaps in a particular order. Which kinds of companies will deliver these capabilities to the market, and in what vehicles, I can't predict. That will likely be decided by the dictates of market position, customer response, and ROI. Finally, I'll also discuss some new business capabilities that may emerge in the near future. With a sense of how ESs are likely to develop in the future, one can consider the impact they will have on the concerns of managers and companies.

COMING CHANGES TO THE BUSINESS ENVIRONMENT

I have no lock on the future of business (or I would be writing novels and occasionally monitoring my vast stock portfolio).

However, several broad trends carry the weight of general consensus. These trends include globalization, rapid sense-and-respond business models, overcapacity and corporate realignment, the growth of virtual organizations, and accelerating product innovation. Enterprise systems serve as platforms from which companies can pursue these sources of future business value, but to truly enable the required business capabilities, ESs will have to acquire new functionality themselves. The gaps between current and desired ES functionalities represent opportunities for the ES industry to expand and to capture some of the value associated with each trend.

RAPID SENSE-AND-RESPOND BUSINESS MODELS

Sense-and-respond businesses provide value by learning what an individual customer wants at a particular time and responding by quickly providing a tailored product or service. The phenomenon has been widely predicted, and is also referred to as *lean production, mass customization, customer-centric,* and so forth.[1] Companies that wish to provide this type of rapid response must maintain a tight link between customer contact and production or service processes in real time. A truly robust sense-and-respond capability also requires process integration throughout the supply chain. Additional capabilities that benefit sense-and-respond businesses are production management and product configuration.

The integrated applications and databases of ESs provide the basis for this level of process integration within individual firms, and supply chain integration is a major area of development for ESs at this time. Production management software has been around for some time, but it is becoming more sophisticated. Mohawk Industries, for example, uses a production model based on chaos theory to schedule production time for special orders even before they are received, which allows a faster response to such orders.[2] Product configuration software, which allows customers to select product options and receive a customized product, is available from bolt-on vendors such as

Trilogy. Enterprise system vendors are also recognizing the value of this kind of flexibility and are creating solutions for industries in which product options are central to the business. SAP, for example, has its own configuration module.

The expanding capabilities of ESs are increasing the speed and flexibility with which companies can respond to their customers, making sense-and-respond processes possible, at least in pilot form. The classic example of this process in the real world is Levi's custom manufacturing of jeans. The company obtains customers' physical measurements via scanning booths placed in retail stores, sends customers' orders, including style, color, and personal measurements, directly to the factory, and delivers the custom-made jeans within several weeks. An example that points to how this process might be extended even further is one clothing manufacturer, cited by Bradley and Nolan, that uses fashion experts with digital cameras to roam the world in search of promising styles.[3] The company receives pictures from the experts over the Internet, uses computer-aided design and computer-aided manufacturing (CAD-CAM) programs to design the garment, and then creates a prototype with fabric prints made with laser printers. Levi's system adapts the cut of a style to an individual customer's measurements. How long before companies allow the customer to create the style itself?

GLOBALIZATION

Perhaps the most obvious and compelling business trend today is globalization—of corporations, markets, and competition. Multinational corporations have existed for a long time, and globalization already has increased as companies seek growth and as regulatory barriers have fallen over the past several years, so ES vendors have had good reasons to address the capabilities required by global companies. Enterprise systems already support obvious, relatively straightforward capabilities, such as allowing transactions and reporting in multiple currency denominations, and reporting on operations by country. However, other capabilities, such as adapting to local regulatory structures or cultural expectations, are more complex and less easily programmed. Indeed, the integrated databases and complex structure of ESs may make it more difficult for companies to adapt their processes to local conditions. This cuts both ways: Standardizing processes tends to make them more efficient overall, but the fit to local requirements and the ability to locally customize products and services may suffer.

In addition to adapting to multiple local conditions, companies that operate globally must manage across the local conditions within countries. An example of how ESs support managing across local conditions is provided by global production management software—currently from third-party vendors, and eventually from ES vendors. This software integrates global data on site capacity, production and transportation costs, tariffs, and demand in order to schedule production across multiple sites, maximizing the cost efficiency of overall operations.

Finally, as markets become more global, companies within those markets tend to consolidate in order to better deal with overcapacity in markets. The increased rate of mergers and acquisitions leads to a need to combine previously separate ESs. Similarities in information and process environments may also lead to business combinations. Integrating information systems from separate companies is similar to integrating systems from separate business units, and so the experience is likely to be similar, as well. If at least one company has an ES in place, the overall choice and configuration of the final system may be a fait accompli, but issues will still remain regarding determining the extent of local changes and merging data definitions and processes (along with managing the usual cultural changes). Additionally, personnel's investment in the old ES may be higher than it is with legacy systems, both because personnel may see the old ES as more valuable and because they likely put in an enormous effort to install the old ES. On the other hand, if the consolidating companies use the same ES package with similar configurations, then merging their information systems could be relatively easy, but detailed analysis and configuration will still be required.

HORIZONTAL CORPORATE REALIGNMENT

While the globalization of markets appears to press for consolidation of industries, the complexity of managing very large, global firms and decreased communications costs across organizations will push corporations to realign themselves horizontally.[4] In other words, companies will split off certain business functions into new firms. The functions that are split off may be noncore functions, or they may be those that are deemed incompatible with each other. Outsourcing represents this kind of corporate realignment in its nascent stages: Call centers provide customer services for many companies from a single site, Federal Express provided inventory management services to companies such as Laura Ashley, and professional employment organizations provide human resources services at a level that smaller companies often are unable to afford on their own.

Given the combined goals of a focused business and global scale, firms must not only spin off certain functions, but the spun-off businesses must combine to achieve critical mass. To accomplish this serial unbundling and rebundling, corporations will have to separate and merge data and processes multiple times. Enterprise systems will undoubtedly make this process easier, but even with them it won't be a walk in the park. Integration across supply chains is becoming better established, but cross-firm integration of other processes lags somewhat. Also, while ESs can in some ways facilitate merging data and processes, as discussed earlier, there are no clear models of how to disaggregate or pull apart data and processes when organizations break themselves up. System integration is a transition cost for every ES installation, and therefore ES vendors have worked to provide integration tools, such as preconfigured packages for particular industries. System disaggregation or disintegration, on the other hand, is only an issue when companies divest, and so until the unbundling begins to occur on a large scale, ES vendors are unlikely to devote much attention to the disaggregation issue.

VIRTUAL ORGANIZATIONS

Virtual organizations could be described as the fluid, flexible combination of components of one or more businesses to deliver value to a market. They are characterized by connections between companies that handle specific portions of a process—connections that change as business opportunities arise, are taken advantage of, then abandoned as their value diminishes. As with the more permanent corporate realignment I've just discussed, integrating (and disaggregating) systems of different firms is an important capability for virtual organizations. However, since the latter organizational forms are more often in a state of flux—bundling and unbundling on a more or less constant basis—transition costs become a bigger component of their business environment. They are thus more of a potential driver for ES vendor efforts to decrease the cost and speed of bundling and unbundling. In addition, since the possible portfolio of relationships is much larger than with permanent realignments, evaluating possible portfolios becomes a much larger, ongoing task. Finally, since virtual organizations are not simply mergers or acquisitions, the range of possible relationship types is greater. To accommodate this range, ESs will need to support different levels of integration of data and processes—from simple interorganizational market transactions to complete integration and sharing—that are appropriate to the kind of relationship between the two (or more) organizations that make up the virtual organization.

One way to imagine the shape of ES-enabled virtual organizations is to see them as extended value chains.[5] Competition would be between different value chains, instead of between individual companies. Organizations would have to evaluate the benefits of participating in alternative value chains, and members of a value chain would have to evaluate the benefits of allowing a potential new partner to participate. Evaluating entire value chains, and the role of any one company within it, suggests a deep sharing of data among the value chain partners. Setting aside the issues of trust with proprietary information, that kind of analysis requires consolidating information across multiple data systems.

A more dynamic view of virtual organizations would portray them not as simple, one-dimensional value chains, but as value networks that pull together capabilities in a nonlinear fashion. Individual companies could participate in multiple virtual organizations, providing capabilities across many value chains. A company might be a supplier in multiple chains, a customer in a different set of chains, and a simultaneous competitor and collaborator in all of them. Competition between entire value chains would still exist at some level (as it does today), but would also exist between individual companies in niches focused on providing specific capabilities. Depending on the relationships between the value network partners, evaluating the value of participating may be based on a straightforward market transaction (e.g., fee for service contract), or it could be extremely complex, based on some calculation of the value of the contribution of each particular partner.

Today's ESs clearly do not support the rapid, flexible, and secure integration and disaggregation of data and processes required by virtual organizations. Neither do they support the kinds of analyses that are needed to evaluate the benefits of participating in particular value networks. The potential value of virtualizing organizations seems very great, however, and these gaps, while not bridgeable in the short term, probably will drive ES development in the longer term.

CURRENT ENTERPRISE SYSTEM CAPABILITIES AND FUTURE GAPS

In the previous section I described several areas of functionality into which ESs are likely to grow as the large-scale changes to the business environment outlined take hold. The future development of ESs is likely to follow a particular sequence that can be laid out in a framework of two dimensions: business scope and information processing sophistication. While this framework does not represent the workings of immutable natural laws, it does suggest that certain developments are more likely to occur before others. Once the framework has been laid out, one can map current ES functionality onto the framework and then point to likely scenarios for future development.

BUSINESS DOMAIN

Business domain refers simply to the general range of business locations in which an ES operates. Borrowing from Brandenburger and Nalebuff's "Value Net" framework,[6] an ES can support three different domains: internal to the firm, along the supply chain (the vertical direction in the Value Net framework), and among a set of collaborative peers. Internal processes can be addressed, either individually or in an integrated manner, by an individual firm. This was, of course, the first domain to which ESs were applied. Supply chain processes, described in the previous chapter, connect a firm to its suppliers and customers. Interpeer processes connect a firm to complementing firms (not directly linked in the supply chain), and potentially to its competitors.

The Value Net framework itself does not imply a particular ordering among these various process domains, but the order—internal, supply chain, peer network—follows from the differing ease of implementation and expected ROI associated with each domain. Individual, internal processes are elemental, and they logically precede processes that integrate across internal processes. Processes that connect the firm to the outside must negotiate management and intersystem hurdles, and thus tend to be more complex than processes that exist wholly within firms. Processes that connect the firm to its supply chain partners and to its customers provide obvious rewards, whereas processes that connect a firm to non-supply-chain peers have less easily measured benefits, so supply chain processes are likely to be addressed prior to peer network connections. Brandenburger and Nalebuff, in the context of the "co-opetition" idea, make the point that individual peer companies simultaneously complement and compete with each other in a variety of ways. Therefore, these peer network relationships are more complex than familiar supply chain relationships, making models for managing processes among peers more difficult to create and validate.

INFORMATION SCOPE

Information scope refers to the level of information processing and analysis provided by the information system. There are three basic levels of business scope: transaction automation, process management, and knowledge management.

Transaction automation refers to the ability of an ES to process data from various internal or external business transactions. The nature of the transactions may involve the sale of a product to a customer, the hiring of a new employee, or the use of inventory in production. The processing of data includes presenting relevant existing data on the relationship, offering options to a user, and updating the data in a database.

For transaction automation to succeed, the system needs a "good-enough" model of the processes in a business domain along with the data management tasks that allow the system to keep its representation of the domain internally consistent and externally valid. For example, when a customer buys a particular item on credit, the ES knows to add the dollar amount to accounts receivable and to lower the inventory level of the item purchased. The system must also incorporate rules that reflect real-world facts, such as "Inventory levels cannot be less than zero" and "The date of purchase cannot be greater than the number of days in the current month." Humans can be involved in transaction automation, but usually only as providers of needed inputs; this is not where the higher-order analytical functions of humans are required. Of course, transaction automation is well established in business, although the breadth and scale of the transactions automated by an ES, and the complexity of the ES business model, put us into new territory.

Process management refers to the ability of an ES-enabled organization to take action on data. Process management begins to put data into context, representing not only the state of the real world and what actions are possible given that state, but also what actions ought to be taken in an algorithmic, computer-based sense. Thus, when inventory is depleted to a critical (nonzero) amount, the system could issue a recommendation that a purchase order be cut, automatically send a purchase order to the appropriate supplier, or, if the ESs of the two companies are integrated, automatically update the amount of the item on order in the supplier's database.

Process management incorporates business rules, that is, a human being's sense of what should happen in a particular business context. Someone—a system designer or process owner—must define these rules on the basis of best or good business practices. The system either incorporates the heuristics that humans previously used to manage the process manually or is augmented by a human user of the system who observes what is happening in a process and intervenes. Just as process control systems automate manufacturing processes in a factory, process management systems automate administrative processes and limit the need for human intervention. Process management was possible prior to ESs, but was never institutionalized. Today, many firms are beginning to operate at the process management level with the help of their ESs.

Knowledge management is the most sophisticated domain in which ESs can operate. Here the interaction between systems and humans becomes more collaborative; while the system itself can have some decision-making capability programmed into it, the system also acts as an extension of the human ability to store and process knowledge. From the standpoint of the system's intelligence, it can begin to transform data into knowledge through complex statistical analyses. Such data-mining capabilities are available today, but typically separate from an ES.

In the knowledge management middle ground between highly structured data and totally unstructured text are documents. Enterprise system vendors are already working with document management vendors to incorporate documents; one application, for example, allows chemical firms to tie structured product information about a substance in an SAP database to the safety documents describing its safe handling that are located in a document management system. Other key documents that could be linked to an ES include invoices, procedure manuals, product specification sheets, and so forth. Increasingly, standard ES functionality will incorporate not only links to documents in other systems, but the ability to handle documents within the ES package itself.

Future ES capabilities will also include the ability to combine data-based information with more value-added observations and insights from human beings. A salesperson visiting a customer, for example, would be able to call up the customer's purchase history with the company, as well as external news reports and discussion items from other sales and service personnel who have dealt with the customer—all in an integrated fashion. A human resources transaction system will also contain detailed information about the knowledge and skills an employee has, would include comments about the person's performance, and could even make recommendations about what educational offerings might be appropriate to advance to the next level of skills.

Companies are increasingly pursuing these sorts of knowledge management applications today, but they are almost totally separated from the systems used to support transaction automation and process management. Successful knowledge management, however, should incorporate knowledge derived from data. The ES capability of knowledge management will unite all of the information processing modes and make ESs a highly useful tool for knowledge workers.

BUSINESS DOMAIN AND INFORMATION SCOPE FRAMEWORK

Figure 9-1 places major categories of ES functionality within a framework of the two dimensions of business domain and information scope. In the context of this framework, ES functionality has expanded over time from the lower left corner toward the upper right. The examples discussed here are meant to illustrate different categories of functionality, and are in no way exhaustive. Indeed, these examples cannot be exhaustive, because new products with more functionality will become available on an ongoing basis. On the other end of the spectrum, though, ES prehistory is, at this point, not very interesting, and so I'll save trees by forgoing providing examples for it.

Transaction automation with internal, integrated processes. As noted in the figure, this combination represents the baseline functionality of an ES database. Any true ES could serve as an example here. Good stuff, but nothing to stir up excitement in the twenty-first century.

Process management with internal, integrated processes. This sector represents the standard functionality of ES packages, and requires the integrated database that also comes with all ESs. The sophistication of process management applications has increased over time, often through the use of company-specific applications or the development of bolt-on applications by third-party vendors. One of the primary areas for advancement in this regard involves embedding more sophisticated algorithms into ESs—from chaos or complexity theory–based models to rule-based artificial intelligence to more traditional operations research techniques.

Knowledge management with internal, integrated processes. Knowledge management entails a more sophisticated use of the data within an ES to manage internal processes, and also entails the use of process knowledge. From one perspective, knowledge

FIGURE 9-1

FUTURE APPLICATIONS OF ENTERPRISE SYSTEMS

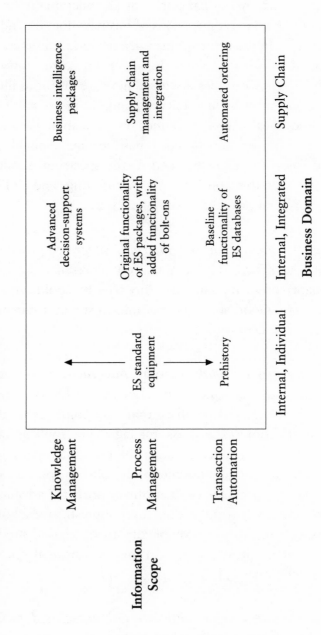

management in this context amounts to an advanced decision-support system, which can present managers with highly refined data on the performance of a process and recommendations for what to do about it. One example of this kind of functionality is PeopleSoft's "My World" concept, which aims to bring together information based on the user's role within an organization.[7] The PeopleSoft system will also reach beyond organizational boundaries to bring information from external sources, such as news wires and supplier databases, to the desktop. Another example is SAP's new "mySAP.com" offering, which also attempts to make ES-derived information meaningful at the individual worker level. However, because such factors as how much the systems will process this information and how integrated they will be with data-derived knowledge are unclear, they may not really reach the level of true knowledge management with supply chain processes.

Another application of knowledge management to internal processes involves the capture, storage, and use of process best practices, workarounds, and shortcuts for use by the human users of a system. If, for example, a system user is called by a customer asking for a product to be delivered three months from today and the system won't take the order because the company's ordering horizon is only for one month, the order taker needs to know what might be done in the situation. Is there a way to enter the order? If not, can I get the system to prompt me at the appropriate time to call the customer and complete the transaction? Even an explanation of why the company doesn't want to take orders three months in advance would at least give the order taker something to tell the customer. Any of these scenarios could be considered process knowledge management.

Transaction automation with supply chain processes. This combination encompasses automated ordering processes, such as centralized purchasing applications. Companies have been doing this with EDI for years, but they can improve upon that activity by interfacing interorganizational communications directly to a system without human intervention, by switching to the Internet as a communications platform, and by working on the efficiency of supply chain business processes as well as by using systems to improve the process.

Process management with supply chain processes. Some aspects of this cell of the framework have been employed for a number of years, such as incorporating automated reorder points or other business rules into logistical applications. Others are available now, but are not yet in broad use. An example of such an application is collaborative planning, forecasting, and replenishment (CPFR) software that allows supply chain partners to share information on marketing, sales, and production. At this point, the major vendors of supply chain applications offer CPFR, although active use of it is largely restricted to the consumer products and retailing industries.[8]

Knowledge management with supply chain processes. This combination represents a more sophisticated use of ES data in managing the supply chain, and is a leading edge for ES development. Such a system would integrate supply chain management with product life cycle and customer management, and would provide tools for executives to consider these processes as a single dynamic system. SAP, for example, is planning to offer a business intelligence package that includes business planning and simulation, a corporate "performance monitor," and stakeholder relationship management. To the degree that these capabilities are used to analyze external relationships, it would be an example of work in this cell of the framework.

Transaction automation with peer processes. Once cross-firm transactions are automated for supply chain partnerships, using this functionality in peer relationships is a small technical step. Although peer-to-peer automated transactions are feasible, the issue is not what is possible, but what value there is to be gained. Another problem is the establishment of the business relationships that would make ES-based automation necessary. Beyond the traditional supply chain, outsourcing other processes, such as human resources management, provides obvious benefits and might qualify to be placed in this section of the framework if the client's and supplier's two systems were integrated to some degree. Integrating the full range of non-supply-chain processes between peers is still off in the future and will likely co-evolve with virtual organizations.

Process management with peer processes. If and when virtual organizations become a reality, ESs (in whatever form they take at that time) will enable peer-to-peer transactions. In addition to automating transactions, though, ESs will need to provide tools to manage interpeer processes and relationships through analysis and control applications that are analogous to the applications used for supply chain relationships. Real-time choices of partners will have to be made on the basis of some factor, be it price, previous history of a relationship, or the unique capability of a provider. Just as some organizations now calculate pricing in real-time yield management systems, the process systems of the future will calculate real-time relationship value. Virtual organizations are likely to exist within a shifting set of relationships, so a particularly important capability will be to analyze the values of partners' contributions to the virtual organization and the value to a particular firm of staying within a specific virtual organization.[9]

Knowledge management with peer processes. This sector of the framework is, of course, the furthest out in the future, and the most speculative. Knowledge management in this context would need to include knowledge management processes developed earlier, and to go beyond them by using the analytic and control applications developed specifically for peer-to-peer processes. Brandenburger and Nalebuff suggest that game theory provides a key analytic framework for companies in the present; perhaps game theory will be incorporated into future knowledge management applications for peer-to-peer processes in virtual organizations.

In addition to the game-theoretical analysis, at this level companies would also collect and analyze knowledge about peers, collaborators, and competitors and combine it with the data on peer relationships to form an integrated picture of the relationship potential. At any moment any employee could come up to speed quickly on who makes decisions within the potential collaborator, what their primary business issues and objectives are, and what their predicted collaborative value might be. Companies scarcely have this information about their customers today, much less their peers or competitors.

TECHNOLOGICAL DEVELOPMENTS

Just as business capabilities evolve over time, the technological capabilities of ESs will change significantly over the next several years. Some of the technological changes will come in response to business need; others may emerge with regard to some other logic, for example, the need for ES vendors to sell more to customers. In this section I'll review a variety of changes that I and other observers—usually employed by technology market analyst firms—anticipate from ES vendors and related third parties. Some of these directions have been mentioned in passing before, but it's probably useful to put them all in one place.

NEW APPLICATION DOMAINS

Enterprise applications vendors can't afford to stand still; they have to come up with new reasons to sell ESs to customers, and reasons for existing customers to upgrade to new versions. Also, they don't want vendors of more focused applications to gain account control. As a result, we will continue to see increasing breadth of ES functionality being introduced over time. The question, then, is in what areas ES functionality will be introduced.

I'm no technology prognosticator, but fortunately it doesn't take much insight to see that the primary ES applications of the near future will be in the areas of customer relationship management, supply chain management, knowledge management, and new product development. I'll discuss each area briefly except for supply chain management, which was covered in the previous chapter.

Customer relationship management is already the focus of ES vendors to some degree. More than one vendor has added sales force automation technology (including such applications as sales call planning, call reporting, contact management, sales team communications, product configuration, time and expense reporting, and sales collateral database) to its applications portfolio; others have purchased vendors of customer service software (including call center automation, field service tracking and dispatch, customer problem tracking and resolution, and product problem analysis and reporting) and are busy integrating that software with their ES packages. Vendors will also begin to offer capabilities for customer self-service over the Internet.

We'll see more of this in the future—more functionality, more integration with the core ES package, more ES vendors adopting this line of work. We'll also see the integration of traditionally marketing-oriented functions into ESs, including tools for the management of marketing campaigns, for the analysis of market data, and for the design and operation of direct marketing programs. Enterprise system databases already contain the "official copy" of customer transaction information, and there is considerable value in combining customer analytics with the records of customer transactions.

Enterprise systems will also become the primary repository of customer knowledge. When a salesperson learns that the customer has a new VP of operations, there will be a way to record it in the ES. Right now customer information and knowledge is scattered throughout various databases, knowledge bases, and paper files; the knowledge is too important to leave in such scattered form.

It's not just customer knowledge that these systems will be used to manage, but rather all types of encoded knowledge. Any knowledge that will fit into a computer repository will be storable and accessible through an ES, or rather an *enterprise information portal* that combines ES data with various types of knowledge, both internal and external. Enterprise system vendors are already exploring how such portals can be a front end to their systems, just as Web sites such as Yahoo! and Netcenter are portals to the Internet. Combined business transaction data and knowledge will be a big step forward when it's available; today they are largely separate. Knowledge about product applications, for example, can be tied to "official" product numbers. Marketing documents can be tied electronically to the products they describe. Business intelligence can be attached to particular companies in the company's customer or competitor database. For the first time in the history of information systems, it will be possible to connect hard data and soft information and knowledge.

Consistent with the overall focus on knowledge, ESs will develop an ability to identify what information is really worth its users' time. Almost every executive today is burdened with more information than he or she can handle. Whether it's through information filters, autonomous agents, or push technologies, there is a great need to help people find the information they need and care about. The earliest days of ES-based information reporting approached this topic in a simplistic way—using green for within-range figures, yellow for borderline, and red for out of range. Future generations of ES information reporting will use more sophisticated approaches.

A third business domain for focus by ES vendors will be product development processes and applications. Product development functionality has only recently been incorporated into ESs, and only to a fairly small degree. However, like other application areas already incorporated, it's useful to have product development data tied to financial data, customer data, and manufacturing data; therefore, we'll see much more of a focus on this area by vendors and customers. There will be ES applications, for example, that allow storage—if not creation in the short run—of CAD documents, with linkages to product data in the overall ES database. Customer complaints about products will be linked back to the development of new products that relate to the old ones. Field engineering applications will be tied to field service systems. The only functionality that may never be added to ESs is product design itself, which typically employs CAD tools, engineering analysis tools, and 3-D modeling capabilities. These are so different from the data-focused applications in ESs that combining them would be extremely difficult.

DECISION AND ANALYTICAL FOCUS

Chapter 7 is all about the use of ES data in management and decision processes. It doesn't happen much today, at least in part because there are insufficient capabilities within ES packages to make it easy. Today, most firms try to extract data from their ESs and then massage it with third-party query and reporting tools, third-party data warehouse management tools, or third-party statistical analysis tools. However, all of the large, mainstream ES vendors have announced new capabilities in the area, and some have even begun to deliver working functionality. Therefore, in the future it's clear that the following will be true:

► All vendors will incorporate increased query, reporting, and statistical analysis capabilities.

► All vendors will link their systems with common performance measurement frameworks, for example, the balanced scorecard.

► Vendors will develop more sophisticated display approaches for executive information system purposes.

► Leading vendors will integrate data-mining techniques into their ESs, including neural network analysis.

A further indication that these capabilities are likely to appear is that there is now a three-letter descriptor of them that seems to be gathering support throughout the vendor and analyst community. From now on, this aspect of ESs will be known as *strategic enterprise management* (SEM).

THE COMPONENT ASSEMBLY MODEL

A commonly held view among ES market analysts is that monolithic enterprise applications will become more modular and flexible. They will, according to this view, evolve to a model in which the basic ES is a backbone into which disparate best-of-breed applications can be plugged and played. This would represent a benefit for ES user companies if it became a reality; companies could choose the best functionality for particular component applications, and they would all fit together seamlessly—or so goes the vision, anyway.

However, it's not clear that this model would benefit ES vendors. Presumably most vendors would prefer to sell a broad suite of applications over selling a backbone system, because they could sell the former at a higher price. Also, for this scenario to succeed, extensive cooperation between different vendors would be required. Each ES vendor would have to work with each component vendor, which would be difficult to imagine.

In the short run, this model is becoming somewhat more feasible through the availability of third-party middleware systems that ostensibly allow different ESs to communicate with each other, or with focused application components. In late 1999, however, this less ambitious version of component assembly is still more vision than reality.

EXTERNAL HOSTING OF ENTERPRISE SYSTEMS

As ESs have become more complex and comprehensive, companies using the systems typically have come to rely more and more on external IT expertise. Enterprise system vendors now design the system, and vendors or solutions integrators partner with clients to configure and implement the system, though clients still must maintain the internal IT infrastructure and provide support functions in-house. Now some service companies and ES providers, such as U.S. Internetworking, Corio, and Oracle, are offering Web-hosted ES services. Other partnerships are emerging between ES vendors, telecommunications service providers, and IT hardware companies to provide such *netsourcing* services, such as a partnership between SAP, Qwest Communications, and Hewlett-Packard.

What these offerings mean is that client companies no longer have to buy, upgrade or support ES packages, but rather can rent them. Companies with limited resources or IT expertise can still receive the cutting-edge benefits of ESs. Clearly, outsourcing a company's ES functionality over the Web involves a strategic decision that must weigh factors such as cost, convenience, management focus, and leading-edge technology against possible concerns with data security, service levels, loss of control, and loss of internal technical expertise. It's also unlikely that a company could make modifications to software that is delivered by an external provider over the Web, unless they were renting their own off-site instance of the ES.

Thus far, few companies have availed themselves of this service, but it's only been available for about a year as I write. Those that ultimately do take advantage of the service are likely to be relatively small or midsize companies who don't consider their information systems to be a strategic advantage. This may be a low-cost option, but it's not likely to be a high-value one. Ironically, when SAP was formed in 1972, the company's original service model involved offering the package over time-sharing networks. In some ways the netsourcing idea is a return to that notion.

Looking to the future, the large-scale changes to the business environment I outlined at the beginning of this chapter are likely to tip the balance of factors associated with outsourcing toward a Web-based, shared-services model for ESs. All of the changes mentioned—sense-and-respond business models, globalization, the horizontal realignment of corporations, and virtual organizations—rely on robust communications and strong data connections between divisions (in the case of globalization) and especially between companies. Intranets have provided this kind of robust connectivity within companies, and *extranets* (intranets that allow access from users outside a company) have allowed small sets of firms to communicate; however, for global companies or interorganizational collaborations these technologies can be prohibitively expensive.

In contrast, the Internet can provide connectivity levels similar to (and even greater than) a proprietary network that only the largest firms can afford, and this fact is already driving ES vendors to make their products Web-enabled, that is, accessible through the Internet and a browser. For firms that remain regional and whose business relationships are few in number and relatively stable, the current client/server model, combined with external extranet connections to supply chain partners, may suffice in the future business environment. However, for companies that either are global, have a large number of suppliers and customers, or have suppliers and customers that change frequently, the connectivity of the Internet will be essential.

To survive in the future business environment, companies will need to combine the connectivity of the Internet with the functionality of ESs across firm boundaries. Enterprise application functionality is derived from the integrated structure that these systems impose on a company's data, and businesses in the new environment will need to have their data in such an integrated structure. It will include not only internal data, but also the data of their partners in a supply chain or value network.

While middleware or "between-ware" vendors are currently trying to address the need for businesses to share data, the increasing benefit of truly integrating data across firms will drive ES vendors to offer a shared-services model in which the vendors themselves run the ESs and host clients' data in large, integrated databases.[10] One vision of this future has entire supply chains being hosted on a particular vendor's ES, with different supply chains competing as whole units against one another—in other words, ES-enabled *keiretsu*. Although it seems unlikely that companies will commit to a single supply chain, integrating data will be easier with companies using the same ES, and so *intra*system partnerships will enjoy an advantage over *inter*system partnerships.

APPLICATION AND INFORMATION STANDARDS

As virtual companies become more prevalent, there will be more incentive to eliminate the cost of integrating across ESs by creating a single standard that all companies can share. Multiple standards could continue to exist, but there are several possible paths to reaching a single standard. One possibility, given the workings of the increasing returns economics and network effects common in the software industry, is that a standard based on a single vendor's product will come to prevail in the marketplace, which would put that vendor in a position with respect to ESs that is similar to Microsoft's position with respect to PC operating systems. A second possibility is that an industry body will develop a standard that companies adhere to, such as was done with EDI.

An additional possibility is that a meta-standard will be developed that will allow ESs to access data definitions dynamically and thus be able to interpret data from other systems correctly. XML, the eXtensible Markup Language, and its associated protocols for accessing data definitions dynamically over the Internet, might provide this kind of meta-standard. Already, some groups, such as librarians, chemists, and musicians, have developed their own sets of data definitions and are using them to share structured data over the Internet. Industry groups, or even individual companies, could create their own data definitions, publish these on the Internet, and reference them when sharing data with other companies. With this type of

290 ◄ *Mission Critical*

meta-standard in wide use, the Internet would come closer to bringing together ubiquitous connectivity and an integrated data structure, making it, in effect, one big database.

POTENTIAL EFFECTS OF ENTERPRISE SYSTEM DEVELOPMENT

ENTERPRISE SYSTEMS AND THE PRACTICE OF MANAGEMENT

Enterprise systems and communications technologies are beginning to enable many of the changes discussed at the beginning of this chapter. I outlined possible corporate realignments—the vertical consolidation driven by globalization and overcapacity, the vertical unbundling and horizontal consolidation enabled by lowered communication costs, and the vertical and horizontal aggregation and disassociation of virtual corporations. These new organizational forms will affect the work of managers within them and will shape the information requirements of various types of businesses. However, views on how technological developments will affect the practice of management vary widely.

Steve Haeckel and Dick Nolan, researchers at IBM and Harvard, respectively, see improved communications and especially ES technologies as enabling "management by wire," which they liken to flying a modern airplane with sophisticated flight telemetry. They expect that with a (futuristic) ES in place, an executive crew would pilot the organization "using controls in the information cockpit of the business. Managers respond to the readouts appearing on the console, modifying the business plan based on changes in external conditions, monitoring the performance of delegated responsibilities, and sending directions to subsidiary units such as manufacturing and sales."[11]

Haeckel and Nolan argue that companies need an "enterprise model" to ensure that information is integrated and consistent across the organization. When they wrote in 1994, this may have been the case, but such enterprise models have largely been superseded by enterprise systems. They do, however, provide a preview of what might happen when an ES doesn't fit the organization well: "Of course, if the enterprise model represents the wrong reality—or is incomplete, out of date, or operating on bad data—the outcome could be catastrophic."[12]

My own view is that ESs certainly make managing by wire a more plausible model for management behavior. Interestingly, some ES vendors (SAP most aggressively) are developing their own visions of what a management cockpit might look like, with screen-covered walls featuring complex graphical displays. However, this approach to management behavior has risks, and I don't mean just the misconfiguration of your system. If managers never step out of their cockpits and never take their eyes off their screens, they may miss important aspects of what's going on in their organizations. For the foreseeable future, not all information and knowledge that's important within—or external to—an organization will be found within an ES database. Interactions with other managers and employees, customers, suppliers, regulators, and so forth will still be critical to any company's success.

In contrast to the picture of executive pilots in an information cockpit, MIT Sloan School professor Tom Malone sees decision making becoming more decentralized.[13] He suggests that decision-making structures move through three stages as communication costs are reduced by technological improvements. When communication costs are high, *independent decentralized* decision makers (whom he labels "cowboys") manage on their own. As communication costs fall, information can be aggregated more easily so that *centralized* decision makers ("commanders") can use a global perspective to inform decisions. He implies that most organizations are in this stage at present, although the model sounds similar to what Haeckel and Nolan expect in the future. When communication costs fall even further, information can be shared throughout a network, so *connected decentralized* decision makers ("cyber-cowboys") can combine the advantages of a global perspective and localized knowledge to inform local decisions.

Malone makes two additional important points: First, localized knowledge is often "sticky"—implicit, contextual, and difficult to communicate—and second, localized control provides benefits in terms of speed of response and the motivation of local personnel. From these points he concludes that a good use of communications technology is to transfer information to places where information is not easily available and cannot be easily communicated.

Even when information is not in short supply, the benefits of local control may outweigh the benefits of central control. Actively involving frontline personnel in decision-making processes gives them ownership, and providing them with centralized information can help them make good decisions. The CVS drugstore chain, for example, has an inventory system that provides advice to the store managers about ordering stock, but has allowed the managers to maintain decision rights about the orders actually placed. The thinking behind this arrangement is focused on maintaining the motivation for high levels of customer service. As the CVS senior vice president for MIS and CIO, Howard Edels, noted:

> If [the store managers] make a mistake [by forgetting to place an order, for example], it's their mistake; they treat you nicely and say, 'I'm sorry, I'll take care of it.' But if they see the computer as having control, the answer becomes, 'I don't know why your order isn't here, the stupid computer didn't bring it.' It changes the whole relationship with customers.[14]

CVS store managers act similarly to Malone's cyber-cowboys, and they are supported—not controlled—centrally by the information provided by the company's integrated ES. Companies with more rigid hierarchies may find it difficult to cede decision-making power to local managers when ESs make it easy to dictate actions from corporate headquarters.

In focusing on communication costs as the major determinant of the decision-making structure, Malone overlooks other variables, such as the limits of management attention and the value of coordinated action, that also affect how decisions are made. Cyber-cowboys must balance maintaining a global perspective against attending to local events, and if maintaining the global perspective takes too much management attention, local decision makers may prefer that a centralized decision maker manage that perspective and make decisions based on it. There are also situations in which the value of coordinated action exceeds the value of local response. To borrow the airplane analogy, how many people would want to ride in a plane controlled not by a pilot and copilot team, but by several dozen cyber-cowboys, each of whom independently controlled a flap, an engine, or a landing wheel? Management theorists may talk about the value of "self-organizing systems," but I for one would rather be flown about by a hierarchical command structure.

Of course, actual future decision-making structures will incorporate elements both from executive pilots in the information cockpit and from cyber-cowboys. The overall costs and benefits (taking into account information encoding, communications, computing, attention, time, motivation, and ultimately money) of centralized versus decentralized decision making, as well as a management team's understanding of the options and consequences of different approaches, will likely determine the locus for making a particular decision.

While almost every situation will be some kind of mix, different types of decision structures are likely to emerge in organizations with different value disciplines. Customer intimacy companies will put a premium on customer knowledge and service, and although many customer attributes can be encoded and placed in a database, the ability to sense and respond to the changing moods and needs of individual customers means that cyber-cowboys may dominate the decision landscape. Operational excellence companies will focus on process efficiency, which can be maximized through an emphasis on standardized data and processes and centralized control. Product innovation companies will focus on sensing environmental signals and on creating new ideas, both of which involve a need for local information and knowledge, and cyber-cowboys are therefore likely to reign. In each case, however, ESs are likely to bring about a higher level of accountability because of their more complete and readily accessible data. Executives in all companies will continue to face the challenge of creating management structures that balance empowerment and accountability in ways that work best for their particular situation.

While no examples of management futures exist in the present, we can envision an environment in which enterprise systems have changed almost every aspect of management. In this final section of the chapter I'll describe a hypothetical ES-enabled executive with thus-far-unknown abilities to manage both internally and externally with high-quality information.

A DAY IN THE LIFE OF AN ES-ENABLED EXECUTIVE

Imagine that you're the president of a division of a large manufacturing firm in the year 2007. Your division manufactures industrial products—let's say electronic process control systems—to process manufacturing firms, such as chemical and oil firms, located all around the world. Your systems aren't exactly commodities, but other companies manufacture similar products. The rest of your company sells other types of industrial products, generally to different kinds of customers.

You like to get to the office early in the morning to see what's happened in Asia and Europe. Your ES screen immediately presents your daily information profile with information you've requested from those time zones, and then updates it throughout the day. In Asia you note that orders are up 10 percent over the daily average for October 17 in previous years. Europe is about average, but you are informed that products manufactured the day before cost 7 percent more than the specification because of some outsourced production of a control unit. You remember that this was to meet high demand for a new product from a single customer, and with two clicks you confirm that the customer took delivery of the products and paid a 15 percent price premium for them.

Your daily scorecard, which takes all of yesterday's performance indicators into account, only shows red (below target) figures for employee learning. This is the third time this week that the learning indicators show a shortfall. You assume that the problem is related to a short-handedness of skilled workers in the Americas—they don't have time to be trained—and confirm that with a few clicks. You quickly review the linkages to temporary employment agencies in the system, and contract on-line for 100 temporary skilled workers so that those in your own company can work on addressing their learning deficit.

After a quick chat with another division president over coffee, you begin a meeting on new product development progress with the head of the division's New Product Development (NPD) process based in Germany. You link your screens so that you can both look at the same information while you talk on a videoconference. As you are presented with several alternative designs for a new form of pump controller developed by NPD, you examine on-line the material and labor costs projected for each design, the percentage of component reuse, and the skill impacts involved in manufacturing, selling, and servicing the controller. You and the NPD process head jointly decide on the pump design that has cost projections 10 percent under the others, and you end the meeting.

After another cup of coffee and a doughnut, you notice that your workstation lists three requests for your confirmation of unprofitable sales. The system has recently begun to calculate whether individual sales are profitable, and you've asked that it be configured to request confirmation whenever a sale is calculated to be unprofitable, since you don't want this to happen often. Two of the sale transactions, you quickly determine, are for customers who are profitable overall, so you approve them. The other one you reject, and you notify the sales rep that ordering a very similar product to one in the order would make the sale profitable. The rep should have known that and checked the system himself; you expect he will in the future, since your message was a bit curt.

You're tempted to have another doughnut, but resist and start dealing with a procurement issue that's come up over the past several days. Your global supply chain management process leader is on vacation, so you have to deal with it yourself. One of your key vendors has noticed that the volume you order electronically from them is declining and has left messages wondering why. You check prices and sources for several automated purchases over the past weeks and note that the system has been relying more heavily on spot market purchases of the vendor's product. You note that the vendor had automatically notified your system of a price increase, and that led to the system's search for alternative suppliers. You call the vendor, relate this information with cool precision, and gently berate your supplier for trying to push through a price increase. You note that the vendor, which has access to your ordering information, could have noticed the reason for the decline himself. After all, your system sent him an e-mail noting the price increase and suggesting that "prices on products tendered may no longer be competitive." As you suspect he'll do, he backs down on the price increase and says he'll have his system send notification to your system. You have perfect confidence that order volumes for this vendor will pick up when the system factors in the new price.

You have a lunch scheduled with the process head of customer relationship management. She has a problem she wants to discuss with you, she said in an e-mail message. After you get your food and sit down in the cafeteria, she says, "I thought I would get to you before you got to me. You may have noticed already that the system says our cost per service call is up." It's really not service cost increases, she argues, but rather investments in service knowledge management that you've already approved. A few of the service reps are entering descriptions of past service cases into the knowledge repository, and the company will be able to resolve customer problems a lot faster after they finish. You do recall agreeing to this arrangement, and then discuss with her how to factor the costs of the knowledge management work into the activity-based costing system for the project.

At 4 P.M. you have a golf date, which you'd feel guilty about if you hadn't been so productive this morning and over lunch.

But before you take off you want to resolve a couple more problems that have been brewing all week. One of your competitors is threatening to drop out of an industry manufacturing consortium that you were instrumental in creating. The consortium runs a manufacturing plant that handles peak demand for process control systems when any of the participating companies runs out of capacity. It uses your brand of ES, so when your system predicts a capacity constraint, orders are automatically shifted to be manufactured at the consortium plant. You're proud of how the consortium saved you from having to build another plant, even though it took special approval from antitrust regulators to work across competitive firms.

Before calling the competitor, you check into the consortium's system to find out what you can about why he might be threatening to withdraw. You're not entitled to see all order information in the consortium system, but it is possible to see aggregate figures on who's using the plant's capacity. The competitor, you note, has been using the consortium's capability on a fairly regular basis, so there must be another reason. When you call you find out what it is: The competitor says there's a good chance that he'll be selling off the process control business, and by the consortium contract he has to give three months' notice before withdrawing. You ask if he might be interested in selling the business to your firm, and set up a dinner meeting at a quiet restaurant to discuss it.

It's 3:30 and you have to get moving if you're going to make your tee time. You are playing with the VP of customer relationship management for your ES vendor firm. It's obvious to you and to the vendor that your use of the system makes you strategic partners, and over a golf game you plan to discuss further ways to cooperate. All in all, your ES has enabled you to have a fruitfully busy day.

APPENDIX: A TECHNICAL OVERVIEW OF ENTERPRISE SYSTEMS

IN THIS APPENDIX A NUMBER OF TECHNICAL ISSUES WITH regard to ESs are discussed. Although the explanations of the technology should be accessible to nontechnologists, the focus of the appendix is on how the technology works and what some of the important differences are between ES offerings, and not on the business implications of the systems. Since technology changes rapidly, let me warn that this section of the book may age faster than other sections, and parts of it will eventually become obsolete. (On the other hand, the rest of the book is timeless!) I'll begin with a discussion of how ESs work.

How Do Enterprise Systems Work?

An ES is a technical tour de force. It combines a very high level of functionality and complexity with day-to-day dependability and robustness. Several technical capabilities are key to how an ES works, including the following:

- ► Modular construction
- ► Client/server architecture
- ► Configuration
- ► Common central database
- ► Variable interfaces

Each of these capabilities is described in detail in the following subsections. Understanding the way that an ES functions is key to knowing how it fits into the organizational context.

MODULAR CONSTRUCTION

Enterprise systems are collections of application modules. SAP, the most comprehensive ES package, has twelve modules; these are listed in table A-1. The modules can communicate with each other either directly or by updating a central database.

Companies can select among the available modules offered by a vendor and install only those needed. Companies can also augment or replace functionality offered by an ES vendor with software from a third-party provider. The goal in such cases is for the third-party software to act as just another module, though this is rarely so straightforward in practice. Some sort of customized interface must usually be developed in order for the bolt-on module to connect with the ES.

CLIENT/SERVER ARCHITECTURE

Contemporary ESs all run on a client/server computing architecture. This means that some part of the processing is done on a server, and some on a desktop personal computer (the client).

TABLE A-1

SAP APPLICATION MODULES

Financial Accounting

Treasury

Controlling (financial control)

Enterprise Controlling (management reporting)

Investment Management

Production Planning

Materials Management

Plant Maintenance

Quality Management

Project System (project management)

Sales and Distribution

Human Resources Management

Advanced Planner and Optimizer

Enterprise systems are large and complex programs requiring powerful servers and relatively powerful PCs. Some brands of ES (e.g., SAP) require two layers of servers—one for the application programs and one for the database.

Earlier versions of ESs (e.g., SAP's R/2 system) ran on centralized mainframes. Some firms still have these mainframe versions installed, but almost every company is moving toward installation of client/server versions (for reasons of technical currency, not really increased business value). In some cases, vendors are withdrawing support for the mainframe versions of their software. To further complicate the issue, a few firms (for example, the postage meter company Pitney Bowes) have installed one layer of their ES on a mainframe computer, but refer to it as a server. Many companies struggle with the technical complexity of the client/server environment and with the scalability to support the required number of concurrent system users (which may range into the thousands). They often seek the most powerful server available to run their systems.

CONFIGURATION

Although an ES is a standard set of applications, individual companies can tailor their ESs to their particular business environment through configuration. A configuration table enables a company to tailor the functionality of the system to the way it chooses to do business. An organization can select, for example, what kind of inventory accounting it will employ (e.g., FIFO or LIFO), or whether it wants to recognize product revenue by geographical unit, product line, or distribution channel. The sequence of configuration is to first establish an unambiguous corporate structure and hierarchy; this affects how results are consolidated. Then for each business process, subprocess, and major activity, the company should answer the following questions:

▶ How are we doing this today?

▶ How would we like to be doing it?

▶ How does the system allow us to do it?

Enterprise system process designs are usually quite rational and typically offer several choices, but they do not encompass all possible ways of doing business. SAP, the most complex ES, has more than 8,000 configuration tables—but even the SAP configuration options are not unlimited. Companies that have idiosyncratic ways of doing business may find that they are not supported in the ES they select. For example, a firm may be able to recognize revenues by either product or geography, but not double-count by both. A company may not be able to give preferential treatment—for example, ship product out of already-promised inventory—to customers based on long-term business relationships. It may require months or even years for a company to decide how it wants to configure its system. Unknown Computer, for example, spent more than a year going through this mapping of processes to system configuration.

However, both ES software vendors and consulting services are increasingly supplying templates for particular industries or company types (e.g., international oil companies, small manufacturers) that greatly shortcut the process of configuring a system—if, of course, the company is willing to take a standard configured system or make only minor changes to it.

COMMON CENTRAL DATABASE

All ESs feature a common central database from which all application modules draw, manipulate, and update data. This is not a new concept, but it has reached its highest level of successful execution in the ES environment. The databases are generally not proprietary, but are offered by leading database vendors (e.g., Oracle, Sybase, Informix). The databases used by ESs are almost always relational; that is, they store data in an easy-to-access format that does not require advance knowledge of all the ways in which the data will be accessed.

VARIABLE INTERFACES

An important aspect of ESs is their global nature. What makes it possible for one system to be used in many different countries is the inclusion of different interfaces for different countries. A user of an ES in Brazil, for example, would look at ES screens in Portuguese and would see financial results in reals. The ES might even be able to apply Brazilian employment law in its human resources system. Of course, not all languages and currencies are supported in all ESs, but there is a good chance that if you are in an industrialized nation you will be able to interface with an ES in your native terms. An occasional error message in the home country language of the ES vendor may sneak through, however!

ORIGINS AND MAJOR VENDORS OF ENTERPRISE SYSTEMS

The modern ES is a creation of software vendors. However, the concept of the broad, modern ES did not spring full-blown from the head of a brilliant entrepreneur. Just as Microsoft incrementally added products, functionality, and profitability to the personal computer market, so did ES vendors start with much less ambitious products. Most of them were focused on a particular function at the beginning, and incremental capabilities were added over time. In some cases these companies grew by acquisition and then integration of the acquired system into the integrated ES.

In large organizations, SAP, Oracle, and PeopleSoft are the clear market leaders (with 28 percent, 9 percent, and 7 percent market share in 1998, respectively, according to International Data), together constituting almost half the market. Other players in the large-customer market include J.D. Edwards, Baan, and Lawson Software. In smaller and midsized companies, the vendor market is much more fragmented. Companies such as Geac, Platinum Software, Ceridian, QAD, and SSA offer enterprise products in these markets, usually on the strength of one particular functional application, such as financial systems or human resources applications. The large-company vendors are aggressively moving into the midsized company market, however, and given their ability to market their products effectively and their greater system functionality, they will probably come to dominate this market eventually.

For some industries there are ES packages that were specifically designed for the industry's process and information requirements (this was originally the case with all ES vendors—most systems originally supported manufacturing companies—but they evolved to support many different industries). Clarus and FlexiInternational, for example, focus on service industries; Marcam focuses on process manufacturing businesses; JDA Software and Richter Systems address retail applications.

SAP

The first firm to introduce a broadly functional ES was SAP AG (Systeme, Anwendungen, Produkte in der Datenverarbeitung—Systems, Applications, and Products in Data Processing), a German company based in the town of Walldorf. Five software engineers at IBM in Germany had the idea for a cross-functional information system. IBM, however, rejected the idea, so the engineers formed their own firm in 1972. SAP's earliest integrated offering ran on mainframes and was called R/2. The client/server version of the system, R/3, was introduced in 1992. SAP has more than 17,000 customers and just under a 30 percent share of the ES market.

SAP's strength is the breadth and extensive capability of its software's functionality; if it has a shortcoming, it is the complexity of the system and of its implementation. SAP, being more than double the size of the next largest ES vendor, spends much more on R&D than any other firm, and is most likely to introduce new functionality as a result. SAP takes a strong industry-specific focus in its marketing; its strongest industries are oil and gas, process industries (e.g., chemicals and pharmaceuticals), and high technology, but it is coming on strong in a variety of other industries, from health care to financial services.

ORACLE

Oracle Corporation was founded in 1977 as a database company, and still is one. Its database offering is the most popular repository of ES data. But in the late 1980s the company began to develop its own computing applications. Early versions of the internal software were then refined in co-development projects with customer companies, such as Millipore. Today Oracle has just under 10 percent of the ES market. Its ES package has almost fifty different modules in six categories: Finance, Human Resources, Projects, Manufacturing, Supply Chain, and Front Office (customer-oriented applications). It also offers industry-specific offerings, most of which were acquired from companies that had developed them to a certain degree (e.g., the Oracle Energy Downstream package obtained from BP).

BAAN

Founded in 1978, Baan is a Netherlands company based in the town of Putten. For its first fifteen years its software was primarily manufacturing oriented. Then the company went public and invested heavily in development of broader capabilities. The company now has more than 3,000 customers and is heavily focused on manufacturing and logistics; its most prominent customers (e.g., Boeing) are complex manufacturing firms. Baan has expanded its capabilities recently through acquisition; it bought Aurum for its customer service software, and Coda for detailed financial reporting capabilities. It's run into some financial difficulties of late, but is generally believed to have a good product.

PEOPLESOFT

Based in Pleasanton, California, PeopleSoft is the newest of current ES vendors. Its traditional strength has been human resources (HR) applications, though it now offers a fairly broad range of software functionality. The company's CEO, Dave Duffield, had led two previous HR-oriented software companies. He started PeopleSoft in 1987 to create a client/server version, and began with such HR functions as employee records, payroll, and benefits. The company developed its own financial applications; later it built manufacturing software, and acquired logistics software when it acquired Red Pepper. Its system is relatively flexible and easy to install, but does not support the scale or complexity of a very large organization as well as, say, SAP. PeopleSoft today has about 7 percent of the ES market; until recently it was growing rapidly.

J.D. EDWARDS

Founded in 1977 by ex-accountants, J.D. Edwards has long been focused on systems that run on midrange computing platforms, for example, the IBM AS/400 series. Today, however, the company's software runs on many different types of systems, but the midrange focus continues with the company's heavy presence in small to midsized companies. Because the company has had a strong focus on application development tools, the J.D. Edwards ES package (called OneWorld) is relatively easy to configure and modify to an individual company's needs.

D&B SOFTWARE/GEAC

D&B Software, now Geac Computer, was one of the early developers of an ES. The company was formed from a merger of firms with financial and manufacturing-oriented software, and offered early promise in integrating these capabilities. However, D&B Software didn't make a successful transition from mainframe to client/server versions of its software rapidly enough, and it has not prospered in the late 1990s.

COMPLEMENTARY SOFTWARE

Implementing an enterprise solution is often not just a matter of installing a single vendor's package. While ES packages typically offer an amazing degree of software functionality, they don't yet do it all, and particular application modules from an ES vendor may not provide the best available functionality. As a result, a series of bolt-on applications are offered by other software vendors. The bolt-on systems usually incorporate some ability to work with the basic ES package and use its data. Enterprise system package vendors are usually working diligently to add the functionality provided by bolt-on systems to their own packages, but they may not have done so yet, or their new offerings may be judged inferior to a special-purpose bolt-on.

Two major types of bolt-on systems are particularly important to companies today. One set involves so-called *supply chain optimization capabilities*. These systems, offered by such vendors as i2 and Manugistics, allow constant fine-tuning of the relationship between demand and supply. If a critical supplier's component becomes unavailable, for example, these supply chain systems can help managers determine the implications of the problem for overall production and perhaps even to plan a way around the shortage. These supply chain capabilities are sufficiently popular that both SAP (through internal development) and PeopleSoft (through acquisition) have added them to their own offerings.

The second type of bolt-on involves so-called *front-office applications*. These are systems that support employees working directly with customers, such as salespeople, customer service representatives, and call center workers. They may also be called *customer asset management systems* because they enable the capturing and analysis of many forms of interactions and transactions with customers. Vendors of these systems include Vantive and Clarify (primarily for customer service applications), and Siebel Systems and Trilogy Development (primarily for sales-oriented applications). Again, these types of systems are growing rapidly in popularity, which has motivated at least one vendor (SAP) to make an acquisition in the area and to incorporate front-office functionality into its ES package.

The specific functions that companies seek in bolt-ons are varied, but most fit into the above two categories. A survey of sixty-two firms that had implemented ES packages suggests that well over half had implemented something other than a basic package, including the following functions:[1]

Electronic data interchange	21%
Distribution/warehouse	18%
Data warehousing	17%
Human resources	16%
Tax	16%
Bar coding	15%
Sales force automation	13%
Planning and scheduling	11%
Transportation	11%

Many other types of software were implemented by less than 10 percent of the respondents, including product data management, forecasting, financial systems, customer information systems, engineering, and shop-floor support.

Why is an ES project such a multivendor undertaking? The survey suggests some answers. Some of the noted software types are included in most basic ES packages, suggesting that companies preferred to use separate software functionality for, say, human resources applications. Some are available today from major ES vendors but were not when the companies began to implement; they may or may not return to their primary vendor's fold when the new capabilities are available and mature. Some capabilities are simply not available from mainstream ES vendors.

ALTERNATIVES TO ENTERPRISE SYSTEMS

There are really only a few alternatives to ESs today for organizations that wish to have up-to-date information systems with some level of integration. Most of these, unfortunately, are unproven or provide few benefits to justify the lack of integration or the increased technical risk. However, in order to help you make an informed choice, I'll describe three alternatives here.

BEST-OF-BREED SYSTEMS

The first and most commonly pursued alternative to ESs, as I've mentioned briefly earlier, is to pursue a best-of-breed strategy. This involves installing systems that are the best available for the particular task at hand. The system selected may be a standalone system or possibly a single module of an ES. For example, some firms have installed only the human resources management component of PeopleSoft's system, believing that it is the best possible system for that application, with no current desire or plan to implement other capabilities and link them together. Some ES vendors are attempting to support this approach by offering the ability to link diverse vendors' systems together under one broad architecture or framework.

Is this a good idea? I think information and process integration are desirable features of ESs, and if you didn't agree you probably wouldn't have bought this book or read this far in it. The additional capabilities for a specific function offered by a best-of-breed system are probably not worth the loss of integration. In general, unless the survival and prospering of your business relies on the functionality supplied by a standalone system, it's not worth the trouble.

MESSAGE BROKERING

A somewhat related alternative to ESs is the concept of message brokering. This systems architecture attempts to achieve integration between diverse systems (either standalone packages or custom-built applications) through the sending of messages between systems. A standalone system that takes an order from a customer, for example, might then send a message to the inventory management system asking it to reduce its level of inventory on hand, and a message to the manufacturing system telling it to build a set of product components. The messaging concept is derived from object-oriented systems, though the systems that send messages back and forth need not be truly object oriented. This is a less ambitious approach to information integration that may ultimately prove to be more flexible and easier to implement than an ES. At the moment, however, it's relatively unproven and technically risky.

One organization that has made a heavy bet on message brokering is Unknown Computer. As I discuss in several chapters of this book, Unknown cancelled most of its initial attempt to install an ES, keeping only the human resources module of SAP as a small legacy of its initial project. The company's new chief information officer helped to kill the ES project and has become an enthusiastic proponent of message brokering. If I used clichés I would say, "Time will tell."

Message brokering can also be used in conjunction with an ES to combine ES-based information with that from other systems. This type of setup is sometimes called *enterprise integration applications* (EIA), and several vendors have begun to offer products that connect multiple types of systems. The idea behind these applications is to reduce the need for customized program code. However, the early implementations of EIA technology themselves require a high level of customization and integration. Some of the EIA vendors focus specifically on linkages between particular ES packages and specific other types of systems, for example, a specific sales force automation tool. If you have that specific combination, it makes it much easier to select an EIA offering.

OBJECT-ORIENTED SYSTEMS

Theoretically, one could use object-oriented systems to accomplish the purposes of an ES. Such systems are, all other things being equal (and of course they never are!) more flexible, maintainable, and simple to understand and install than an ES. It's beyond the scope of this book to describe them in any detail, but if you are interested in learning more, check out the useful endnote.[2] In some industries there are already object-oriented systems that will do some of what an ES will do. In the process manufacturing industry, for example, a company called Marcam will sell you an object-oriented ES called Protean that is supposedly the wave of the future. How future oriented do you feel? Suffice it to say that it has not yet caught on in the present.

Object-oriented systems have been hyped as the wave of the future for the twenty years or so that I have been involved with information technology. As a friend and SAP project manager recently noted to me, "If object-oriented was really going to revolutionize the world, it would have already done so." I agree. It is conceivable that ES vendors will use object technology to build their own systems, but this will not be of great relevance to the user except for possible improvements in ES flexibility.

CONCLUSION

The ES technology environment is changing rapidly, with vendors adding functionality all the time, and with everyone adjusting to the role of the Internet. I discuss some specific technology futures for ESs in chapter 9. Here I'll simply note that these systems will continue to get bigger, will stay integrated, and will evolve to be more flexible and easy to fit to your business. The underlying technology may change, but the basic functionality won't.

Enterprise systems may be complex, difficult to install, and inflexible, but then information systems have never been noted for their simplicity, ease of development and installation, and flexibility. Slow but steady progress will be made on these fronts. Enterprise systems will remain the most capable, integrated systems in the history of the world. They may have their flaws, but they are also the answer to our information systems prayers.

NOTES

CHAPTER 1 WHAT ARE ENTERPRISE SYSTEMS AND WHY DO THEY MATTER?

[1] Andersen Consulting LLP in cooperation with *Chief Executive* magazine, "Enterprise Business Solutions: The Andersen Consulting Survey of Chief Executive Officers," 1999.

[2] Christopher A. Bartlett and Sumantra Ghoshal, *Managing Across Borders: The Transnational Solution* (Boston: Harvard Business School Press, 1989).

[3] I suggested that this was a good idea in the first book on reengineering, *Process Innovation: Reengineering Work Through Information Technology* (Boston: Harvard Business School Press, 1993). At the time, however, the notion was not a popular one.

CHAPTER 2 THE PROMISE AND PERILS OF ENTERPRISE SYSTEMS

[1] Information about the Bay Networks implementation was obtained primarily from a case study by Benchmarking Partners of Cambridge, Massachusetts ("Bay Networks SAP R/3 Implementation Case Study," 1997). The case study was partially funded by SAP.

[2] Information about Elf Atochem comes from interviews with company executives, a case study by Benchmarking Partners ("Elf Atochem North America, SAP R/3 Implementation Case Study," 1997), and an article by Craig Stedman, "ERP Pioneers," *ComputerWorld,* 18 January 1999, 1.

[3] Information and quote from PE Biosystems come from "The *Chief Executive* Guide to Enterprise Business Solutions," a supplement to *Chief Executive,* May 1999.

[4] The workshop was organized by the Concours Group in August 1997.

[5] Andersen Consulting LLP in cooperation with *Chief Executive* magazine, "Enterprise Business Solutions: The Andersen Consulting Survey of Chief Executive Officers," 1999.

[6] The Farmland case is described by Vinnie Mirchandani in a research note entitled "Delivering Promised Packaged-Software Benefits" (Stamford, CT: Gartner Group, Administrative Applications Strategies, 1997).

CHAPTER 3 SHOULD MY COMPANY IMPLEMENT AN ENTERPRISE SYSTEM?

1 Andersen Consulting LLP in cooperation with *Chief Executive* magazine, "Enterprise Business Solutions: The Andersen Consulting Survey of Chief Executive Officers," 1999.

2 Benchmarking Partners, "ROI Strategies: Enterprise Applications" (Cambridge, MA: Benchmarking Partners, 1999).

3 Ken Sansom, "The Case for a Business Case," *Context,* Spring 1998, 58.

4 Martha Amram and Nalin Kulatilaka, *Real Options: Managing Strategic Investment in an Uncertain World* (Boston: Harvard Business School Press, 1999). For a discussion of real options from an IT perspective, see Martha Amram, Nalin Kulatilaka, and John C. Henderson, "Taking an Option on IT," *CIO Enterprise,* 15 June 1999, 46–52.

5 This list is modified from one found in "ERP Systems—Making the Business Case and Selecting the Right System," *Management Advisory Guide,* Canadian Society of Management Accountants, 1999.

6 Vinnie Mirchandani, "Ten Ways to Justify Acquiring Packaged Applications" (Stamford, CT: Gartner Group, Administrative Application Strategies, 1997).

7 Cisco information comes from conversations with company managers and a Harvard Business School case study: Mark Cotteleer, Robert D. Austin, and Richard L. Nolan, "Cisco Systems, Inc.: Implementing ERP," Case 9-699-022 (Boston: Harvard Business School, 1998).

8 Chevron information comes from e-mail communication with company managers and a Benchmarking Partners case study, "Chevron Corporation SAP R/3 Implementation Case Study" (Cambridge, MA: Benchmarking Partners, 1997).

9 Benchmarking Partners, "Corinter SAP R/3 Implementation Case Study" (Cambridge, MA: Benchmarking Partners, 1998).

10 Information about PC Connection comes from Derek Slater, "The Ties That Bolt," *CIO,* 15 April 1999, 64.

11 Benchmarking Partners, "Bay Networks SAP R/3 Implementation Case Study" (Cambridge, MA: Benchmarking Partners, 1997).

12 Robert Rubin, interview by author, May 1998.

13 Craig Stedman, "Retailers Adopt Different Strategies for Installing SAP R/3," *ComputerWorld,* 25 January 1999, 9.

14 Susan Reda, "The ERP Dilemma: Packaged Solution or Best-of-Breed?," National Retail Federation, October 1998 <http://www.stores.org/archives/oct98cover.html>.

15 Ibid.

16 Benchmarking Partners, "Hoechst Marion Roussel (Venezuela) SAP R/3 Implementation Case Study" (Cambridge, MA: Benchmarking Partners, 1997).

[17] Data is from an "ERP Payback Study" of sixty firms that had recently implemented ESs, conducted by the Meta Group, Stamford, Connecticut, 1999.

[18] Andersen Consulting LLP in cooperation with *Chief Executive* magazine, "Enterprise Business Solutions: The Andersen Consulting Survey of Chief Executive Officers," 1999.

[19] Information about Air Products comes from interviews with company executives.

[20] Information about Nike comes from interviews with company executives by Susan Cantrell. Information from Reebok comes from interviews with company executives and a presentation by a Reebok IT executive at Boston University in March 1999.

[21] Marianne Kolbasuk McGee, "Nike CIO Plots IT Strategy," *InformationWeek*, 13 April 1998, 40.

[22] Ibid.

CHAPTER 4 LINKING ENTERPRISE SYSTEMS TO STRATEGY AND ORGANIZATION

[1] The concept of lean production and its automotive manifestations are described in James P. Womack, Daniel Roos, and Daniel Jones, *The Machine That Changed the World* (New York: Rawson Associates, 1990).

[2] Most information about Compaq's SAP implementation came from an interview with John White, former chief information officer of Compaq, in 1997. I added some more recent information from Bill Gates, *Business @ the Speed of Thought* (New York: Warner Books, 1999).

[3] Eryn Brown, "VF Corporation Changes Its Underware," *Fortune*, 7 December 1998, 115.

[4] Suzanne DuBois, "SAP at Amoco—From Business Case to Rollout" (paper presented at the Information Management Forum Meeting, Charlotte, NC, April 1997).

[5] I discuss the idea of federalism from an "information politics" standpoint in *Information Ecology: Mastering the Information and Knowledge Environment* (New York: Oxford University Press, 1997), 68–72.

[6] For information on corporate federalism, see James O'Toole and Warren Bennis, "Our Federalist Future: The Leadership Imperative," *California Management Review* 34, no. 4 (Summer 1992): 73–90.

[7] A similar situation to this one is described in Andrew McAfee, "Vandelay Industries, Inc.," Case 9-697-037 (Boston: Harvard Business School, 1996).

[8] See, for example, one of the many change management books, David A. Nadler, *Champions of Change* (San Francisco: Jossey-Bass, 1998).

Chapter 5 Linking Enterprise Systems to Business Processes and Information

1. This book, the first on reengineering, is called *Process Innovation: Reengineering Work Through Information Technology* (Boston: Harvard Business School Press, 1993). You are probably already familiar with Michael Hammer and James Champy's *Reengineering the Corporation: A Manifesto for Business Revolution* (New York: HarperBusiness, 1993).

2. Davenport, *Process Innovation*, 5.

3. My favorite source on the distinction between process and practice is John Seely Brown and Paul Duguid, "Organizational Learning and Communities of Practice: Towards a Unified View of Working, Learning, and Innovation," *Organization Science* 2 (1991): 40–57.

4. For a good description of the gap between process design and implementation, see Sirkka Jarvenpaa and Donna B. Stoddard, "Business Process Redesign: Radical and Evolutionary Change," *Journal of Business Research* 41 (1998): 15–27. Unfortunately, by the time this important work appeared, many companies had already abandoned their reengineering efforts!

5. Charles G. Cobb and Donna B. Stoddard make this point in "Enterprise Resource Planning Systems" (Wellesley, MA: Center for Information Management Studies, Babson College, 1998).

6. Michael Hammer, *Beyond Reengineering: How the Process-Centered Organization Is Changing Our Work and Our Lives* (New York: HarperBusiness, 1996). This is a good overview of how process-centered organizations might work (if they ever come about).

7. Information from Owens Corning comes from discussions with company managers and a case study by Carol V. Brown, "Advantage 2000 at Owens Corning" (Indianapolis: Kelley School of Business, Indiana University, 1998). The quote in the text is from the case study, p. 2.

8. Hammer and Champy, *Reengineering the Corporation*, 49.

9. More detail about the Visio situation can be found in an excellent article by Christopher Koch, "The Big Uneasy," *CIO*, 15 October 1997, 41–52.

10. Information about Dow Corning's process knowledge management was obtained from the Phios Web site (<http://www.phios.com>) and interviews with Dow Corning and Phios executives.

11. For the MIT research that led to the Dow Corning implementation, see Thomas W. Malone et al., "Tools for Inventing Organizations: Toward a Handbook of Organizational Processes," *Management Science* 45, no. 3 (1999): 425–443.

12. Information about Millipore was obtained from interviews with company executives and a case study. See Sandy E. Green and Nitin Nohria,

"Millipore: A Common Language for Common Systems," Case 9-494-011 (Boston: Harvard Business School, 1993).

13 Both quotations are from Green and Nohria, "Millipore: A Common Language," 11.

14 I wrote a book about this issue entitled *Information Ecology: Mastering the Information and Knowledge Environments* (New York: Oxford University Press, 1998).

CHAPTER 6 ACHIEVING VALUE DURING ENTERPRISE SYSTEM IMPLEMENTATION

1 Robert D. Austin and Richard L. Nolan, "Effectively Managing ERP Initiatives," working paper, Harvard Business School, Boston, MA, October 1998. Quotation appears on p. 3.

2 See Jeffrey Liker, David Roitman, and Ethel Roskies, "Changing Everything at Once: Work Life and Technological Change," *Sloan Management Review* 28, no. 4 (Summer 1987): 29–47.

3 Benchmarking Partners, "Realizing Value from ERP" (Cambridge, MA: Benchmarking Partners, 1998).

4 See Craig Stedman, "ERP Pioneers," *ComputerWorld*, 18 January 1999, 1, 24.

5 Bay Networks information comes from interviews with company managers, Andersen Consulting materials, and a case study by Benchmarking Partners, "Bay Networks SAP R/3 Implementation Case Study" (Cambridge, MA: Benchmarking Partners, 1997). Quote is from the case study, p. 8.

6 Information about the Cisco experience comes from conversations with company executives and a case study by Mark Cotteleer, Robert Austin, and Richard Nolan, "Cisco Systems, Inc.: Implementing ERP," Case 9-699-022 (Boston: Harvard Business School, 1998).

7 Cotteleer, Austin, and Nolan, "Cisco Systems," 3.

8 Cotteleer, Austin, and Nolan, "Cisco Systems," 9.

9 In Focus comments come from Derek Slater, "Business Line Backers," *CIO Enterprise*, 15 March 1998, 25–32.

10 The same "underpromise and overdeliver" strategy was praised by respondents in an Oxford University study of international companies. See Geoffrey McMullen and David Feeny, "International Companies and Common Administrative Information Systems" (Oxford Institute of Information Management, 1996).

11 Michael Hammer, *Beyond Reengineering: How the Process-Centered Organization Is Changing Our Work and Our Lives* (New York: HarperBusiness, 1996).

12 Dow Corning information comes from case studies by Jeanne W. Ross, "Dow Corning Corporation: Business Processes and Information Tech-

nology" and "Dow Corning Corporation (B): Reengineering Global Processes" (Cambridge, MA: Center for Information Systems Research, Massachusetts Institute of Technology, 1997).

13 Benchmarking Partners, "Bay Networks SAP/R3 Implementation Case Study" (Cambridge, MA: Benchmarking Partners, 1997). Quote is from case study, p.5.

14 Jeanne W. Ross, "Dow Corning Corporation (B): Reengineering Global Processes" (Cambridge, MA: Center for Information Systems Research, Massachusetts Institute of Technology, 1997), 17.

15 For more on knowledge management, see Thomas H. Davenport and Laurence Prusak, *Working Knowledge* (Boston: Harvard Business School Press, 1998).

CHAPTER 7   TRANSFORMING THE PRACTICE OF MANAGEMENT WITH ENTERPRISE SYSTEMS

1 The study was sponsored by SAP and presented at that company's annual U.S. user group meeting; company managers allowed me to be perfectly objective and did not try to influence the study's results in any way. The study was first reported at the Los Angeles Sapphire user group meeting in late 1998.

2 Since the study, I have added several other firms to it informally. I found out about them in the context of another research effort at the Andersen Consulting Institute for Strategic Change. This latter study, called "Extracting Value from Business Transactions: Data to Knowledge to Results," seeks to understand the organizational factors involved when companies successfully transform transaction data into knowledge that is used for decisions and increased performance. Enterprise system data is, of course, transaction data. Some of the companies contacted in the context of this research include Earthgrains, J.D. Edwards, and Boston Scientific.

3 Robert Kaplan and David Norton, *The Balanced Scorecard* (Boston: Harvard Business School Press, 1996).

4 A draft of this case was originally written by David D. De Long, a research fellow at the Andersen Consulting Institute for Strategic Change.

CHAPTER 8   USING ENTERPRISE SYSTEMS TO MANAGE THE SUPPLY CHAIN

1 Information on Colgate comes from interviews with company executives and an article by Linda Grant, "Outmarketing P&G," *Fortune*, 12 January 1998, 150–152.

2 Jeff Sweat, "ERP: The Corporate Ecosystem," *InformationWeek*, 12 October 1998, 42–52.

3 The categories as labeled here are those used by Forrester Research. See, for example, J. T. Gormley III, S. D. Woodring, and K. C. Lieu, "Supply Chain Beyond ERP," *Forrester Research Report on Packaged Application Strategies,* Vol. 2, no. 2, May 1997.

4 Randy Weston, "ERP Vendors Eye E-Commerce," *CNET News.com,* 8 July 1998, <http://www.news.com> (8 July 1998).

5 Ron Margulis, "Jo-Ann Stores Fabricates Simplicity with ERP," *Retail Information Systems News,* <http://www.risnews.com/archive/Jan99/Jan99_10.shtml> (January 1999).

6 SAP, "Homepage," <http://www.sap.com/press/magnews/special/scope_e/s20.htm>.

7 The possibility of increased interenterprise computing leading to "lock in" around one or two ESs in an industry is not wholly remote. It's been observed that whereas a decade ago IT people were likely to identify their organizations as IBM or Digital shops, now they're describing themselves as SAP or PeopleSoft shops. Even the perception of an advantage from standardization may drive sales away from all but the market leader.

8 Information about the Reebok/VF consortium comes from interviews with Reebok managers and an article by Craig Stedman, "Strong Links in the Chain," *ComputerWorld,* 25 January 1998, 59.

9 For one account of the Nabisco/Wegmans pilot of collaborative planning, forecasting, and replenishment, see Nancy Dillon, "Story Link in the Chain," *ComputerWorld,* 25 January 1999 <http://www.ComputerWorld.com>.

10 General Electric did, in fact, greatly expand the number of small suppliers it could buy from when it established its Trading Process Network—a Web-based procurement application. Texas Instruments is well known for its commitment to dealing only with suppliers who can interact with it electronically.

CHAPTER 9 THE FUTURE OF ES-ENABLED ORGANIZATIONS

1 Many of these concepts are discussed in Stephen P. Bradley and Richard L. Nolan, eds., *Sense and Respond: Capturing Value in the Network Era* (Boston: Harvard Business School Press, 1998), 263–284.

2 Steven L. Goldman, "Enabling the Next Generation Enterprise," Management Accounting Guideline focus group, meeting of the Society of Management Accountants of Canada, Jersey City, NJ, March 1999.

3 Bradley and Nolan, *Sense and Respond.*

4 John Hagel and Marc Singer argue that this disaggregation will yield three different types of organizations. See "Unbundling the Corporation," *Harvard Business Review,* March/April 1999, 133–141.

5 Andersen Consulting Enterprise Resource Planning Forum, July 1997.

6 Adam M. Brandenburger and Barry J. Nalebuff, *Co-opetition* (New York: Doubleday, 1996).

7 PeopleSoft presentation at Boston University, 15 April 1999.

8 Jennifer Bresnahan, "The Incredible Journey," *CIO*, 15 August 1998, 38–46.

9 Goldman, "Enabling the Next Generation Enterprise."

10 Craig MacDonald and Rick Lawlor, "Wanted! CFOs with ERP Experience: Enterprise Resource Packages Now Dictate the Structure of Finance" (paper presented at the World Research Advisory Trend Teleconference, 12 November 1998).

11 Stephan H. Haeckel and Richard L. Nolan, "Managing by Wire," *Harvard Business Review*, September/October 1994, 122–132.

12 Haeckel and Nolan, "Managing by Wire," 23.

13 Thomas W. Malone, "Inventing the Organizations of the Twenty-First Century: Control Empowerment, and Information Technology," in *Sense and Respond: Capturing Value in the Network Era*, eds. Stephen P. Bradley and Richard L. Nolan (Boston: Harvard Business School Press, 1998), 263–284.

14 Bresnahan, "Incredible Journey," 44.

APPENDIX A TECHNICAL OVERVIEW OF ENTERPRISE SYSTEMS

1 Benchmarking Partners, "Realizing Value from ERP" (Cambridge, MA: Benchmarking Partners, 1998).

2 A good overview of object technology is provided by David A. Taylor, *Object Technology: A Manager's Guide* (Reading, MA: Addison-Wesley, 1997).

INDEX

ABOUT THE AUTHOR

THOMAS H. DAVENPORT is the Director of the Andersen Consulting Institute for Strategic Change, a research center in Cambridge, Massachusetts. He is also a Professor at the Boston University School of Management and a Distinguished Scholar in Residence at Babson College. His books *Process Innovation: Reengineering Work through Information Technology* and *Working Knowledge: How Organizations Manage What They Know* (with Laurence Prusak) were bestsellers. He is also the author of *Information Ecology: Mastering the Information and Knowledge Environment* and coauthor of *Reengineering the Organization: Transforming to Compete in the Information Economy.*